If you enjoy Bach cantatas, Mozart concertos, Beethoven sonatas, Tchaikovsky symphonies, Verdi operas, or Bartok quartets—this is one of the most stimulating books you will ever pick up.

If you would like to understand more about the music you love, here are the basic facts about music and the significant facts of music history.

If you would like to discover more music for yourself but don't know where to start, here is an introduction to a whole wealth of new music.

If you would like to increase your listening pleasure, A POPULAR HISTORY OF MUSIC is one of the most rewarding books you will ever read.

The author, Carter Harman, is both composer and critic. A group of his songs for children have been recorded by Mary Martin. He was formerly editor for TIME and a music reporter for THE NEW YORK TIMES.

A POPULAR
HISTORY OF MUSIC

by Carter Harman

A Laurel Edition

Published by
DELL PUBLISHING CO., INC.
750 Third Avenue
New York 17, N.Y.

© Copyright, 1956, by Carter Harman

Laurel ® TM, Dell Publishing Co., Inc.

Designed and produced by
Western Printing & Lithographing Company

Cover design by Jerome Kuhl

First printing—October, 1956
Second printing—January, 1960

Printed in U.S.A.

To PALMER and HELEN HARMAN

CONTENTS

INTRODUCTION

In MID-20TH CENTURY, music literally surrounds us. Phonograph styluses, tape recorder pickups, radio microphones and the photoelectric eyes of film soundtracks conspire to make music as familiar as the ticking of a clock, commonplace as a singing commercial. It blares or whispers from railway terminal public address systems, pedestrians' portable radios, restaurants' Muzak, beer joints' juke boxes.

The bright side of this situation is that Americans are becoming a race of music-lovers beyond compare. We have more than a thousand symphony orchestras and uncounted amateur choruses and instrumental ensembles, and we pay more cash admissions for music per year than we do for professional baseball. Less bright is the fact that much of the music that surrounds us lurks unobtrusively in the background and tends to become a mere series of sensations without conveying any sense of significance or even of continuity. It is no use to congratulate ourselves on the fact that millions of people are becoming accustomed to music if they get nothing more out of it than sound effects.

Since music deals with the very fabric of our world, nobody should be surprised to find it a complex subject, all but indescribable, elusive even to the men who create it. Rhythm not only ticks off units of time but seems in some mysterious way actually to control the speed with which time flows. Melody has been peered at, dissected, and even graphed, but to this day nobody has unraveled the secret of its impact on human listeners; all we can say is that a melody is a single row of notes tautly or loosely related, depending on the width of its intervals and its speed.

Music is at once the most subtle and the most precise method men ever developed to communicate with one another. It is subtle in its ability to suggest the fleeting whispers and nudges of unconscious thought, the nuances of vaporous moods, the colors and textures of forgotten scenes. Its precision lies in the immutability of tone and of the intervals created when two tones are sounded together or in turn. Unlike words, which can be utterly changed by context, musical intervals are unchanging no matter in what musical context they appear. Of course, the music of the past two centuries or so gains in precision as a direct result of its complexity: the more parts there are to a structure, the fewer there are that are absolutely essential. From one performance to another there can be variations in the fabulous wealth of detail contained in a mere phrase of a symphony, but the essential expression will shine through unchanged. It is no easier for a beginner to sit down with a symphony and perceive that expression without help than it would be for him to read French without a dictionary. On the other hand, once he begins to understand the methods and objectives of composition, his enjoyment soars.

Music has been a force in human affairs ever since the first man raised his voice in song. But it has taken its largest strides since the development of abstract, instrumental music, i.e., music without words. Such music became fully coherent only about 300 years ago in Europe, and it is the subsequent developments of abstract music that are the chief concern of *A Popular History of Music*.

I have told the story in terms of the men who lived it, selecting as protagonists those composers who left music somehow different from the way they found it. If others, such as Handel, Brahms and Tchaikovsky, are included here, it is because, although they have not really altered the course of music, they have nevertheless made it richer by their contribution.

Running through music literature is a thread so tenuous that many writers about music ignore it altogether, but so powerful that it has affected—positively or negatively—the work of literally every composer from Bach to 20th-century modernists. The thread is tonality. Despite its sound, this word does not refer to "tones" as such, but to the elusive emanation described as "key-feeling," a quality that seems to be a locus in space, a sense of home base. The most positively tonal music is the music of Haydn and Mozart, to whom the prospect of starting in a key, venturing as far as possible from it, and returning to affirm it, was the highest kind of adventure. From their time on, tonality began to lose its grip on the imaginations of composers until, eventually early in the 20th century, a group of Viennese, known as "atonalists," actively tried to negate the home-base principle in their compositions. It is my hope that the reader will get a sense of how tonality works as he follows this story. Still more, it is my hope that *A Popular History of Music* will stimulate the reader to seek out the music in question, for reading about music is no better than reading about a delicious meal.

CARTER HARMAN

PART ONE

ORIGINS AND ORIGINATORS

ORIGINS AND ORIGINATORS

No ONE IS CERTAIN what the earliest music was like. As a matter of fact, we are not even sure how Bach's orchestra sounded, only ten generations ago. But we can be quite sure that primitive men discovered rhythms from the movements of their bodies and melody from the changing pitch of their own voices. When they recognized the power of these elements of music, they made them tools of incantation, sorcery and exorcism. As people became more familiar with the musical magic, they became aware of musical patterns. In the pattern of rhythm, they discovered two fundamental pulses: double, or march, time (naturally derived from the act of walking), and triple, or waltz, time, a more sophisticated discovery. In the pattern of melody the basic discoveries were: (1) that repetition of a note gave it significance; (2) that a high or loud note, because of the strain it took to sing it, produced a strong effect; and eventually (3) that certain melodic intervals were disturbing, or restless, while others were satisfying and solid.

To the Greeks, many centuries later, music was both a part of everyday life and a manifestation of the divine. In a civilization that we remember for its plastic art, there was no god of sculpture who ranked with the music god, Apollo, no artist-hero as popular as Orpheus and his heart-shaped lyre. The Greeks held annual Olympiads of music that had the status of a World Series, and a virtuoso on the reed-pipes or the lyre was the equivalent of a modern home-run king. The Greek word for "distinguished man" also meant "musical." There was never a comedy or tragedy staged without its chorus, singing and dancing as the action proceeded on stage; and all of the great poets were actually minstrels who played the lyre as they recited their verses.

Music in Greece progressed, as it later did in Europe, from the purely vocal with words, to vocal with instrumental accompaniment, to purely instrumental, or abstract. The earliest known instrumental work was a descriptive piece called the *Pythic Nome* (585 B.C.) which depicted in five movements, on the shrill and penetrating reed-pipes, a fight between Apollo and a dragon. To modern ears, this composition would undoubtedly sound thin and meaningless, because Greek music was purely monodic, i.e., all voices and instruments produced the same tune. When there was any accompaniment for a human voice, it duplicated the melody and added only an occasional arabesque to underline a particularly poignant moment. But the subtleties of the *Pythic Nome* were readily apparent to ancient listeners, who found the Apollonian battle as vivid as we find the adventures of *Till Eulenspiegel* in the richly scored Strauss tone-poem.

Like Greek philosophy, Greek music was organized into an order of harmonious proportions; like its science, into purposeful numbers. One important Greek discovery (Pythagoras was the discoverer) was the relationship between the length of a vibrating string, or a column of air, and the pitch it produced. This was the beginning of the science of acoustics. It continued with the discovery of harmonics, those faint overtones that appear with any tone and give it its characteristic color. This discovery led directly to the realization that the pitch of the first overtone is virtually the same as the fundamental note. The note at that pitch is called the octave (from the Latin word for the number eight), and thus every eighth note on the piano looks alike in the pattern of black and white keys.

Disciples of Pythagoras continued to investigate the science of music and found that there were other natural acoustical strong points, notably the fourth and fifth notes, within the octave. This became the foundation for the whole Western theory of music, but the Greeks were content to let others develop the implications of their discoveries.

They themselves divided their scales into eight modes and ascribed to each a characteristic quality. Any melody that fell within the scale pattern of the Dorian mode, for instance, had for the Greeks a manly effect, while one in the Lydian was certain to be lascivious. We can get a fairly clear idea of the Greek modes by using the white keys of the piano. Starting on any note and playing down to the octave below we can reproduce one or another of the modes. The difference between them is slight, and today we rarely try for anything subtler than major (C-C) and minor (A-A) modes.

Greek modes survived the decline of Greek civilization and turned up in the Holy Roman Empire with many of their qualities intact. But, although we know something about Greek theories, we know nearly nothing of how their music sounded.

MASSES, MOTETS, MADRIGALS

A VISIT TO THE EARLY CHRISTIAN CENTURIES would give the horrors to a 20th-century musician—or even a layman. As nearly as anybody can reconstruct the situation, music was in a state of chaos. There was no regular meter, no bar lines, no established scales and, at a time when music was still primarily vocal, there was not even stable language to sing in; Latin was disintegrating, and the Romance languages—Italian, Spanish, French—had not yet become fixed.

It remained for the Church to put things in order. The monasteries had built up a large body of music, gathered from sources sacred and secular, oriental and occidental. In the sixth century, Pope Gregory the Great decreed that it should be written down and codified, and for the next 1,000 years the hollow and severe-sounding unisons of Gregorian chant were the musical basis of all Catholic services. It was a remarkable collection and one that solved theological, theoretical and formal problems.

The Mass was the fundamental source of all medieval lyrics, and there could hardly have been a better source, for it contained natural elements of form: e.g., the thrice-repeated words *Kyrie eleison* suggested repetitions of the musical phrase, and the words' return, following the contrasting *Christi eleison,* practically demanded a return to the original musical phrase. In the freer recitational sections, too, where the words suggested no repetitions, composers of the Middle Ages began to apply the principle of recurring melodic patterns. Meanwhile, the more daring soloists began to experiment with florid ornamental passages—singing many notes on one syllable—thus taking the first steps away from the bondage of words almost before the bonds were established.

Gregorian melodies had to be sung in one or another of eight church modes. These bore the same names as Greek modes, but they were differently conceived: the scales were counted upward instead of downward, and each was a steady progression of all eight notes, rather than a pair of four-note tetrachords. Every chant was in one of these modes, in the sense that its tune was chosen from the notes of the indicated scale and ended with a carefully approached home-tone. This music has a plaintive, antique sound to our ears. It has no recurring pulse-patterns, and its endings seem indecisive. The half-step interval was shunned everywhere, strange as that seems today, either as a matter of taste or as a matter of superstition. Less strange is the reason why the augmented fourth, the awkward interval from F to B, was regarded as the "devil's interval"; it still bothers us.

Although music had been subjected to a certain amount of codification and organization by the eighth century, it was still a far, far cry from the music of later centuries. It was, after all, never more than a single tune sung by many men. But something remarkable was about to happen, something that seems natural to us, but which was all but inconceivable to medieval musicians, circumscribed as they were by clerical restrictions: men were about to sing different tunes simultaneously. The age of polyphony was beginning.

In the sixth century, a philosopher named Cassiodorus had given the first opinion on record that separate but simultaneous sounds were agreeable. He invented a name for the effect, "symphonia"; by which he meant the combination of high and low notes. The origin of such an innovation may be imagined. Men and boys (women were not permitted to sing in church) were accustomed to singing the same tune together, doubling the tune eight notes apart. This octave interval sounds, to the unwary, like the same note. Actually, it bears the acoustical ratio of 2 : 1 (the higher note contains exactly twice as many vibrations per second as the lower), and so its sound is similar. The conclusion that the octave interval is not harsh marked the first step toward ensemble music.

It was not much of a jump to the discovery that two other intervals within the octave are also fairly easy on the ears, or "consonant." These are the other so-called "perfect" intervals, the fourth and fifth. After that discovery, it was possible for a style of group singing called "organum" to become popular in the ninth century, a style in which the melody was doubled at the fourth or fifth, note for note, syllable for syllable, until the final cadence. Organum sounds curiously glassy and unstable today; parallel fourths and fifths are forbidden in our harmony. It must have soon grated on medieval ears too, and it certainly made it difficult to conform to the rules of modal writing. Composers soon began to experiment with voice parts that were not strictly parallel, and true counterpoint was born.

The next steps toward abstract musical expression were fairly complex. They took some 200 years, until the 13th century, and they included the use of two and then three and four voices, all singing different tunes simultaneously, all linked by strict rules. They were held together by the rhythm of their words, which theorists divided into six "rhythmic modes" and which, when combined, invariably had the effect of a ponderous triple rhythm.

The most popular form in the 13th, 14th and 15th centuries was the motet, a variation form in which one voice, the tenor (from the Latin *tenere,* "to hold"), intoned a severely narrow melody while two or three others spread their 13th-century-style arabesques about it, sometimes in several different languages at once. Flemish and French composers filled their motets with great vitality, and one, GUILLAUME DUFAY, dared to introduce the use of popular tunes for his tenors. Once this heterogeneous counterpoint was accepted, musicians took another significant step: they gave one or more of the florid vocal parts to instruments. The melodies often became quite exuberant, so far as we can tell by studying the rather puzzling notation, for another change was taking place: instead of chilly, mathematical counterpoint, music began consciously to express human emotion.

A case in point is the most famous of all medieval compositions, *Sumer is icumen in.* This was probably written about 1300, some time later than scholars originally placed it, but still early enough to be an astonishing bit of virtuosity for its time. It has six parts (four was usually regarded as the technical limit), four of them singing the melodic parts and two low voices plodding along in what was called "feet" *(pes).* The tune is as gay as the words:

> *Sumer is icumen in,*
> *Lhudè sing cuccu;*
> *Groweth sed and bloweth med*
> *And springth the wudè nu.*
> *Sing cuccu!*
> etc.

One of the most remarkable aspects of this tune, considering its antiquity, is that it is a strict canon, and this requires a word of explanation. To begin with, early polyphonists discovered a powerful principle to unify the effect of various voice parts. It is called "imitation." Imitation is a kind of musical follow-the-leader, in which the second, third and subsequent voices enter in order and tread note-for-note in the steps of the leader. Sometimes the imitation is literal—each successive voice sings identical notes—in which case the piece is called a "strict" canon. *Three Blind Mice* and *Row, Row, Row Your Boat* are strict canons. The difficult part about writing canons in the Middle Ages, when musical possibilities were fewer, was to make all voices sing the same notes at different times and still conform with the rules that governed the counterpoint.

Shortly after the turn of the 14th century, another development was made, and its innovators were so impressed that they called it *Ars Nova,* the new art. (From that day to this, composers have proudly called their compositions "modern music.") The basic improvement was the perfection of a system of notation, which helped composers to free themselves from the conventional triple rhythm. Its simple secret was to divide the standard note of previous usage into four faster notes. This was enough to start musicians thinking in four-beat time and in faster tempos. *Ars Nova* was not only radical rhythmically, but also harmonically: it used chords that included intervals of a third.

The written notes themselves started out as mere accent signs, indicating more or less stress and, consequently, higher or lower pitch. Gradually, these developed into more complex shapes resembling modern shorthand, indicating up-and-down movements of notes but still failing to depict pitch. Each note was called *punctus,* and our word "counterpoint," comes from *punctus-contra-punc-*

tus, note-against-note. But the whole process of writing down something as fleeting as musical pitch was not so simple, and a third level of abstraction had to be mastered before any real accuracy could be assured. This was the application of an alphabetical letter to each note, and then the assignment of that letter to a place on a lined graph called a "staff."

Many refinements in notation were tried; lines of the staff were given different colors to distinguish them, notes were given different shapes to stand for different lengths, and eventually—of utmost significance for ensemble music—vertical bar lines were invented. The space between two bar lines, called a measure or bar, thereafter contained a specified number of beats, and singers at last could be sure they were singing together. Music became more rigid as it became measured—notes had to have a specific duration to make the system work—flexibility would come later. But the new technique was a milestone.

Meanwhile, the eight modes were breaking down. Never very distinct to untrained ears, they were made even less so by a musical device called alteration. This is the process of raising or lowering a note—raising an F to F sharp or lowering a B to B flat—and thus introducing accidentals into the scale. These were the first of what are now black notes on the piano. Composers used alteration for the simple reason that it heightened expression, as a "blue note" heightens a jazz tune. Eventually, the differences in the modes, small enough to begin with, disappeared, and there remained only those modes known today as "major" and "minor." The major has an effect of brightness and cheer, is suitable for marches and waltzes and joyful moods. When a work switches to the minor, the effect is like that of a cloud passing over the sun.

By the 14th century, the popular art of song was flour-

ishing in taverns and castles, on village greens and squares
—everywhere, in fact, outside the restrictive walls of the
Church. The men who made the popular songs were
called troubadours and trouvères in France, according to
which part of the country they came from. (Both words
mean "to find" or "to invent.") In Germany, the most
famous minstrels were called minnesingers because their
songs celebrated true love (*minne* is an old German word
for "love"); their successors were the meistersingers
(*meister* means "master"), whose pleasure it was to apply
numerous rules to the art of music. Their ballads and
roundelays were improvised, or at least were reproduced
from memory, and never properly written down; consequently this improvisatory art is almost totally lost. But it
was bound to have its effect on the studious musicians of
the Church, and, in fact, a number of popular 14th-century
songs have been immortalized as the subjects of motets.

By the late 15th century, Flemish musicians had established themselves as the finest polyphonists in the world,
and the finest of them was JOSQUIN DES PRÈS (1450?-1521).
At the peak of his career, he was the idol of Europe, including distant Italy, where another proud school of composers was establishing its own claim to immortality.
Even the great evangelist MARTIN LUTHER (1483-1546) had
words of praise for Josquin. "Others follow the notes," he
said. "Josquin makes them do as he wishes." Josquin was
a fully accomplished contrapuntist, able to invent refinements that were miracles of ingenuity and a dazzling setting for his own lofty sentiments.

Among the polyphonists' devices were augmentation,
in which the tune was extended by lengthening its note
values; diminution, in which it was condensed by shortening its note values; inversion, in which it was turned upside down; and *cancrizans* (crab-wise), in which it was

sung backwards. The trick was, of course, to employ these devices without changing the theme by a single note, keeping the effect harmonious and pleasing to the ear. Josquin also made important discoveries in the realm of musical expression; his music, more than any which preceded it, was strikingly appropriate to the words. He was aware of the emotional possibilities of music.

In describing a piece of 15th-century polyphony, Luther wrote: "Is it not remarkable and admirable that one voice can sing a simple tune while three or four others, singing along, joyfully enfold this simple tune, playing and leaping around and embellishing it wonderfully, skilfully as if they were leading a heavenly dance, meeting and embracing each other amiably and cordially." Luther himself left his musical mark as the composer of hymns. These were sturdy, simple, even severe tunes that were the antithesis of counterpoint. They were to establish congregational singing and to become a focus of the early Protestant movement. They achieved a double immortality, for they became the foundation for much of the music of Johann Sebastian Bach.

One of Josquin's pupils was ADRIEN WILLAERT (1480-1562), who studied in various European centers before he finally settled in Venice. There he became organist in the great church of St. Mark's and founded what is known as the Venetian School. His most striking contribution to music was a device called "antiphony," which he developed when he realized what spectacular acoustics the great church possessed. The church was built in the form of a Greek cross, and its four equal arms suggested to Willaert the idea of having choruses sing back and forth from opposing positions. The result was the famous echoing effect. Willaert's music was not only theatrically impressive but so lovely to hear that one local admirer called it "drink-able gold."

One of Willaert's choirboys was ANDREA GABRIELI (1510-86), who felt strongly that music should be the "power of words expressed in tone." He improved on Willaert's invention and wrote for three antiphonal chor-uses, high, middle and low. His nephew, GIOVANNI GA-BRIELI (1557-1612), is more familiar to 20th-century lis-teners, if only because we have the chance to hear more instrumental music than choral. Giovanni was one of the first to discover the possibilities of brass choirs. He wrote his music almost as if it had words but wrote it to sound from horns instead of the throats of singers. By his time, listeners were so used to the sound of polyphony —and so resigned to the fact that they could not under-stand the words anyhow—that they accepted instrumenal music quite readily.

In the 16th century the two greatest composers were ORLANDO DI LASSO of Flanders (1520-94), often called Or-landus Lassus, and GIOVANNI PIERLUIGI DA PALESTRINA (1524-94), whose accepted last name is actually the name of his birthplace outside of Rome. Lasso was a brilliant and facile musician who received a worldly education, in-cluding visits to all of Europe's most important musical centers. He composed no less than 2,500 works, including Masses, motets and those newer, secular pieces, madrigals (see below), many of them of extreme beauty even to modern listeners. His most famous compositions are the *Seven Penitential Psalms,* which took him seven years to complete and which are still occasionally performed. Among his contributions to the development of music, the most distinctive is his tendency to weld contrapuntal lines into the appearance of block chords. This meant that composers were beginning to think of their music in terms of the sound at any given instant—in other words, vertically. It was an important step toward the music of a later day, a step away from polyphony and toward harmony.

Palestrina was organist and choirmaster in his native town at the age of 20 and was married at 23. Despite the fact that he was not a celibate, he became choirmaster at the Pope's *Capella Giulia,* where he found himself right in the midst of a musical revolution. The Popes, who were succeeding each other in rapid succession at that time, all felt that church music was in need of reform; particularly, words should be more clearly heard, and nothing impure or "lascivious" should be allowed into music for either choir or organ. Although it is likely that the Church was referring to infractions of its own multitudinous rules for composition, the edict indicates that composers had gone pretty far in evoking human states of mind in musical sound.

At any rate, Palestrina's *Mass for Pope Marcellus* was accepted as the model of the desirable new style in which the words could be understood. Palestrina still has a reputation for otherworldly purity of style, a style which comes from his ability to polish his harmonies to glowing beauty. Palestrina seems to have been a shrewd and worldly fellow who knew how to use his connections with the Church when conditions were right and when to turn to other patrons. After the deaths of his first wife and his children, he actually decided to take holy orders, but instead of completing this step he married again only eight months later. His demands on patrons were so outrageously high that at least two music-loving noblemen who might have employed him broke off negotiations. He eventually made such a success at the skin and fur business that he was able to publish 16 collections of his own music.

As the Renaissance blossomed, composers began to feel the impact of literature. They became fascinated by classical stories and set out to heighten the effect of the words by means of appropriate music, probing to find the musical phrase that would best express a line of poetry. One of their most popular forms was the madrigal, a four- or five-voice composition—usually sung by soloists rather than by a large chorus—that made use of polyphony as well as simple chords. The finest madrigals were cunningly devised so that a key word or phrase—often amorous or naughty—would suddenly stand out in the sonorous web of counterpoint like a patch of blue showing through a cloudy sky—and then the busy, often jolly counterpoint would close in again. English madrigals playfully imitated natural sounds, notably the call of the cuckoo.

There were madrigalists in all major musical centers of the 16th century—Italy, Flanders, France and England —who made important discoveries about expression and carried them over for use in Masses, motets and psalm settings. Lasso and Palestrina both liked to compose madrigals, and Palestrina is supposed to have lost at least one ecclesiastical job because of his interest in this secular form.

One of the most important of all English composers, WILLIAM BYRD (1543-1623), was himself a great madrigalist. He was a pious Catholic—a fact not to be underestimated in a land where the Anglican Church was the law of the land—and his madrigals often show a distinct, if subtle, pathos. He was also an innovator in instrumental music, writing some compositions for strings and many for the virginal, that delicate keyboard instrument which resembles the European clavichord. He is often credited with the invention of the solo song, which he set to lute accompaniment, or which he wrote to be sung in stage plays, thus foreshadowing in style, as well as in concept, Italian opera.

ENTER THE DRAMA

IN 16TH CENTURY FLORENCE, instrumental music was a lively salon topic. It was just the thing, thought some young radicals, to be combined with plots based on Greek tragedy, for intensifying the emotional impact of the drama. Unlike many amateurs, those Florentines believed in suiting the action to the words and soon were writing their own monodic songs. They were, in fact, beginning to write arias. But they felt the need of a kind of singing that would move the action forward, as their reflective songs could not. The result of their experimentation was recitative (or Italian: *recitativo*), a kind of super-declamation punctuated by simple harmonies. The recitative was followed at length by the more lyrical song, much in the way the verse of a modern show tune is followed by the more familiar refrain. Many years later Mozart and his contemporaries began to write orchestral accompaniment to their recitatives and to give the recitatives themselves more tunefulness. Eventually, in the music dramas of Richard Wagner, the recitatives became so closely woven into the musical fabric that they were indistinguishable from the rest of the music.

The young Florentines who first turned their discussions into music were JACOPO PERI and GIULIO CACCINI, who collaborated on *Dafne* in 1594 and have the honor of being the first opera composers. Later both men composed operas on *Euridice,* and Peri's was performed in 1600, the date of the first public operatic performance. It is possible that another and even more talented young composer—this one a professional madrigalist, singer and organist—was in the audience: CLAUDIO MONTEVERDI (1567-1643). He soon was composing his own first opera, *Orfeo.* It was produced in 1607, and his second, *Arianna,* the following year.

The difference between Monteverdi and his predecessors was enormous. Instead of a simple accompaniment, played on a keyboard instrument and a motley array of viols, Monteverdi for the first time specified which instruments were to play what notes. Instead of stiff recitatives designed to imitate the inflections of speech, he composed recitatives with emotional impact. The audience for this music was different too—4,000 to 6,000 people are said to have attended each of the premières—and the "Lament" from *Arianna* became so popular that Monteverdi had to arrange it as a madrigal. After this success, the composer underwent a series of ups and downs before he became Music Master of the Republic of Venice; and his madrigals, Masses, and particularly his operas, became the object of admiration throughout Europe.

Now we must pause for a look at the technical innovations that made Italian opera—and after it, all of Western abstract music—possible. The basic innovation was figured bass or *basso continuo.* This was a kind of musical shorthand invented for the benefit of the keyboard musician, who had to fill in the harmonies left bare by orchestra and soloist. The only notes on his score were the soloist's melody and the notes played by the bass instruments. Between these were short columns of numerals that represented harmonies in relation to the bass notes. The task of the keyboard player was to fill in the remaining notes as indicated by the numbers: e.g., ¾ above a bass C meant the accompanist's chord would also contain F (four notes above) and A (six notes up). Since he was also usually the leader, the keyboard player embellished on this skeletal part at will. Basso continuo sounds square and bottom-heavy, especially compared with the more economical bass writing of later periods. The technique was developed partly because copying out the whole score for a single keyboard player was expensive, and partly because it allowed him free rein in the ever more popular art of improvisation.

The use of basso continuo freed melodic parts more than ever, and one result of this freedom was the establishment of the solo virtuoso. He was the dazzling personality who could perform miracles of technique; he soon took the spotlight from the composer and to this day represents musical glamour to the public.

In 17th-century Italy, singers were trained almost from the time they could talk, and their voices were capable of feats that seem incredible today. Sons of the most ambitious parents were castrated so they would retain their high female vocal range as they grew older, and many of them developed such power and technique they became the most famous opera stars of their day. The finest *castrati* could run scales, arpeggios, trills and other ornamental passages with the agility of a wind instrument. They became so popular that they were allowed to interpolate their own flashy, show-stopping cadenzas and even whole arias whenever they pleased. This decorative kind of singing is known as "coloratura," and although the castrati lost favor before 1800, Italian operas were written in that style right up to the time of Giuseppe Verdi, in mid-19th century.

With vocal virtuosity as a model, it was no great step for Italian composers to start writing purely instrumental music. It was the violin, the most sensitively expressive of all instruments, to which they turned. The violin movement centered in the northern town of Cremona where the proud Stradivari, Guarneri and Amati families were turning out hundreds of matchless instruments. Experts are still trying to determine the secrets that made those instruments so resonant, so sweet, so even-voiced across their entire range. Scholars can only speculate that the soil possessed just the right amount of acidity; the climate, the precise ratio of sun and rain; the lumber merchants, the patience and understanding for proper seasoning of the wood; the glue and varnish makers, the perfect materials; and the craftsmen themselves, a superlative degree of skill at refining the proportions of the instrument.

Of course there would have been no reason for all this activity without a market for fiddles. The big buyers were virtuoso performers: ARCANGELO CORELLI (1653-1713), GIUSEPPE TORELLI (1650-1708), ANTONIO VIVALDI (1675-1741). Each of them was a man who considered himself primarily a performer, but whose imagination was so far ahead of his time that he was forced to become a composer as well. They specialized in concertos, which featured a violin soloist with a small orchestra in the background, and concerto grossos, which had more than one featured player in a group called the "concertino," opposing the whole orchestra, called the "tutti."

The concerto grosso and the solo concerto contained movements that were longer than any instrumental music had ever been, and this length raised two basic problems. These problems were to keep the listener interested—ten minutes of sheer display or even of beautiful melody

turned out to be boring—and to give him some method of
keeping track of the progress of the music. The latter was
solved by providing the listener with something he recognized, usually in the form of literal or nearly literal repetitions—and with this the foundations of modern musical
form were laid.

One 17th-century form repeated itself from beginning
to end, with a concluding flourish to make it sound more
finished the second time around. This was the binary
form, used from the time of the Italian concerto composers
through the first sonata composers, such as DOMENICO
SCARLATTI (1685-1757) and J. S. Bach himself.

Opera composers developed a three-part ("ternary")
form (writing the words *da capo*, "from the beginning,"
over the last note), which required singers to repeat only
the first half of the aria. The second part of the composition, being different from the first and sung only once,
provided the contrasting section for the identical first and
third parts. This form, diagramed by the letters "A-B-A"
(B stands for the contrasting section), is the foundation of
a vast body of music: most of the first, second and third
movements of classical and romantic sonatas, string
quartets and symphonies—and, of course, today's popular song.

Although the B section provided contrast of musical
material, 17th-century composers had yet to discover the
subtleties of dynamic contrast. For all their dexterity,
performers were still on uncertain ground when it came
to control of loudness and softness. So far, the concerto
provided the best solution with its alternating sections
of tutti and concertino producing sharply defined levels
of volume and intensity.

But the concerto was not the only instrumental form
in Italy. Orchestral accompaniments to early operas be-

came more and more important until there were whole scenes where, listeners complained, the voices could hardly be heard over the din in the orchestra pit. The overture, under the stimulus of an Italian musician in the court of Louis XIV, JEAN BAPTISTE LULLY (1632-87), grew longer and better organized until it became a full-scale composition in its own right and was the most successful of the early attempts at purely instrumental composition. The overture was also produced outside of the theater as the introductory movement for orchestral suites of six or eight dance movements, which were a direct ancestor of the symphony.

The Italians' facile melodies became the rage of Europe —and the despair of serious composers in the cooler countries who had begun to use their newly discovered ability to express in sound the deeper human feelings. The northerners began to curtail virtuoso display for display's sake and substituted more detailed writing. As they did so, they found that some of the frills and arabesques of the virtuoso style were useful for more serious purposes as well. A trill, for instance, when spun out at the proper moment, could produce a feeling of tense expectancy; the up-down-up convolutions of a turn, when wrapped more slowly around its fundamental note, could result in a deliciously languorous effect; a rapid scale passage could be made to indicate anger or ecstasy or a storm at sea. Other decorative devices, such as delaying a harmonic point of rest, proved to be emotionally disturbing.

At this point in music history the fundamentals of music as we know it were all present and accounted for.

THE ORGAN

WHILE ITALY WAS ESTABLISHING THE OPERA CAREER that was to be its steady contribution to music for the next 200 years, the countries to the north were perfecting their more serious kind of music making. Aside from the unrecorded songs and dances of the peasants, most of the early music of central Europe was made for and in its churches. The noble art of polyphony had reached a point where its forms were so familiar that Germans began to use them without the assistance of words, writing for the organ.

The organ is a series of pipes of fixed lengths (unlike a whistle, which is a pipe of variable length, depending on how many holes are uncovered), through which air is passed to obtain one note per pipe. The organ's earliest ancestor was probably the syrinx, a bundle of reed whistles of the type that Pan used to hypnotize nymphs. This handy little instrument was limited to six or seven notes. Men who wanted to improve it connected a larger number of pipes to a mechanical source of wind and found they could make more noise than a mere man could make by blowing.

The first organ to use a mechanical source of wind was the hydraulis (water organ), which was in function 200 years before Christ. An inverted cone was fixed in a receptacle; water was poured in, compressing the air in the cone, which was connected to a wind chest on which the pipes were mounted. When valves were opened to let the

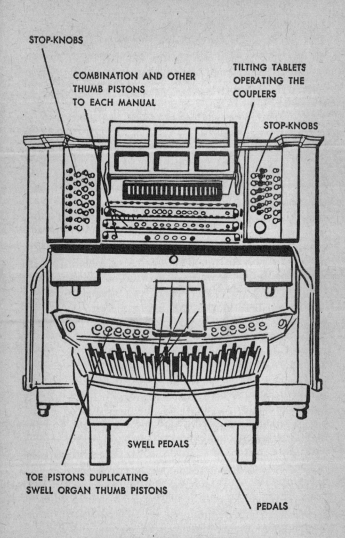

STOP-KNOBS

COMBINATION AND OTHER
THUMB PISTONS
TO EACH MANUAL

TILTING TABLETS
OPERATING THE
COUPLERS

STOP-KNOBS

SWELL PEDALS

TOE PISTONS DUPLICATING
SWELL ORGAN THUMB PISTONS

PEDALS

PIPE ORGAN CONSOLE

air into the pipes, the sound was tremendous. By 400 A.D. enormous water and pneumatic organs were pumped and played by crowds of people; the one at Jerusalem could be heard a mile away on the Mount of Olives. To sound a tone on such monsters the players pulled out a slide at the base of a pipe, which allowed the air to rush in. Later, as men began to appreciate fast-moving notes, the slides were attached to heavy control levers, which the players knocked down with their fists; and thus organists came to be called "organ beaters." For centuries, these instruments were banned from churches but eventually were considered just the thing to throw the fear of God into congregations and became fixtures in all European churches that could afford them. In the 10th century, there was a 400-pipe organ in Winchester, England, that required the perspiring efforts of 70 strong men to supply enough wind and the efforts of two others to work its keys. It made so much noise that local observers proudly claimed nobody dared come too near, for fear of tympanum rupture.

Gradually the great mechanism was improved as music itself became better organized. By the 12th century some organs had two keyboards to control the different ranks of pipes and even boasted a rudimentary pedal system for the lowest notes. Two hundred years later, keyboards contained all twelve notes of the chromatic scale, and the keys were flexible enough to permit the organist to play both the melody and a primitive descant simultaneously. By the 15th century, organ builders were discovering that, by shaping the pipes differently, or by covering the open ends, or building out of wood instead of metal, different tone colors could be produced, roughly resembling those of the different wind instruments in an orchestra. Eventually, ingenious connecting devices (stops) were invented to turn on these different tone colors, and the organ began to resemble the musical and mechanical giant it is today.

By the 17th century, the organ was a highly developed mechanism. It contained as many as 3,000 separate pipes, each handmade out of sheet metal or wood, emitting some 60 different tone colors. Its keys were almost as easily worked as those of a modern piano, although they did tend to stick and produce a squealing sound. The instruments still relied on manpower for wind, usually through the reluctant efforts of a team of sweating teen-age boys, who heaved the pump handles and worked supplementary bellows with their feet.

Aside from the familiar set of ornate pipes—today, these are usually dummy pipes—that fronted the organ loft, all that was visible of the organ was the console. This contained as many as three separate keyboards, one above the other. Above the manuals was a row of stop plungers, which could be pushed or pulled to connect any set of pipes with any keyboard. Under the organist's feet lay a row of movable slats, laid out like an oversize piano keyboard. They were the pedals, constructed with enough space between for his dancing toes and heels to play distinctly. The 17th-century baroque organ, with its low pressures, was hardly able to rattle church windows; its beauty lay in the distinctness of its voices and the colorful contrasts of its tone—especially its nasal reed sounds, with their curiously scintillant overtones added above, and its haunting trumpet stop.

With bands of musicians playing together more and more often, and with organists tolling out preludes and other keyboard pieces in the churches, the time was at hand when purely instrumental music was to leave vocal music behind. This was some 85 years after Italy saw its first opera, and troupes of Italian singers and players were charming the European public—and irritating European composers—with their melodies. Germany was charmed, too, though still suffering from the effects of the disastrous Thirty Years' War, and its people had turned wholeheartedly toward the Reformation, with its stern emphasis on simple living and the honest fear of God. This was the world into which the great Johann Sebastian Bach was born, the composer who inherited all the glory of the polyphonic era and transformed it into a foundation on which future composers would build.

THE BIRTH OF MODERN MUSIC

BACH

JOHANN SEBASTIAN BACH was born in the North German town of Eisenach on March 21, 1685, into a particularly musical family of town bandsmen and church organists. His was a world where composing was as respected and earthly a craft as carpentry. It was a world where every hamlet worthy of the name had its own church, a choir and often an instrumental ensemble—hence, its own musical director or capellmeister. Young Sebastian, who became a competent fiddler almost as soon as he could draw a bow, learned to help out in the town orchestra as today's teen-ager might help out with the family dishes.

His mother died when he was nine; his father remarried and then died himself a few months later. After a short time with his stepmother, the boy left home, trudged the 30 miles to a town called Ohrdruf, and placed himself in the tenderer care of his older brother. It was there, according to the legend, that he used to steal precious musical manuscript scores from their locked cabinet and copy them by moonlight, in order to unravel their delicious intricacies the next day. Bach's musical curiosity was bottomless, and how better could he learn than to study the music of his elders? By the time he was 15, he was an accomplished musician with a pretty singing voice, a good fiddle technique and a better one on the organ. But he realized he was becoming a burden to his brother, and so, almost in storybook fashion, he set off to seek his fortune. The first thing he did was hitchhike the 200 miles to Lüneburg where he enrolled as a chorister and was able to sing and play for his keep.

In the next three years, the youth developed a strong technique and a level-headed way of judging the qualities of an organ. He became such an expert, in fact, that when he was 18 a messenger arrived from the neighboring town of Arnstadt with a command from the reigning nobleman for young Bach to come and test the new town organ. Bach played the instrument so beguilingly that the count appointed him official organist. His contract required him to care for the organ, as well as play it at church services, and in his "daily life to cultivate the fear of God, sobriety and the love of peace."

It looked like a fine position for a beginner, with a salary, that, with the expected raises, could make him as comfortable as an ordinary musician could hope to be for the rest of his days.

But Bach already knew he was no ordinary musician. What was more, he had little respect for those that were. One day, goaded beyond his rather short patience, he called a student in the orchestra a "nanny-goat bassoonist." The offended student complained, and Bach received an official reprimand. As he was to do often in the future, he began to look around for a better position.

He thought he saw his chance when he was 21. Only 50 miles away, in the neighboring town of Lübeck, lived one of the world's most famous organists, the Swedish-born Dietrich Buxtehude. Young Bach, so gossip said, lusted to be his successor, and we have reason to believe he was confident and ambitious enough to do so. Arnstadt town records show that he was granted a month's

leave of absence. We know that he walked the long journey. He studied the old master and was so bemused by
what he saw and heard, and was so eager to learn while he
had the chance, that he stayed four months.

When he finally got back to Arnstadt, the town fathers
were shaking with anger. Not only had he overstayed his
leave, they charged; he also had a backlog of misbehavior:
(1) he had neglected the training of the choir; (2) he had
played "unseemly" variations on the organ while the congregation was trying to sing its chorales; and (3) worst of
all, he was reported to have allowed a "stranger maiden"
in the church while he was practicing. Bach may have
talked his way out of the first two charges, but the last
was true, all too true. He made the scandal worse by
quitting his post and marrying the girl, who was his pretty
cousin, Maria Barbara Bach.

Bach spent the next year or so as organist in the town
of Mühlhausen. His salary was 85 gulden a year, plus the
"added emoluments of 54 bushels of grain; two cords of
wood, one beech, one other; and six-times-three score
faggots, delivered to the door." Bach thought he deserved
more; besides, he was not happy with the condition of
the organ at Mühlhausen, and the city fathers were reluctant to improve it. This, to a rising virtuoso, was grounds
for resignation. The next year he was offered the job of
court organist at Weimar, and he took it.

At that time, as during most of his life, Bach was regarded—and undoubtedly regarded himself—primarily
as a virtuoso organist. When he got settled at Weimar, he
began to write his most famous organ pieces, the brilliant
toccatas and fugues. These magnificent works served a
double function, first to excite, then to exalt the listening
congregation. Bach's toccatas ("touch pieces") are virtuoso pieces designed to keep the performer's fingers and

feet flying and the listeners' ears dazzled. But Bach's greatness, for all his ability to make a fine display, lay in his ability to create a sense of musical destination, a sense that leaves the listener with the impression that the music has meaning; that the trip has not only been a delight but has taken him where he has wanted to go. When a Bach toccata piles up tension on tension and then releases them at last in an achingly prolonged cadence, even sophisticated musicians sigh with satisfaction. But then, after rousing his listeners with the toccata, Bach goes further and gives them something to solace their souls: one of his great organ fugues.

Bach fugues have come to be regarded as the ultimate in the art of counterpoint. Fine fugues have been written since, but like Beethoven symphonies and Strauss tone-poems, Bach fugues have never been surpassed.

The fugue form is based on the old contrapuntal principle of imitation, with an elaborate set of rules: (1) the "subject" (tune) is expected to outline the three basic harmonies of the key (tonic, dominant, subdominant); (2) the "answer" enters with the same tune but at a different pitch level, five notes up or the reciprocal four notes down, while the first voice continues in a passage known as the "counter-subject"; (3) the third voice enters on the same notes as the first, etc., and the process often goes on until as many as five or six voices have joined in. Bach managed to give this rigid-sounding scheme a tremendous impact, building up emotional tension by various fugal devices. One of them was the stretto, in which the voices of the fugue appear to pile up like people eagerly interrupting each other in a conversation; another was a penultimate pedal point (or "organ point"), in which the bass holds one note while the voices above seem to try to break away from its influence, until at last they capitulate, and the tensions are released in the final cadence.

After Bach had spent nine years at Weimar, the little town became too small for him. His renown as a keyboard virtuoso was growing. There is the story of his visit to Dresden, when he was 32, to play before the king and court. It happened that a noted French harpsichordist, Marchand, was there too. Bach judiciously evaluated the Frenchman's performance from a place of concealment, then sent him a courteous challenge: he would execute on the spot any musical task Marchand could devise, offering in return to devise a few problems of his own to test the Frenchman's keyboard ingenuity. Marchand accepted graciously enough, but when the contest time came, he was nowhere to be found. It turned out he had left town, apparently intimidated by Bach's reputation.

Back in Weimar, Bach's employer had decided to give the valued capellmeister position to another musician, a move that insulted and angered Bach. But in 1717, Prince Leopold of Anhalt-Cöthen offered him a good post as his capellmeister, and in November of that year Bach took the job—after receiving an "unfavorable" discharge and spending a month in Weimar's jail, "for too obstinately forcing the issue of his dismissal."

Although the move meant an advance in salary and prestige, it had a serious drawback for an organ virtuoso of Bach's stature: there was no organ adequate to his needs at the Cöthen court. But Bach was willing to tackle any musical problem, and he enthusiastically set about composing and performing music for other instruments. He astonished his audiences. One eyewitness wrote home, excitedly describing Bach's playing on the clavier "with all the fingers of both hands ... and, at the utmost speed, with his feet"; and describing Bach's ability to direct an ensemble, "playing his own parts, watching over everything and bringing back to the rhythm and the beat, out of thirty and even forty musicians, the one with a nod, another by tapping his foot, the third with a warning finger, giving the right note to one with the top of his voice, to another from the bottom and to a third from the middle of it—all alone, in the midst of the greatest din made by all the participants, and although he is executing the most difficult parts himself, noticing at once whenever and wherever a mistake occurs, holding everyone together, taking precautions everywhere and repairing any unsteadiness, full of rhythm in every part of his body. . . ."

One of the first instrumental works that Bach completed at Cöthen was a collection of keyboard pieces called the *Little Clavier Book (Clavier Buchlein)*, which he wrote for his oldest son, Carl Philipp Emanuel. The collection is a treasury of perfectly formed little pieces, including several of Bach's most famous *Two-Part Inventions* and several pieces that later turned up in an even more famous collection called the *Well-Tempered Clavier*. The music was as useful for the developing performer as it was appealing to listeners, and it is not surprising that Carl Philipp became the greatest keyboard virtuoso of his generation. The secret lay in a radical new method of fingering the keys.

The word "clavier" was used in Bach's day to represent any keyboard of black and white keys; even the organ console was called the clavier. Like most instruments in the 18th century, keyboard instruments had not become standardized. Each one was made large or small, with more or less carving, to order, and there were several generic types. Most familiar was the harpsichord, and next came the clavichord. The latter was the smallest and most intimate clavier of the age; its single strings were vibrated by means

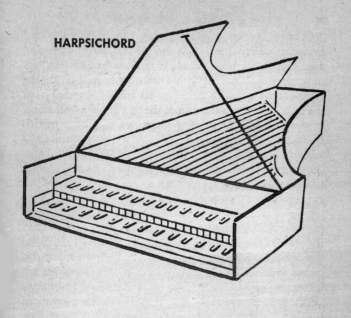

HARPSICHORD

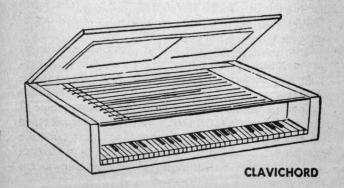

CLAVICHORD

of small, wedge-shaped tangents that rose as the keys were depressed and struck them to produce sweet, tiny sounds. The instrument was capable of great expressiveness, including a plaintive vibrato that could be induced by a rapid vibration of the finger on the key.

The harpsichord was sounded by quills which rose to pluck the strings. It could be made to sound twangily assertive or as hushed and intimate as a ukulele, and it could deliver astonishing volume when its mechanical couplers were hooked in: one finger could then produce notes in two and even three octaves simultaneously. With the exception of the clavichord family, 18th-century claviers had one thing in common: unlike the modern piano, the initial volume could not be varied no matter how hard the keys were struck. Since the strength of the finger was not important, performers tapped the keys with flat fingers and rarely used their thumbs because those digits simply did not reach the keys. To play scales, they passed their long middle fingers over the shorter index or weak fourth ones, and when the thumb *was* employed (as it had to be for big stretches) it was also passed clumsily over the other fingers. In the *Little Clavier Book,* Bach numbered some of the fingerings in such a way that it is certain he advocated the then radical, now commonplace, method of keeping the fingers arched and passing the thumbs beneath. That way he developed far greater speed and the continuous use of all ten fingers.

Besides composing music for his young prince's private orchestra—and playing in it—Bach continued to make contacts in the outside musical world. One of them was a certain Christian Ludwig, Markgraf of Brandenburg, who made a snobbish hobby of collecting concertos by famous composers (he owned no orchestra). It was for him that Bach in his 36th year composed a set of six concerto grossos which are known today as the *Brandenburg Concertos*.

Making a shrewd guess that the Markgraf really wanted the concertos to grace his library table and would probably never have them performed, Bach allowed himself an impractical luxury: he composed each concerto for a different set of instruments. No. 1 is written for strings, three oboes, two horns and bassoon; No. 2, for solo violin, flute, oboe, high trumpets and strings; No. 3, for strings; No. 4, for two flutes, solo violin and strings; No. 5, for solo harpsichord, violin, flute and strings; No. 6, for violas, two violas da gamba, cello, harpsichord and strings.

Although it was certainly meant to be a show of virtuosity, this variety of instrumentation does not mean that Bach treated each instrument with much distinctiveness. He was as backward as his contemporaries about ascribing individual personalities to orchestral instruments and made no attempt to write music that "lay well" for one or another of them. Counterpoint was counterpoint; he wrote trumpet parts in the flute range, so high that scarcely a trumpeter alive is able to play them on the bulkier modern trumpet; his violins play the same kinds of figuration as his winds, while basses and cellos bumble along with the harpsichord.

Nevertheless, his treatment of the form was extremely flexible; where most concertos mechanically alternated brilliant solos with crashing, commonplace tuttis, Bach applied some of his finest invention to the tutti and democratically allowed it to banter on something like equal terms with the soloists. His ear for dissonance, which got him in so much trouble with church congregations, induced him to write one of the most poignant movements in all music, in the slow movement of *Brandenburg No. 1*. There, entranced with the conflicting sounds of major and minor modes, he actually allows the two to clash head-on when the bass viol (in one of its earliest uses as a solo instrument) moves down the minor scale, while the higher instruments climb upward in the major.

Chances are, no modern ears will ever hear Bach's instrumental music as he himself did, if only because our great homogenized orchestras make more noise. But we can get some idea of the quality of the sounds he heard when we play on the dulcet wooden pipe known as the recorder. Bach scored for it in several of the "Brandenburgs." As for the Markgraf, there is nothing to indicate that he ever heard his new compositions. Bach never wrote another concerto grosso, although he did write a pair of melodious violin concertos and one for two violins and orchestra, as well as several fine clavier concertos.

Bach's wife died unexpectedly while he was away on a trip with his prince. A little more than a year later, he married Anna Magdalena Wülcken, at 21 the possessor of a clear, true soprano voice and a respectable performer on the clavier. It was for her that he put together the delightful collection of keyboard pieces called the *Little Anna Magdalena Book*. We know that he liked five of the pieces so well that he arranged them as movements in orchestral dance suites.

The year 1722 was important in the history of music, for only a few months after Bach completed the *Little Anna Magdalena Book*, he finished the first book of preludes and fugues in that landmark of music, the *Well-Tempered Clavier*. Its importance lies in the fact that it helped to establish tonality; but before we examine that elusive subject, let us see what the music of the *Well-Tempered Clavier* was like.

A prelude is a style, or rather a method, of composing that derives from the nature of the harpsichord and clavichord. Unlike the organ, which has a box full of wind to

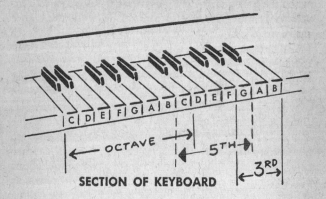

SECTION OF KEYBOARD

keep its notes sounding as long as the keys are held down, stringed keyboard instruments have no way to increase the volume or even sustain a note once it has been struck. Eighteenth-century claviers, weak-voiced to begin with, were especially lacking in sustaining power; and so 18th-century composers worked out a way of breaking up a chord into its separate notes (making an arpeggio out of it), thus sustaining the harmony. Basically, a prelude is a system of arpeggios (or related musical figures), smoothly and carefully extended to make a comprehensible form. One of the simplest and most perfect examples is No. 1 in the *Well-Tempered Clavier*—the one that Gounod "improved" by adding a melody to it and naming it *Ave Maria*. In the two volumes of the *Well-Tempered Clavier* there is a wide range of musical expression, from reflective-ness, even melancholy, to exuberance. Because its musical interest is so great, the collection established the keyboard prelude as a distinct form: almost every composer since (notably Chopin and Debussy) has written some of his best music in prelude form.

When Bach called his collection "well-tempered" he was not referring to the placid nature of the clavier, but to the fact that the instrument had to be tuned to tempered pitch, if the collection was to be played through without retuning for each prelude and fugue; for each piece was in a different key, and each book encompassed all twelve major and all twelve minor keys. Tempered pitch is a minute tuning adjustment that makes all steps of the chromatic scale exactly the same distance apart. (Modern pianos are tuned to tempered pitch.) Untempered or "natural" tuning causes several of the black notes to be noticeably out of tune.

Until a century or so before Bach, music was written diatonically, as if for the white keys of a modern piano. Instead of writing in the basic major and minor scales, composers wrote in the ancient modes. The white keys form an unequal pattern of notes; the five that are separated by black keys are called whole steps, the other two, half steps. To the sensitive ears of 18th-century listeners, the patterns caused by these uneven groupings were quite distinct. The effect of a scale starting on D, for instance, was entirely different from the one starting on A, although we find the two effects almost identical. We can imagine the excitement of the ingenious composer who first discovered how to insert an occasional F sharp or B flat among the white keys; the effect must have been as startling as the discovery of perspective in painting, creating a whole new world of possibilities in music.

Besides new expressive effects, the addition of sharps and flats made possible that smooth transition from one key to another known as modulation: F sharp has a distinct urge to move toward the note G, and therefore the key of G. When F sharp appears in a piece written in C (which contains no black notes at all) the whole locus of key-feeling shifts toward the new center, G, and lends a contrast that makes the eventual return to the home key, C, more satisfying and final.

Gradually, as composers explored the possibilities of the black notes, all five of them assumed importance. There was only one trouble: if a chromatic scale was played (all half steps in order) as it was ordinarily tuned in those days, the steps would not come out equidistant; some would sound sharp, others flat. A common chord in, say, the key of C sharp, with its many black notes, would sound grotesquely, painfully out of tune. The same chord a half step lower, in C, with none of the troublesome black notes, would sound perfectly all right.

A good many musicians were aware of this difficulty by Bach's time, and many of them favored "equal temperament," which artificially equalized the intervals. Bach himself was notoriously finicky about tuning, and when he was invited to test a new organ, became the terror of organ builders, who very likely would have to go into the loft and adjust the tuning plugs on upward of 600 pipes. The *Well-Tempered Clavier* was his credo for the new tuning and is usually recognized as one of the factors in stabilizing it.

When Bach was 37, his young patron, Prince Leopold of Anhalt-Cöthen married a lady who had no taste for music, leaving the composer with the unhappy conviction that he would soon be out of a job. In the same year, Johann Kuhnau, the famed cantor of St. Thomas Church in Leipzig, died. Bach applied for the position and got it —after George Phillip Telemann, equally famous and a proponent of the popular new Italian style, as well as another organist named Graupner, turned it down. A year later he moved into the post he was to hold for the last 27 years of his life. At Leipzig he was to compose most of his 400-odd cantatas, his monumental *St. Matthew Passion* and *B Minor Mass* and those remarkable testaments to the dying art of pure counterpoint, the *Musical Offering* and *The Art of the Fugue*.

Although Leipzig was a large, cosmopolitan center and St. Thomas was its finest church, Bach was not headed for a life of musical luxury. Under his contract he was required to act as a kind of housemaster for the 70-odd unruly boys who were sent to the church school and train them to sing in his choirs and play in his orchestras. He had to supply music for four Leipzig churches and even teach the choirboys a certain amount of Latin. Among other matters he agreed not to play too long during church services nor to permit his music to make "an operatic impression." He was also required to treat his superiors on the town council with proper respect and obedience, a point which must have rankled, because those honorable men made it painfully evident that they thought Bach a mediocre choice for their new cantor.

When he arrived, Bach found that his orchestra was a motley array of town bandsmen who commanded among them a total of two trumpets, two violins, two oboes and a bassoon. Seven years later, he complained to the council: "discretion deters me from revealing anything near the truth as to their quality and musical knowledge," and asked for a better balanced, abler orchestra. What he got was permission to divert some badly needed choirboys and train them to play the necessary instruments.

One of Bach's most important musical jobs in Leipzig was composing cantatas. (The word "cantata" refers to a sung piece, as the word "sonata" does to a played piece.) The form of a cantata is a more flexible thing than any sonata form, for it depends primarily on words. Bach obtained original texts from local librettists and used them almost as if he were writing operas. His cantatas run from ten to 40 minutes in length (almost the size of a dramatic oratorio) and have four to a dozen movements. He wrote almost 300 ceremonial cantatas, including one for each holy day in the church calendar.

To provide the proper atmosphere for his sung stories, Bach usually began each cantata with a noble introductory movement or overture for orchestra. The rest of the composition was comprised of three kinds of music: (1) solo arias for reflective moments * (Bach's favorite voice was the low female range, called "contralto," or simply "alto," and he loved to pair it off with the reedy tones of an oboe); (2) recitatives in which the singer narrated the story with many words to a note and with very little instrumental accompaniment, much in the manner of Italian operas; and (3) massed choral movements. The last were almost always based on the familiar, stately Lutheran chorales, usually set in four-part counterpoint but sometimes blown up to near-heroic proportions by orchestral interludes of free fantasy.

At the end of his first year in Leipzig, Bach composed the first of his large church compositions, the Latin *Magnificat.* Before the year was out, he had put the finishing touches on a still larger work, the *St. John Passion,* which told the final episodes of the Gospel tragedy for the St. Thomas congregation to contemplate on Easter. Like the

---

* A Hamburg music lover, Johann Mattheson, who published the first musical periodical in any language, poked fun at Bach's setting of words, in 1725, by quoting directly from one of the cantatas ("etc." is used for repeats): "I, I, I, I had much grief, I had much grief in my heart, in my heart, etc., I had much grief, etc., etc., I had much grief, etc., in my heart, etc., I had much grief, etc., in my heart, etc., etc., etc., etc., etc., I had much grief, etc., in my heart, etc. . . ."

monumental *St. Matthew Passion,* which was to follow
four years later, the *St. John* gives one singer the role of
the Evangelist and allows him to tell the narrative in
highly expressive recitative. Other soloists take the parts
of the principals in the story, while the chorus assumes
the role of the populace, commenting and reflecting as the
tragedy unfolds. Occasionally the chorus breaks into the
action, as it does in the Golgotha solo with cries of *"Wohin? Wohin?"* (Whither? Whither?).

By 1729, when Bach was 44, he was distinctly unhappy
with his life in Leipzig. Many of the fees he had earned
were not forthcoming, the year was poor in funerals
(from which the cantor derived as much as a fifth of his
income), the cost of living was high and, as Bach wrote to
a friend, "the authorities are odd and little interested in
music, so that I live in almost continual vexation, envy
and persecution." And yet, with the mysterious strength
that many composers have, he continued to turn out music
that grew in depth and power. It was the same year, 1729,
that he finished the greatest musical monument to Christian worship the world has even known, the *St. Matthew
Passion.*

The Passion takes four hours to perform and requires
the services of two orchestras, organ, two four-part choruses, and a separate chorus of boy sopranos, in addition to
a corps of soloists. The huge opening chorus sets the tone
for what is to come: both choruses and orchestras build
their interweaving counterpoint until they reach a peak of
shouting intensity. Then, floating clear and serene over
the tumult, the boys' chorus sings the tune of the "Passion
Chorale." From then on, Bach reveals the story in tones
of utmost beauty, in solo laments of surpassing sadness, in
contemplative moments of choral hymn singing, and in
climaxes of raging energy such as had never before been

heard in music. Through it all, Bach makes use of his own language of musical representation, of falling cadences of sadness, leaping shouts of anger, rising lines of exaltation. A century later, Wagner was to become famous for his own use of similar devices, called "leitmotifs." The Passion was performed on Good Friday, 1729, and drew the acrid comment of one Leipzig housewife that it sounded to her like a musical comedy. Bach made some improvements before the next performance, the following year, and it was performed in Leipzig several times after his death. Then it disappeared, as new cantors supplied their own music, until it was discovered by Felix Mendelssohn 100 years later.

During the last decades of his life, Bach wrote several other works that apparently were never intended for public performance, at least not in their complete state. One is the *B Minor Mass,* the mightiest choral work ever written. Since the words are in Latin, it was probably not intended for Lutheran services, and since it lasts two and a half hours, it was hardly suitable for any ordinary Catholic service either. Its immediate function was to impress King August III of Saxony, to whom Bach sent portions, along with an appeal for an official position to supplement his meager earnings. To modern listeners its massive choral movements have less appeal than the more dramatic Passion music, but the splendors of individual numbers are among the most magnificent ever conceived.

In 1740, Bach's son, Carl Philipp Emanuel, became court accompanist of that musical monarch Frederick the Great at Potsdam and seven years later persuaded his aging father to accept a royal invitation to visit the court and display his ability for the king. Bach arrived in town just as the king was warming up his flute for his regular evening of concerto playing. When he heard the news, he stopped everything with the announcement, "Old Bach has arrived," and sent for him forthwith. The royal party spent the rest of the evening wandering from one palace room to another, while Bach tried several of the newfangled instruments called "piano and forte" ("soft and loud") built by an inventor named Silbermann. Frederick was impressed with the ease of Bach's improvisation and finally sat down himself and made up a complicated fugue subject on which he asked Bach to improvise then and there. Bach delivered himself of fugues in three and four parts, much to the delight of everybody present, but when Frederick asked for a six-part fugue, Bach, to his embarrassment, had to use his own subject for the improvisation.

When he got back to Leipzig, he brooded about his failure. He wrote down from memory the pieces he had improvised, calling them by the more ancient name, "ricercar" (they are freer in construction than academic fugues), and added a beautiful sonata, several canons and, as a crowning number, a fine six-part fugue, all on the difficult royal theme. Included was a "perpetual canon," or "puzzle canon," in which only one line of notes was written down. The performer was obliged to figure out how the few notes could be developed into a full-scale piece without using additional notes.

Apparently intrigued with his own ability to solve the most complex contrapuntal problems, old Bach sat down to write one of the most amazingly ingenious compositions (though not the most attractive) in all music: *The Art of the Fugue.* It consists of 13 fugues, without any indication of instrumentation. Each is more complex than its predecessor. The last two are complete "mirror" fugues, one the literal inversion of the other, not only capable of being played separately but also simultaneously. One fugue was left uncompleted. It is a monster fugue with three subjects and a counter-subject which contains the notes B-A-C-H (H means B flat in German notation).

But old Bach had worn out his eyes from too much squinting at notes. After personally engraving *The Art of the Fugue,* he went almost completely blind and became too weak to compose regularly. He died in 1750 at the age of 65.

————————

Contemporary with the great Bach lived GEORGE FREDERICK HANDEL, not an important musical innovator, but one of the most spectacularly successful of all the world's serious composers. Born in Halle, Germany, just a month earlier than Bach, he became a fine organist, violinist and composer. When he was 26, he moved to England and turned his energies to the composition of vocal music: first Italian opera, then the idiom in which he remains the master, the dramatic oratorio. He also Anglicized his name (from Händel) and became a member of the *haut monde,* earning and losing fortunes as he merchandized the music he wrote.

Handel started his composing career in Hamburg at the age of 20, when he brazenly accepted the job of composing an opera which his employer had agreed to write and then failed to deliver. This was *Almira,* which turned out to be such a success that Handel eventually had to leave his jealous master and move to Italy. There he made the acquaintance of such important musicians as the violinist-composer Arcangelo Corelli and the two Scarlattis, Alessandro and Domenico, uncle and nephew, who were making important contributions to opera and the oratorio. Handel made the best of their examples, and by 1710 his ability was so widely admired that he was summoned back to become court conductor in Hamburg. Almost simultaneously, he was asked to produce an opera in London. The opera, *Rinaldo,* was received with great enthusiasm; and Handel, ever alert to opportunity, then and there made up his mind that England would be his home. He abandoned Hamburg and settled down in London for a gaudy career.

His impulsive move caused him almost immediate embarrassment for the Elector of Hamburg became King George I of England. The canny Handel is said to have won back his monarch's good will by beguiling the royal ear with his *Water Music,* one of his few orchestral compositions to survive the years. Its 21 pretty movements were played so the story goes, on a barge that followed the royal float down the Thames, and the king was charmed out of his pique.

Handel then became codirector of the Royal Academy of Music—actually an opera-producing organization—and turned out at least one opera a year for its stage. His total output of operas was 46 all of them examples of the formalized Italian style and none of them in today's American repertory. For 20 years he lived high; winning battles with his operatic rivals, going to the Continent to engage new stars, and even being offered an honorary doctorate at Oxford, which he declined.

During the second decade of Handel's operatic career, however, London began to lose its infatuation with Italian opera. The temper of the times was indicated by the appearance of John Gay's *Beggar's Opera,* a rude parody on the operatic customs of the day and a bitter satire on the society that practiced them. Its broad, folksy tunes were a welcome contrast to the starchy airs of Handel and his colleagues; its tattered characters a ribald caricature of the egocentric castrati of the operatic stage. Londoners flocked to hear it. (Oddly enough, this work keeps turning up in one form or another in places where its satire is effective; in the 1920's, a new version by the German-American composer, Kurt Weill, took Berlin by storm, and a translation of it had a long run in New York, 30 years later.) Three times Handel tried to recoup his operatic fortunes; three times he failed.

But he was not defeated. In 1732 he staged his oratorio *Esther,* and its reception showed him the way to a new future. The oratorio is a form of musical drama without stage action. Like opera, it emerged from ancient masques; its name comes from the church oratory, where it was fir performed. In its most developed form, oratorio substitu the words of a narrator for the action and scenery of op Its story line may be Biblical, but is not necessarily e astical. The narrator sings and declaims in recitati his words are answered by the songs of other princi and the chanting of the massed chorus. H e 32 of these large works, the most fam urable —being *The Messiah,* comple ess instinct was still sharp, a once again lay at his feet. In dition thus established by this re oser flourished in Britain for the next 1 years, its massed harmonies and sturdy modulations affecting almost all of the nation's musical output.

Handel, a grand old bachelor, accustomed to success, was working on his penultimate oratorio, *Jeptha,* when blindness began to overtake him. The same English surgeon who operated on Bach's eyes tried to save Handel's, with as little success. Handel lived on, composing and revising his early works, aided by his devoted companion, a fellow ex-German named J. S. Schmidt. Handel died on April 14, 1759, and was buried with reverence in Westminster Abbey.

PART TWO

CLASSICAL MUSIC

CLASSICAL MUSIC

J. S. BACH, to the few contemporaries who were aware of him at all, was a throwback, a heavily talented supernumerary, and the world of music was scarcely affected by his death. His sons and their colleagues of the revolutionary new generation faced a fact that he never admitted, if indeed, he even realized its presence: that music without words, if it were to fulfill its promise, would have to assume a personality quite distinct from the smooth logical flow of polyphony. The dramatic impact of simple ideas, starkly contrasted, had been already felt by some Italian composers; it was still an exciting discovery to Bach's sons and their contemporaries. Instruments, those radical musicians were convinced, had a richer potential than merely substituting for the human voice or for making contrapuntal parts move along. The composers of the late 18th century were fairly bursting with the unformed conceptions of the symphony, the sonata and the string quartet, the forms of the music of the future. They followed up the leads they found in operatic overtures and orchestral dance suites, found ways to express dramatic ideas in abstract sound, and toyed with tempos. Eventually, they discovered that it was best to start with a brisk opening section, relieve it with a slow, melodious aria and wind up with a rousing conclusion. In that simple pattern lay the seeds of the formal discoveries that would soon revolutionize musical Europe.

The word classical (or "classic") is about as abused as any word in the music world. In its general sense, it is used to describe any music that has a serious or authoritative quality, and in particular, music that has withstood the "test of time." More specifically, it is used as a term distinct from popular, romantic or modern music. In its most restricted use, it refers to music written during the period of roughly 30 years, between 1790 and 1820—especially most of the music composed by Haydn and Beethoven and nearly all of the music by Mozart.

When we use the word "classical" in the last sense, we refer to a state of mind in which the artist is more or less consciously attempting to emulate Greek ideals of formal beauty, clarity, balance, and perfection. Artists of the Italian Renaissance were more aware of these ideals than composers of the classical period, but the fact that musicians were aware of them is confirmed by the appearance of such personages from Greek mythology as Orpheus, Dido, Idomeneo, etc., in the operas of the day. We think of classical music as courtly, elegant and cool, mostly because later composers were so much more bombastic and assertive. It is, however, a mistake for us to focus on the superficial mannerisms of the style if we thereby miss its essential expression. The mannerisms were partly cultural residue but also a formal necessity; classical composers were for the first time in history making music that was completely comprehensible without using words. Their music *had* to be formal if it was to be made comprehensible through form alone. As it happened, their music was so comprehensible that the world's musicians have been either following their paths or specifically contradicting them right down to the present day.

THE ORCHESTRA

FIVE YEARS BEFORE BACH DIED, a Bohemian composer named JOHANN STAMITZ (1717-57) settled in the South German town of Mannheim and found it alive with musical activity. Gradually, by force of his vigor and originality, he became the major figure in the influential Mannheim "school" of composition, and conductor of the Mannheim Orchestra, which soon became the marvel of the civilized world. Its methods—and its extravagances—were to shape for a full century the symphony orchestra and the music it was to play.

The most startling innovations of the Mannheimers were the swelling crescendo and the dying diminuendo, powerful contributions to the emotional aspect of music. All publicly performed keyboard music in the 18th century was played, as we know, on organs, harpsichords and their mechanical relatives. Except for the toylike clavichord, which was capable of a subtle control of volume, when a key was pressed it either opened a valve or zipped a quill across a taut string. No matter how hard or softly the performer struck the keys, he could not change the volume. By mechanical coupling, he could make other strings or pipes simultaneously sound the same note, and terraces of volume could be achieved by suddenly adding or subtracting a new "rank" or "stop," but there was no such thing as a sloping path between the terraces. Only the human voice and the members of the bowed viol family made use of such delicate gradations.

Stamitz and his colleagues were aware of the emotional effects on listeners when a singer or a fiddler gradually increased or decreased volume; a crescendo carries with it a sense of anticipation, of growing excitement and purposefulness, of inhalation; on the other hand, a diminuendo is a musical exhalation, a sigh, a relief, and carries a sense of wistfulness. To achieve a crescendo, Mannheimers started with a minimum ensemble, added one instrument at a time and made each instrument play gradually louder until a crashing climax was reached; for a diminuendo, the process took place in reverse. The resulting emotional effects were the pride of Mannheim. As for musicians, they began to see how human drama could be extracted from purely musical patterns.

The Mannheim Orchestra made another great contribution to music—it made the orchestra into a dependable instrument: each section or choir became a distinct personality, the woodwinds specializing in mellow harmonies, the brass in blaring punctuation, the strings in melody. Balance of volume between the sections quickly became standardized as well. Strings were established as the softest-voiced in the orchestral family, so more of them were used in unison to stand up against the doubly powerful woodwinds and the still more powerful brasses and percussion. The seating arrangement included a harpsichord (or, soon afterwards, a piano) centered in the position now occupied by the conductor's podium. The harpsichordist, who sat with his back to the audience, was the leader; he not only held the musicians together but played his instrument to fill in empty spaces in the musical fabric. The string section was seated to his right and left while the heavier instruments were gathered across the middle distance.

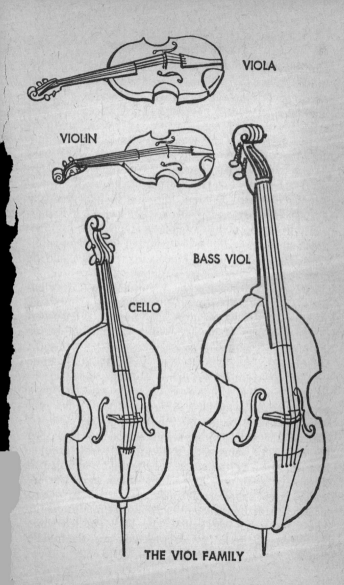

VIOLA

VIOLIN

BASS VIOL

CELLO

THE VIOL FAMILY

The instruments that made up the Mannheim Orchestra are generically, if not always specifically, the same that make up a "classical" orchestra, the nucleus of today's symphony orchestra. They are:

THE STRINGS. As many as 20 instruments, divided into five parts: first and second violins, violas, violoncellos (an obsolete name usually shortened to "cellos") and string basses. The faces of the instruments are shaped into a decorative figure 8. Their tops and bottoms are fully formed to provide resonant boxes full of air to amplify the thin string sounds; the waists are narrowed to leave room for the bow to pass without touching wood. All of them are constructed with four strings stretched across a bridge which is arched so that the roughened bow hairs may scrape each string without touching the next. All but the basses are tuned (by tightening and loosening their strings) five scalewise notes apart; basses are tuned in fourths. Fingers of the left hand are used to "stop" the strings by pressing them against the smooth, ebony fingerboard and thus, by shortening their vibrating length, causing them to rise in pitch. The right hand holds the bow. As its name indicates, this was originally shaped like a bow for shooting arrows, strung with a ribbon of rough horsehair roughened still further by application of rosin. Its purpose is to scrape the strings and keep them vibrating as it rubs across them. Today's bow is slimmer and easier to handle than the old arched bow. The fingers of the bow-hand may also be used to pluck the strings, an effect that is called "pizzicato."

THE VIOLINS (often called fiddles, without any sense of deprecation) are tucked under the performer's left jowl and supported by his left shoulder (not by his left hand, which must remain free for fingering). The physical

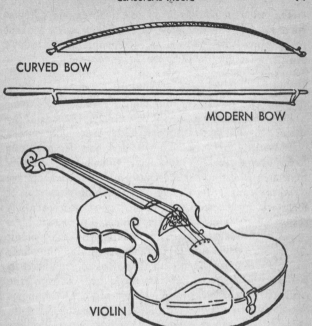

CURVED BOW

MODERN BOW

VIOLIN

marks of a professional fiddler are an ugly callus under his left jawbone, an occupational malady that nobody has ever quite overcome, and short fingernails on his left hand. Violins are the soprano voices of the orchestra. They are divided into two sections, of which the firsts ordinarily play the higher notes. There is a slight sense of superiority among first violinists, but a high ranking second actually outranks a low first. The first-chair first violinist is the assistant conductor, known in the U. S. as "concert master," in Europe as "leader."

THE VIOLAS are the violins' alto cousins. They are slightly

larger but are held and played the same way. It has always been the curse of the viola to play fill-in parts: e.g., the "after-beats," the "pah" of an "oom-pah" in waltzes and marches. Despite the fact that the viola's voice has a rich, haunting quality, the poor violist is only occasionally blessed with solo melodies or with doubling the violins an octave lower or sweeping along with the whole string section in unison passages. Even today, violists are the rarest of string players, many of them ex-violinists who turn to the lower instrument because it is less rigorous. Sadly enough, violists often leave viola playing in favor of such other musical activities as conducting, or they even abandon music altogether in favor of business careers.

THE CELLOS stand on pins and are as big as ten-year-old children. The body of the instrument rests between the knees of the seated player; the fingerboard juts up beside his left ear. Cellos are the rich, sentimental tenors of the string section. In Mannheim days, and for another half century, their biting tone was used almost exclusively to reinforce the thicker, rumbling tones of the basses. It was not until the romantic era that composers fully appreciated the cello's ability to generate sentiment—and cellists themselves developed a reputation as sentimentalists.

THE STRING BASSES are also called "double-basses," "contra basses," "bass viols" or, more descriptively, "bull fiddles." They are the musical foundation upon which the whole orchestral structure rests, and their voices are so low that their music is written an octave higher than it sounds so it can be more easily read. Basses stand as tall as a grown man and rest on the floor like outsize cellos; the players either stand up to play them or sit on high stools. Their strings are so thick that players seem to grip them with their whole hands instead of pressing them with a single finger as a fiddler might. Their tone also is thick and lacks distinctness but can be very rich and rewarding under the sound of a whole orchestra.

THE WOODWINDS are so called because the instruments were originally hollowed out of wooden cylinder The physical principle of their operation is that a column of air, inside the tube, is set into vibration when the player blows the mouthpiece. When the player lifts his fingers from the holes along the cylinder, one by one, he lets air escape and thus shortens the air column and raises the pitch. The lowest note goes through the full length of the tube (all holes covered); the highest notes are produced by a complicated system of cross fingering. Early woodwind instruments were clumsy performers, but musical engineers gradually found ways to increase their flexibility by covering holes with pads instead of fingers and then adding additional holes whose pads were controlled by levers or keys. All woodwinds are held with the left hand closer to the mouthpiece. In the classical orchestra, they usually appear in pairs.

THE FLUTE, like its shrill baby brother, the piccolo, is held transversely. It is sounded by blowing across an open hole, the way a boy blows across a pop bottle. Its tone is the purest of any instrument in the orchestra, judged both subjectively by ear, and scientifically by the simple shape of its acoustical curve; it is delicate in its middle range, piercing on top and its lowest notes have an otherworldly quality.

THE OBOE (from the French *hautbois*) is called a double-reed instrument because of the construction of its mouthpiece. This consists of two narrow (1/4-inch) slivers of tapered bamboo, bound together by silk threads, forming a tiny orifice for the player to breathe through and thus create a buzzing vibration. Oboists carry little kits with razor blades, sandpaper, spare bamboo slivers, etc., to make their own reeds. Before it is ready to be used, the reed must be moistened by holding it in the mouth, then cleared by tooting through it, which accounts for the thin Bronx-cheer sound that accompanies an orchestra tuneup. The oboe is regarded as the instrument of stablest pitch and is the one asked to "sound your A" for the other players to tune to. Its sound resembles a harsher, more penetrating violin tone. When played solo it can be raucous and highly irritating. Since so little air can pass through the orifice between the reeds, the player constantly has the sensation of holding his breath, which abets the rumor that oboists are crazy—if not before they take up the instrument, then soon after. The instrument is one of the most difficult to control and was the first to be called "an ill woodwind that nobody blows good."

THE CLARINET is called a single-reed instrument because its bamboo sliver (considerably larger than the oboe's) is strapped under a beaklike mouthpiece of wood, metal or plastic, rather than being doubled against its twin. It is descended from the ancient chalumeau, and its sweetly rich lower register still bears that name. Its middle register sounds something like an edgier, sandier flute, and its top notes can be shrill and penetrating. It was sparingly used by 18th-century composers (Mozart used it occasionally and wrote solo pieces for it), although it was included in the Mannheim Orchestra. It reached the peak of its popularity in the hands of swing band leader Benny Goodman, when it became known, temporarily, as a "licorice stick."

THE BASSOON is the lowest pitched, ugliest looking and most recalcitrant of the woodwinds. It is a double-reed instrument that resembles its German name, *Fagott* (bundle of sticks), and bears the not altogether affectionate American nickname, "the fighting bedpost." It is a thick

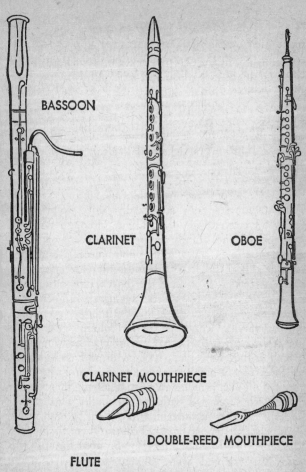

BASSOON

CLARINET

OBOE

CLARINET MOUTHPIECE

DOUBLE-REED MOUTHPIECE

FLUTE

THE WOODWINDS

tube some four feet in length, supported, like a saxophone, by a strap around the player's neck; the butt dangles below his right thigh. It is capable of a beautiful singing tone, with a thin and distant quality, like a saxophone with a cold in its nose. Mannheimers used it mostly to strengthen the cellos, while later composers like Mozart and Beethoven sometimes took advantage of the humor of its popping, rollicking attacks and made it the orchestra's comedian.

BRASSES also produce their tones by causing a column of air to vibrate. They are usually bent into paperclip shapes for convenience of handling, although there are the four-foot-long straight trumpets for such showy occasions as the opera *Aïda*. Brass mouthpieces should, perhaps, be called "lip-pieces," because they are cup-shaped metal pieces that fit against the player's lips rather than between them. The lips vibrate against each other (literally a Bronx cheer) as the air passes into the instrument, and the varying length of the air column controls the pitch. The earliest brasses were similar to hunting horns or bugles: they were plain tubes with no keys or valves. Each instrument had a fundamental tone and could play a limited number of notes above it, following the overtone series. Bach succeeded with fairly complex passages for the high trumpet because he wrote them so high in the overtone series the player could control them by lip pressure alone. But Mannheimers saw no need for such virtuoso displays and were content to use brasses in their middle register for merest punctuation. Their trumpets were little more than noisemakers—along with the kettledrums. Valves, introduced soon afterward, changed the length of the air column in a brass instrument by switching in or out additional tubing; and eventually

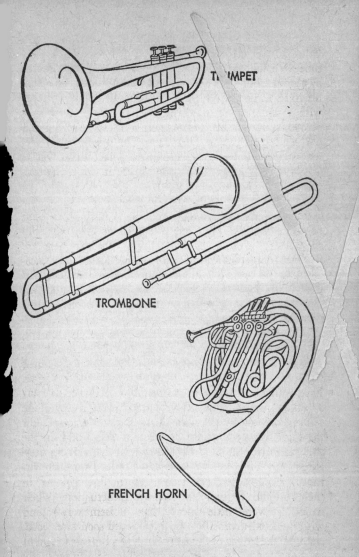

TRUMPET

TROMBONE

FRENCH HORN

THE BRASSES

brasses could play almost as flexibly as woodwinds. Warm, moist air from the player's lungs naturally condenses on the inside walls of brass instruments and puddles in the loops. For drainage, brasses have special "spit-valves" through which the players blow periodically; except French horns which, being more complicated, are drained by being revolved until the moisture runs out the mouthpiece opening.

THE TRUMPETS are the sopranos of the brass section. Today's models are about two feet long, with three piston valves worked by the fingers of the player's right hand, thus giving him eight possible lengths of tubing for eight fundamental tones, each one with a complex of usable overtones. Trumpets are capable of flutey sweetness when used melodically, but Mannheimers used only their blaring, military fortes.

THE TROMBONES are the tenors and baritones of the brass section. They are sometimes found with valves, but the most familiar type is the slide trombone, known in medieval days as the "sackbut." It is shaped like a four-foot hairpin, whose rear loop extends over the player's left shoulder; its bell projects forward just ahead of his face. The variations in length are controlled by the slide, which sticks out in front and is moved by the player's right hand. The trombone is less agile than the trumpet, partly because of the time it takes to move the slide between positions, partly because of the heavier, thicker quality of its voice. It sounds mellow and noble, occasionally martial, and sometimes (because it can "smear" a glissando) humorous. More than any orchestral instrument its sound resembles the human voice. Its performers, according to orchestral humor, are phlegmatic. It is not certain whether this is due to the nature of the music they are given to play or to the nature of the trombone itself.

FRENCH HORNS are the hybrids of the brass section. The occasions when they sound brassy are rare; on the other hand, their more mellifluous, woody qualities are limited by the physics of the same overtone series that governs trumpets and trombones. As a result, they are usually used as go-betweens. They are circular instruments with three valves (on modern instruments), fingered by the left hand. The right is splayed into the bell, which faces to the rear, at about the level of the player's seat. Wrapped into its winding coils are no less than twelve feet of conical brass tubing. Partly because it travels so far, the tone is one of the sweetest—and the instrument one of the trickiest—in the entire orchestra. Where the string and woodwind player, and even the trumpeter, can finger his instrument with fair confidence that the proper note will emerge, the hornist must literally hear every note in his head before he plays it. Otherwise, he is more than likely to come out with a muffled burble or an embarrassing brassy blat. Before valves were invented, horn players lowered pitch artificially, by plugging up the bell with their right fists. This technique permitted the accomplished hornist to produce practically any note he wished; but the results were far from satisfactory, since the so-called "stopped" notes were dim and muffled and uncertain in pitch. Mannheim composers generally wrote simple hunting-call parts for their French horns and hoped for the best.

THE TIMPANI (often misspelled "tympany") were, for many years, the only orchestral drums. They are called kettledrums (in some quarters, "nakers") because of their shape: copper hemispheres with the flat side (the drumhead) on top. Unlike most other drums, the kettles are tunable, within narrow limits, and can thus be used to

KETTLEDRUMS

PADDED TIMPANI STICKS

support the orchestra's most important bass notes. The tuning is accomplished by a system of screw-clamps around the rim of the drumhead; the tighter the sheepskin is stretched, the higher the pitch becomes. Timpani are generally used in groups of two or more to provide a wider variety of notes, and the characteristic sound is a roll (or trill) made by rapid, alternating blows of the two padded sticks.

THE SCORE, technically, is the complete book of notes, in which every sound to be played is written down. In polyphonic music, the voice parts themselves were far more important than their coloration or articulation; even Bach wrote music in which there was no indication of

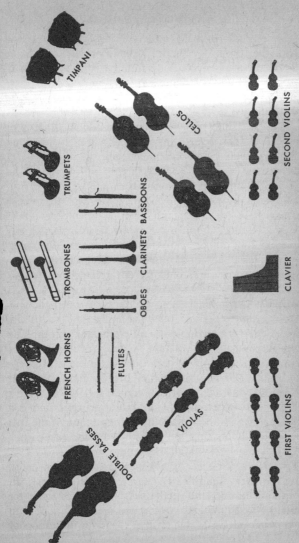

THE CLASSICAL SYMPHONY ORCHESTRA

TIMPANI

CELLOS

TRUMPETS

SECOND VIOLINS

TROMBONES

BASSOONS

CLARINETS

OBOES

CLAVIER

FRENCH HORNS

FLUTES

VIOLAS

FIRST VIOLINS

DOUBLE BASSES

which instruments were to play what parts (and little as to whether the music was to be loud or soft). With the Mannheim school, instrumentation became standardized, and scores began to show similarity in layout. They were written out in ink on sheets of paper which had been ruled into a dozen or more five-line staffs, one for each instrument. The order of instruments, which still rules today, reads downward: flutes, oboes, clarinets, bassoons, horns, trumpets, trombones, percussion, piano (or voices) and strings (first and second violins, violas, cellos and basses). The score is the conductor's part.

THE PARTS. It would be inefficient for each player to have a complete score on his stand when he only needs to read one line of notes; and it is too expensive to have so many copies written out by hand. Efficient shortcuts for reproducing musical notation, usually based on a form of photographic process, are comparatively recent, and still not entirely satisfactory. So a copyist, often the composer himself, must sit down and, selecting one instrument at a time, copies its notes down on separate sheets of manuscript paper. These are known as the instrumental parts. A musician who is familiar with the language of musical notations studies the time signature (which usually indicates two, three, four or six beats per bar), the key signature (the number of sharps or flats indicating which key the movement is to be played in) and can then read the notes. If he is an expert, he instantaneously translates them into fingering, bowing or lipping. If he is a composer, he also "hears" the notes, with all their colors and combinations, inside his head.

Such was the setup of the famed Mannheim Orchestra, whose performances astonished and delighted musicians and laymen of the whole civilized world, and whose influence has affected all concert music since. Mannheim composers and performers found they could move strong men to tears, and they did so at every opportunity. Some listeners said they overdid their abrupt contrasts of loud and soft and their pulse-bumping crescendos, much in the way a modern dance band discovers a pleasing style and works it to death. Nevertheless, Mannheim's theatricality, its blazing orchestral colors and its thumping accents first emancipated Western music from the monochromatics of polyphony, then led it straight toward the violent, personalized conflict of romantic music. Meanwhile, it helped form the classical style.

FATHER OF THE SYMPHONY

HAYDN

ONE WARM EVENING IN VIENNA, a band of young musicians roamed the streets, stopping wherever they thought they saw a likely spot to unsling their instruments and play a serenade or two. If they were lucky, their melodies reached the ears of one of the city's fast-growing population of music-lovers, who might toss out a few coins.

At one point in its wandering, the band halted before the house of a famous clown and ran through its repertory. The comedian poked his head from the window and asked who had written the music. "I did," shouted a stubby, pockmarked youth. "And what is your name?" asked the clown. "Josef Haydn," answered the youth. With that he was ushered up the stairs, and when he returned to his companions, he carried the libretto of a skit for which he had agreed to write the score—for the clown thought his music was very good listening indeed and wanted to hear more of it.

When that incident occurred, Haydn was in his early 20's, living in a sixth-story garret and beginning to make his way around the world of music. By coincidence, for example, one of his cotenants was the famous Italian poet Metastasio, who helped him find a few paying pupils. These were usually young ladies whose parents reasoned that they should learn to accompany themselves on the clavier while they sang, if they expected to make advantageous marriages.

Such good luck would have meant little had Haydn been less energetic. During a typical day, he would rush from one musical meeting to another, first playing fiddle in an early morning church service, then the organ in a nobleman's chapel, then singing tenor in a cathedral service, finally trudging homeward to spend his evening composing and practicing at his harpsichord. This fairly rugged pace was to be characteristic of Haydn's life for the next 55 years, during which he became his world's most renowned composer, and eventually, with Mozart, a synonym for the classical style.

FRANZ JOSEF HAYDN was born on March 31, 1732, and inherited much of his dogged determination and ambition from his father, a master wheelwright in the Austrian town of Rohrau on the Hungarian border. This good man was a fair performer on the lap harp, and he spent many an hour accompanying his own singing—and that of his son, Josef. A cousin noticed that the boy had exceptional musical talent and persuaded the father to pack him off for formal studies before he was six. Josef worked at the violin, the clavier, and at singing. He also played kettledrums in processionals, so legend says, having the bulky instruments strapped to the back of a tiny hunchback so that he could reach them. He paid for his lessons by being handy boy around his teacher's house. His life was so full of chores, both musical and household, that he had little time to himself.

When Haydn was eight, a musician from Vienna's St. Stephen's Cathedral heard him sing and took the boy along to the city of Empress Maria Theresa and of dozens of musical salons. In return for his keep in the choir school and a musical education, Josef sang soprano in the cathedral. The music lessons, unfortunately, were few and far between; Haydn's new benefactor was more interested in furthering his own career than in teaching musical theory to any dirty little choirboy, no matter how beautiful his voice. As a result, Josef learned most of his music by ear.

Fortunately, there was plenty to be heard. Vienna in those days was fairly bursting with late-blooming nobility, composed of sharp-witted merchants who had bought their titles or secured them by cunning, rather than by inheritance. As today's newly rich tycoon might fill his living-room with music from a costly high fidelity phonograph because it is fashionable (and costly), so Vienna's new nobility populated their salons with live musicians. The boys from St. Stephen's were invited to perform often, and Josef managed to station himself close to the tables and feast himself in preparation for the famine he faced back at the cathedral.

Although his profession was, for the moment, singing, the music that fascinated young Haydn was pure or "abstract" music. This music was in the so-called "gallant style"—courtly, decorative, mostly superficial, often high-minded. Vienna's musical heroes at that time were such great composers of the previous generation as the Italian-Spaniard, DOMENICO SCARLATTI (1685-1757), and the Frenchmen FRANÇOIS COUPERIN LE GRAND (1668-1733) and JEAN PHILIPPE RAMEAU (1685-1764). These men filled their scores with frothy decorations in the fashionable manner, but they also experimented with the new methods of evoking emotion in music—methods that included dramatic contrast of light and heavy, loud and soft, major and minor, fast and slow. One of their most important discoveries was the changeable theme that started out gayly, only to change mood midway and end with a

sorrowful cadence. This may seem like a simple eno 'rh
business today, but in a society accustomed to ev ·
tempered counterpoint, which rarely seemed to expr
any feelings at all, it had a startling impact.

In the 1740's, Haydn probably heard little of Scarlatti
music, but he certainly heard plenty of music by one o
the great man's great disciples, CARL PHILIPP EMANUEL
BACH (1714-1788). This was Johann Sebastian Bach's
second and most famous son, whose position as court
harpsichordist to King Frederick earned his music a wide
audience. Haydn, Mozart and Beethoven all spoke of
their debt to this imaginative composer. He wrote more
than 200 brilliant solo clavier pieces, 52 clavier concertos
and 17 "symphonies." History credits him with many important advances in clarifying the formal problems that
beset composers of that unsettled period, but he was
equally interested in stirring his listeners' feelings. He
filled his scores with sighing echoes, tearful effusions and
sudden, surprising twists. Haydn, at least during his youth,
imitated C. P. E. Bach shamelessly.

At the choir school, Haydn suffered from comparison
with his brother Michael, five years his junior and possessor of an especially beautiful voice. When Haydn's own
voice changed, he was evicted from the school. He was 17,
poorly trained and penniless. He was also stubborn; he
refused to hire himself out as a footman or lackey who
could also make a fourth in a string quartet, although
such servants were much in demand. He was, he later recalled, forced to "wander around sorrowfully" until he
could find friends and learn his trade. Wherever he settled, he composed furiously in every form he could imagine or remember.

Haydn's early keyboard sonatas, which he sometimes
called "partitas," closely reflect the fashionable music he

heard in the salons. His melodies are so lyrical and direct they might have been written first for violin and then transferred to the keyboard; his accompaniments are typically the "Alberti bass," a kind of rudimentary boogie-woogie of broken chords; his music often sounds as if it were meant for dancing, but its concert intentions are indicated by the fact that the minuets contain extra "trio" sections, too calm and too slow for dancing.

At the same time Haydn was experimenting with keyboard sonatas, he got started on a medium that fascinated him for the rest of his life: the string quartet. It was a strange hybrid form at that time, derived directly from old-time trio sonatas, which were trios in name only, since the two high voices (usually two violins) and the low cello were spread so far apart that they required the services of a fourth instrument—a clavier—to fill in the gap. Haydn's first string quartets had no keyboard; their primitive filler material was allocated to the viola.

When Haydn was 27, and beginning to whirl in the better musical circles, he had the good fortune to be employed as court composer to a certain Bohemian count. Early in his employment, he composed a little instrumental piece with a resounding title: *Symphony No. 1.* In the noble audience at its first performance was a Hungarian prince named Paul Anton Esterhazy, whose approval was to affect Haydn's career for the next 30 years. One year after the première (and after Haydn's Bohemian patron decided a personal composer was too great a financial burden), Prince Paul remembered that pleasing symphony and signed the composer up for his own court. Haydn became assistant conductor of the court orchestra at Eisenstadt. The contract was signed on May 1, 1761, and its conditions were many:

(1) The aging, incumbent capellmeister would retain

his rank so far as the choir was concerned, but Haydn would preside over the orchestra and "everything else relating to musical performances." (2) As a privileged official of the princely household, "Heyden" agreed to be "temperate, not overbearing toward his musicians but mild and lenient, straightforward and dignified." His uniform in company was to be "white stockings, white linen, and either a powdered queue or a tie-wig." (3) he was to refrain from "undue familiarity" with his musicians and to try and preserve harmony in their ranks. (4) He was to compose on his Serene Highness's command, preserve the resulting music for the princely court exclusively and not to compose for anyone else without the prince's permission. He was to arrange performances, daily if necessary, see that they started punctually and that the band was all present and rehearsed. Also he was to settle its disputes, take charge of its instruments, practice on his own and coach singers. In return, Haydn was to receive a respectable 400 florins a year for three years (the nominal duration of many a modern conductor's contract) plus board at the "officers' table."

Only a man of prodigious energy and human understanding could have carried such a load, and sometimes even Haydn staggered under it. (Once, copying out a new score in the small hours he mixed the staves. When he reached the end, he apologized wryly to himself with the words "written while asleep.") His first job was to improve the orchestra, which had wheezed along for years under the old conductor. Haydn replaced men wherever necessary and drafted the finest talents, starting with the famous violinist Tomasini—whom the prince had hired as a valet—for concert master. When he was through, he had a band of between 16 and 20 players, trained into a competent, homogeneous ensemble.

Once he had the orchestra in hand, Haydn found himself in a position few composers have ever equaled: he was not only paid to compose but had at his service the instrument on which to test every musical experiment as soon as he wrote it down. Today, a 30-year-old composer who hears his latest orchestral music played even once a year considers himself incredibly fortunate.

In the fastness of Eisenstadt, Haydn found himself fairly cut off from the mainstream of music, but in the end, the effect was beneficial. "I was forced," he said later, "to become original." He made early discoveries about the way to write a true string quartet: in his Op. 3, No. 1, he began to free the viola, daringly let it take the melody an octave below the first violin. Elsewhere, feeling the need for closer integration in his scores, he discovered ways to relate secondary themes with the main ones: e.g., by including harmonic or thematic reminiscences and echoes, rather than taking the easy way and simply setting down brand-new ideas one after another. Writing for woodwinds, he began to perceive that each instrument had its own personality and found that those crisp-sounding and unemotional instruments could be made to sing sweetly in slow movements. After experimenting with various numbers of movements for his symphonies and sonatas, he settled on four, and the number became standard for all classical composers.

Prince Paul died just a year after installing his new capellmeister. He was succeeded by his brother Nicholas who was, with good reason, nicknamed "the magnificent." Nicholas was one of the wealthiest men in Europe and liked to wear a diamond-studded coat on state occasions. He traveled far, read widely and was an admirer of—and participant in—the fine arts. For his grand entry into the family castle, he required Haydn to compose no less than five Italian operettas and saw to it that his composer's music graced every other important occasion for the rest of his life.

Prince Nicholas's major plaything was a "castle," designed to rival Versailles, which he built at a cost of more than five million dollars, in the middle of a fever swamp in Hungary. It was named Esterhaza. The climate was foul and the location remote, but the prince was determined to make it a center of culture where he would entertain the world's royalty. Here are excerpts from the prince's own brochure describing Esterhaza.

"In an alley of wild chestnut trees stands the magnificent opera house. The boxes . . . open into charming rooms, each luxuriously furnished with fireplaces, divans, mirrors and clocks. The theater easily holds 400 people. Every day at 6 p.m. there is a performance of an Italian opera *seria* or *buffa,* or of a German comedy, which is always attended by the Prince. . . . Herr Haydn himself conducts. . . . Opposite the opera house is the marionette theater. . . . The puppets are beautifully formed and magnificently dressed. In addition to farces and comedies they also play *opera seria.* The performances in both theaters are open to everyone." The other indoor and outdoor attractions had less to do with the daily routine of Herr Haydn, who was just one of the ranking servants, a peer of the two full-time painters, the librarian, the director of the picture gallery and the landscape gardeners.

Haydn's lack of physical charm was a source of irritation and doubt to him, and so, when the girl of his heart, a pretty young thing named Therese Keller, rejected him in favor of the convent, he wrote an organ concerto for her and married her sister. His mistake was soon apparent, for Anna Maria Haydn was homely, unmusical and barren. Haydn was a middle-aged man of 47 before he encountered the first of his known extramarital loves, an olive-skinned, 19-year-old soprano named Luigia Polzelli. She was inept enough as a singer to require the music master's special attentions and willing enough to deceive her own husband to become Haydn's mistress. Since this relationship began when Haydn was on the threshold of great productivity and inspiration (around 1780) the more generous of Haydn's biographers give her credit for awakening his dormant emotions and opening for him new vistas of musical expression.

There were times when, despite its comforts, the seclusion of Esterhaza was galling to Haydn and even more to his orchestra musicians, who were not allowed to bring their famili s with them. The prince, entranced with his fabulous y, was not concerned with their personal welfare; b Haydn was. To bring the matter discreetly to the ntion of his Serene Highness, Haydn staged one of s subtler practical jokes. It was called the *Farewell* nphony (1772), and it made its point in the last movement. As the piece neared its end, the players finished their parts one by one, snuffed out the candles on their music racks, picked up their music sheets and walked quietly off the stage. Finally, only the concert master remained in the gloom, plaintively fiddling the dying tune. The prince got the point.

Whether or not Luigia was responsible for his romantic crisis, Haydn began to write music that rejected the glimmering past and reached toward the future. He discovered ways to relate separate movements of his works until whole piano sonatas became emotional entities; even the finales became strong, dramatic movements instead of the carefree romps of earlier days. In his Quartet Op. 17, No. 5, he dared to write instrumental recitatives and arias into the slow movements, confident that his musical language was as coherent as if it had words. He filled his scores with interpretive directions such as *affettuoso* (with feeling), *mancando* (dying away) and *scherzando* (sprightly), but even these words were too vague to describe the precise way in which he felt his music should be performed. Once, when he was unable to rehearse a cantata for its première, he wrote out a detailed sheet of instructions for the conductor. Among them: (1) his tempo marks were to be carefully observed, except for the cheerful allegros, which were to be speeded up a bit to add brightness, in deference to the festive occasion; (2) the instrumentalists were on no account to begin their tuttis before the singers had finished their solos; (3) dynamic signs were to be followed right down to the small differences between loud *(f)* and very loud *(ff)*, soft *(p)* and very soft *(pp)*; (4) the conductor was requested to obtain more than one viola, since Haydn now attached greater importance to the inner parts; (5) the works should have at least three or four rehearsals; and (6) he suggested that a bassoon be used to play along with the strong basses, since he had discovered that adding the woodwind gave the part more distinctness.

In 1781, when Haydn was 49 years old, he made an acquaintance that was to have a powerful influence on his future creative life—and indeed, on all European music: he met Wolfgang Amadeus Mozart. The two men were at opposite poles of temperament and experience. Haydn was countrified, clumsy and conscious of his homely, pockmarked appearance; Mozart was only 25, half Haydn's age, a city dandy by comparison, a brilliant success as a clavier player and a man of nervous, high-strung temperament. Nevertheless, the two great men were devoted friends from the time they met, and they saw each other at every opportunity. One of their favorite

pastimes was playing each other's music together at the
keyboard. By some miraculous creative give-and-take, they
supplemented each other, and both of them took huge
musical steps. Mozart insisted that Haydn taught him
how to compose string quartets and dedicated six of his
finest to Haydn in 1785. When he heard another composer
scoffing at a particularly daring passage in a Haydn movement, with the words: "I would never have written that,"
Mozart replied, "Neither would I, and do you know why?
Because neither you nor I would have had such a fine
idea." As for Haydn, he once took Mozart's father aside
and told him, "I say before God as an honest man that
your son is the greatest composer I have ever known,
either in person or by reputation."

By this time, Haydn, Mozart and a score of other composers around Vienna were thoroughly aware that they
were facing an esthetic problem. Back of it all was that
brand-new aural experience, tonality, the sense of key-
feeling that Bach had limned in his *Well-Tempered Clavier*. Tonality was both a challenge and a promise to those
men—a challenge to write purely instrumental music that
could be as big and important as the majestic vocal works
of the past; a promise of a method that could be as comprehensible as written language. To liberate and make use
of the unguessed potentialities of tonality, these composers
evolved a method of composing, a pattern that we call,
confusingly enough, "sonata form." This in its simplest
aspect, is the thematic outline for the first movements of
all classical symphonies, sonatas and string quartets.

On the most obvious level, the sonata form movement
is divided into three parts. The divisions are so clearly
marked that even the inexperienced listener can spot them
with little trouble, for each division starts with the same
(or almost the same) musical idea. The divisions have ac-

quired names that are well-known to students of music appreciation. The exposition contains the first theme, then a transitional bridge passage and a contrasting second theme that is often quieter and more lyrical than the first; the exposition in the works of Haydn and Mozart is generally repeated verbatim. The development follows without pause, usually picking up one or more fragments or sections of the exposition, turning them over, savoring them under different harmonic and rhythmical circumstances, and seeing how far they will go—ideally to the point where the material seems to be used up. The recapitulation, as its name implies, is thematically almost exactly the same as the exposition, and the movement ends with a thorough affirmation of the home key. As this rough outline indicates, the thematic aspects of sonata form are only general; in practice they vary widely.

The harmonic structure of the sonata form was something far more subtle and gripping than the thematic—it was actually the language of tonality. To Haydn and Mozart, the whole idea of tonality was a fresh and urgent matter; the purpose of their sonata form movements was to express tonality.

The foundation of tonality is the overtone series, that amorphous halo of tones that sounds over any musical note in a mathematical pattern. The first few overtones are literally the notes of a major triad, and thus that basic harmony is implied in every single note of the scale. (It is also literally, if faintly, *heard* above low notes, and there is a simple experiment to prove it: play a low C on the piano. Hold the key down as the tone fades away, and listen carefully for fainter notes above. You will distinctly hear a G, an octave and a half higher, and an E a sixth above that. Even musicians of the mid-20th century, who no longer feel the grip of tonality so powerfully, are impressed by this demonstration; it certainly shows the acoustical basis for the triad and for the key-feeling it symbolizes.)

All classical symphonies, string quartets and sonatas were written in and for the thing called tonality. Harmonically, the sonata form expressed tonality in this manner: its first theme was ordinarily in the tonic or home key, often stating the three notes of the triad as an integral part of its theme. The answering theme contrasted not only in mood but in key: it was usually built on the fifth note of the scale (the dominant), and was designed to express the dominant harmony almost as fully as the first theme expressed the tonic. To sensitive 18th-century listeners, this contrast of keys was highly dramatic; for within a scale, five notes is as far away as one can go. On the other hand, the dominant harmony naturally gravitates toward the tonic.

The tonic and dominant are sometimes called the two poles of a tonality, but it may be more descriptive to call the tonic the equator, toward which all other notes tend to slide in the centrifugal course of the music; and the dominant, the north pole. The south pole, then, is the subdominant; its fundamental note is the fourth in the scale; it gets its name from the fact that it is five notes from the tonic, counting downward. It is the third gravitational center in any key. The subdominant harmony is the first chord of the "Amen" in congregational singing, and its peculiarity is that the tonic leads toward *it,* while it continues to lead away from the home-feeling. Sometimes it has to be forcefully brought back by the composer's strength of character. The subdominant in classical sonata form did not ordinarily rate a theme of its own but made its appearance whenever the composer felt the need for a powerful emotional contrast.

Haydn, having outlined the fundamental structure of a key in his opening statements (the exposition), would begin to explore the tonal implications of his thematic material (in the development). He might, in a daring move, concentrate on a section of his melody that was not even a part of the triad, a section whose melodic tensions led the harmony to distant points. He would allow the music to modulate and actually arrive at a new key—perhaps a key that had very few notes in common with the original tonic scale. The fewer notes the new key had in common with the old, the more "distant" it was and the more daring his explorations. Eventually, he concluded his harmonic adventures and returned to a point where he could restate his original themes (in the recapitulation) and wind up safely in the home key, leaving no listeners feeling lost in the harmonic byways of his imagination. Just in case some might not have the home-feeling fixed in mind, Haydn would usually hammer out the last chords at full volume, over and over, until it was clear to everyone that the end was secure.

During the 1780's, Haydn wrote his six quartets, Op. 33, called "Russian" because they were dedicated to Russia's Grand Duke Paul, with the comment that they were "composed in an entirely new and particular manner " By this Haydn meant that he was able to give all four strings equal importance, even the benighted viola playing music that took its shape from some aspect of the main themes. This was, in a sense, a return to polyphonic methods, for Haydn was well aware that horizontally flowing counterpoint could never be replaced as a method of urging music through time. Sometimes, in the 18 quartets that he was still to write, Haydn built whole new movements out of single subjects, reverting to "horizontal thought" in the highest polyphonic tradition.

By the mid 1780's, Haydn had written some 75 of his 104 symphonies. Some of them reveal their charms today only after familiarity and an effort of study; like oriental faces to occidental eyes, works written in a preclassical or even an early classical idiom tend to seem indistinguishable to postromantic listeners. Many of Haydn's symphonies, however, sing with ineffable beauty in any age. Among them are the six *Paris* symphonies (Nos. 82-87), written at the request of French publishers, one symphony improbably nicknamed "The Bear" because of its bagpipe dance finale, another "The Chicken" for its clucking second theme.

One of the many personages who commissioned Haydn was the Canon of Cadiz. His was a special request. Each Lent, from the pulpit of the great cathedral, the Bishop pronounced Christ's seven dying sentences, descending after each to prostrate himself before the altar. The Canon asked Haydn to supply the music for the interludes. With characteristic energy, the composer not only wrote orchestral interludes but set the words as well for baritone solo. "It was no easy matter," he wrote later, "to compose seven adagios lasting ten minutes apiece, one after the other, without tiring the listeners." Nevertheless, the *Seven Last Words of Christ on the Cross* turned out to be a huge success. Haydn later arranged it for string quartet. It was played across Europe soon after its première, and even in the fledgling United States, as early as 1793.

The benevolent Prince Nicholas died in 1790 and, although his successor asked Haydn to stay on, the composer no longer felt obliged to seclude himself. He was well aware that he belonged, by then, to the whole world. As soon as he could decently leave, he fled to his beloved Vienna. In that city one day he received a visitor who introduced himself as Johann Peter Salomon, a leading concert manager from London, who offered to take Haydn to London for a series of public appearances.

Haydn happily spent most of his trip across the channel on the pitching deck but admitted that he was "seized with slight alarm" and "a little indisposition" when the wind and waves became very strong. He gazed at sprawling London with awed eyes and wrote in his diary the astonishing fact that in 31 years, 38,000 houses had been built there, and that the city annually consumed 800,000 cartloads of coal. He found the din of the street hawkers unbearable. When he received a British "hip-hip-hurrah!" at a fashionable dinner party, another guest reported, Haydn put his hands over his face and was disconcerted for several minutes.

No matter how trying its social life, London's musical life was anything but disconcerting. Haydn found himself the center of attraction. Salomon had scheduled a series of gala concerts in which the master was to preside at the keyboard (the days when a conductor stood alone and directed the players by waving a baton was yet to come), but Londoners were much more experienced concert-goers than continentals and were not to be conquered by advance publicity alone. Among the competing attractions of a busy season, including performances in two opera houses and a series of "ancient" concerts, Haydn was faced with a rival orchestral series. Feeling ran high between Haydn's camp and the opposition. Some newspapers, no less prone to partisan reporting than they are today, pointed out unkindly that Haydn was an old man and probably well past the crest of his powers.

Nevertheless, Haydn's debut at the Salomon concerts was a spectacular success. Dr. Burney, an omnivorous dilettante who documented an incredible amount of 18th-century music, was there, and reported that Haydn's "electrical" effects aroused the crowd "almost . . . to frenzy." Another reporter called him the "first musical genius of the age" and expressed the hope he would follow Handel's example of 75 years before and settle in England for good. The orchestra that Salomon had engaged for the series was a powerful body compared to Haydn's relatively small ensemble at Esterhaza. It had 16 violins, four violas, three cellos and four basses, in addition to woodwinds and brass. The volume and perfection of its performance impressed the composer strongly and undoubtedly left him with a more ambitious approach to his future compositions.

Another new influence on Haydn was Handel's music, which he first heard, appropriately enough, in Westminster Abbey, where an ensemble of 1,000 performed *The Messiah*. Haydn listened and marveled. When the climactic "Hallelujah Chorus" rang out, he burst into tears, exclaiming, "He is the master of us all."

Honors kept coming his way, among them a rarely offered doctorate at Oxford University. He accepted gratefully; his "thesis" was not, however, the misnamed *Oxford* Symphony, but another (No. 92) of the twelve he composed for his two visits to London.

These stirring experiences combined to work a change in old Haydn. All his life he had been turning out music to order, and doubtless he thought of it primarily as a commodity: once performed, its usefulness was over, or at least seriously diminished. But now he began to think in terms of writing for posterity. After all, the English still listened to Handel and they were calling Haydn, too, a "great" composer.

Strangely enough, this realization, which might have made a lesser man turn back on himself to become repetitious and conservative, made Haydn more radical than ever. He composed carefully, but he felt free to make more and more daring musical experiments. He abandoned the practice of literal repetition in his recapitulation and continued to compose new music right down to his climactic codas. His finales contained as much dramatic excitement and thematic development as his first movements, foreshadowing the massive symphonies of Beethoven himself. Harmonically, he ventured into more distant keys and playfully interjected strange harmonies here and there.

Still not above playing jokes on his fashionable audience, Haydn wrote a prankish experiment in the slow movement of his Symphony No. 94. After the fairly stringent opening movement, at a moment when the audience could be expected to be relaxing to the accompaniment of a pretty melody, the full orchestra lashed into a fortissimo chord that must have startled the last nodding listener. Naturally, everybody stayed awake to see if it would happen again, but with sure artistic judgment, Haydn never repeated the blast. Inevitably, the work was called the *Surprise* Symphony.

The improvements Haydn made in his symphonies after that were all in the direction of added compactness and coherence. By now fully capable of carrying out any innovation that occurred to him, he began to tie all his movements together by interlocking references to early themes. Hearing a fragment of the allegro during the adagio, the listener seems to recognize an old friend, and the work becomes more unified.

Haydn constantly created new effects. In the minuet of No. 100 (the *Military*) he dared to let two flutes and an oboe carry the trio without any accompaniment whatsoever. The symphony's nickname comes from Haydn's use of extra percussion instruments (triangle, cymbals, bass drum) and from the solo trumpet call at the end of the slow movement. In the slow movement of the *Clock* Symphony (No. 101), he created a ticking accompaniment of bassoons and pizzicato strings. In No. 102 he scored for muted trumpets and timpani. He opened No. 103 (the *Drumroll*) with a roll on the timpani.

All of these works are rich in the kind of warmth that is sometimes thought to be Mozart's private property. It is true that Haydn liked to compose with bland good humor, but more and more he turned to musical introspection and melancholy. One of his most somber symphonies is his No. 97, which he wrote after news reached him of Mozart's premature death.

Increasingly convinced that his music had elements of immortality, Haydn began to feel the stirrings of a masterpiece. But before he was ready for it, he had a lot of living to do. Remote as ever from "that infernal beast," his wife, and separated physically from Luigia, he found a new attraction in the person of a Mrs. Schroeter. She was the widow of the "Queen's Musick Master," and Haydn was so devoted to her, he declared he would have married her if he had been single. As it was, he saw her often and between times wrote letters that, if not actually passionate, were certainly indiscreet. In addition to constant composition and public appearances, Haydn found time to travel about the countryside and be incredibly social, despite his sketchy understanding of English. He remained in England for 18 months and when he left, it was with the promise to return.

Back in Vienna, Haydn found everything changed. Mozart was dead, and Marianne von Gensinger, a very dear lady friend, died not long after his return. He continued a nominal relationship with Esterhaza, but there

was little pleasure in it for him. He also continued to teach a little. Among his pupils in 1794 was an arrogant young man, Ludwig van Beethoven, who had traveled to Vienna to study with Mozart and accepted old Haydn as second choice (he did have the grace to keep the fact from Haydn). Haydn endured Beethoven's stormy temperament as best he could, although he called him "that great mogul" behind his back.

Back in London in 1794, Haydn led a fine, big orchestra of 60 players with tremendous success. In the fall of that year, tardily enough, his triumph was confirmed when he was officially introduced to King George III. But Haydn's earlier enthusiasm for London began to fade. The music he heard sounded terribly flawed. "One young fellow sang an aria so dreadfully that I began to perspire all over my body," he wrote in his diary. Finally, when still another Prince Esterhazy (a second Prince Nicholas) asked him to return to his court, the composer prepared to make his last channel crossing. He returned to Eisenstadt in the summer of 1795, determined, he said, to write a work that would give permanent fame to his name.

The work was a full-scale cantata, *The Creation*. Its text, from the book of *Genesis* and Milton's *Paradise Lost,* was translated and arranged by the same irascible but talented Baron von Swieten who had advised Mozart's widow to bury him in a pauper's grave to save money. When the words were arranged to Haydn's satisfaction, he sat down and for three years labored over his score. They were years of great happiness for the master. Although he had always written *laus deo* at the end of a composition, he had never before been able to sing the praises of God so specifically and at such length. When he felt his inspiration waning he left his piano and his composing desk to say his rosary, with, he reported, consistent success.

The Creation was first presented at a concert in 1799, with such public excitement that mounted police were called in to control the crowds. To tell the story of the world's beginning, Haydn used three narrators: soprano, tenor and bass. The music has much of the majestic simplicity of Handel's oratorios. At times it sounds naïve, sometimes it froths with earthy humor, sometimes it is as reverent as Bach. *The Creation* could hardly have failed. Actually, it was soon repeated and continued to be performed before enraptured crowds. Haydn himself was handsomely paid in cash.

Although he had thought of *The Creation* as his last big work, Haydn continued to compose on the grandest scale. Two years later, at great cost in health and energy, he finished another large-scale oratorio, *The Seasons,* which bubbled even more with the joy of creation. During that period, one of fervent nationalism, Haydn was inspired to compose the song *(Gott erhalte)* that was immediately adopted as Austria's national anthem.

In the year 1801, tired and arthritic, Haydn was convinced that his creative life was over. He made occasional appearances as conductor of his own works when his swollen legs permitted him, but spent most of his time talking with biographers and preparing an exhaustive, if not quite accurate, catalogue of his compositions. In 1805 a rumor circulated that he was dead. His friend Cherubini and the violinist Kreutzer composed memorial music, and Mozart's *Requiem* was being rehearsed for a funeral service in Paris when word arrived that the old man was still very much alive.

By the time the Napoleonic armies bombarded Vienna in 1809, Haydn had already read his generous will to his household. As explosions shook the area he gathered his friends and servants around him and told them, "Don't be frightened, children. Where Haydn is nothing can happen to you." Nothing did, as it turned out, and Napoleon saw to it that a guard of honor was placed around the composer's door. A few weeks later Haydn died, and a warring continent took time off to mourn him.

His body was not to rest in peace. Shortly after his burial, outside the Esterhazy estate, his grave was opened by a pair of students of phrenology, who decapitated him because they wished to caliper his skull and take the measure of genius. The loss was not discovered for many years, not, in fact, until the Esterhazy family was finally convinced their erstwhile servant was indeed a great man and decided to move his grave to a more honored spot. The headless skeleton was discovered, and there followed a comic opera plot of intrigue: the Esterhazys trying to reunite skull and skeleton in their grave, the possessors of the skull refusing to relinquish their treasure. For nearly a century the skull reposed in a glass box in a Vienna museum while negotiations and threats raged. In 1954, the Communists who controlled the Esterhazy grounds in Hungary concluded an agreement with the possessors of the head, and Haydn's skull and bones were at last reunited in their crypt.

A TOUCH OF THE INFINITE

MOZART

WOLFGANG AMADEUS MOZART was one of the world's first free-lance composers, though not entirely by his own choice. Society did not know how to support such a being —and still does not, for the most part—and that fact is at the core of Mozart's tragedy.

He was one of those men who turn up at the proper moment in history to fill out and refine ideas initiated by others; not to invent new forms or a new language but to enrich and expand the language that already exists. His language was the classical style. Without ruffling its placid surface, he warmed its graceful musical forms with his energy, his joys and his sorrows. Before he died, he had written down some 600 compositions, many of them works of perfection and few of them less than first-rate music. The world he left, at the age of 36, barely knew how much richer it was.

Mozart was born in Salzburg, Austria, on January 27, 1756, six years after the death of Bach, and possibly during the same year that Haydn's serenade so pleased the Viennese comedian. The child was starred for a musical career. Leopold Mozart, his father, was an excellent musician with a steady job as assistant capellmeister in the court of the Archbishop of Salzburg. When Wolfgang was three, he began to duplicate his 7-year-old sister's keyboard lessons by ear. Leopold noticed this and soon found that Wolfgang had a most sophisticated ear indeed; not only could the boy tell when a violin was a fraction of a note out of tune, but he had a clear idea of which combinations of notes were pleasant to hear, and which clashed. The good—if overambitious—Leopold recognized a marketable commodity when he saw one and prepared the boy and his talented sister, "Nannerl," for public appearances. Thus began a life of traveling in search of wealth and renown that was as successful in public acclaim as any man could ask—but more frustrating financially than any should deserve.

It began with two tours of Europe, including a visit to England, during which the seven-year-old "prodigy of nature" repeatedly astonished crowds of music-lovers with his technique on the harpsichord, his musical memory and his ability to improvise sonatas, fantasias and fugues on themes presented to him by strangers. Royalty was entranced by the youngster's performance; in London he was examined at length by learned professors, who stared at his answers to their tests, conferred together incredulously, and finally pronounced him a true prodigy.

In spite of long hours of weary coach travel and a busy schedule of appearances, the lad seemed never to lose his buoyant spirits or his endearing charm. He heartily kissed the Empress Maria Theresa, chided Madame Pompadour for being too standoffish and rebuked a famous fiddler for careless playing—all without serious repercussions. In Vienna he was so much in demand his visits were scheduled a week in advance. As reward for his genius, he was loaded down with watches, snuff boxes, a toothpick case and clothes, to the chagrin of Leopold. "Neither the innkeeper nor the postmaster can be paid in kisses," he complained.

In Bavaria, aged seven, "Wolferl" saw his first pipe organ and astonished everybody by walking up and down on the pedals and playing it professionally—"as if," his father wrote, "he had been practicing a long time." The next year, four of his piano sonatas were published in Paris, while society marveled that a lowly German child could display so much of the passion that music-lovers liked to think was the private property of Italians. Young Wolfgang, in fact, was already composing constantly, if not yet perfectly (his sonatas of 1762 contain examples of those slithering nightmares of the beginning counterpoint student called "parallel fifths").

Leopold was diligent in his efforts to win a big success for his son while the boy was young enough to attract attention. In Vienna, he wangled an imperial request for Wolfgang to write an opera. "Where is my boy more likely to succeed than in the theater?" he wrote. The work was called *La Finta Simplice,* but it was not performed because of an epidemic of smallpox, which the 13-year-old Wolfgang duly caught and threw off. But that summer he wrote another opera, and this one was performed. It was a pretty trifle called *Bastien und Bastienne,* and it was played in the Viennese garden of the discoverer of animal magnetism, the same Dr. Mesmer who contributed "mesmerism" to the world.

Mozart's next concert tour was just as impressive as the first in terms of public recognition, and more so in terms of experience; for it was a tour of Italy, the birthplace and home of opera. He continued to astonish musicians who heard him. He was just 14 when he went to hear the Papal choir sing the famous *Miserere,* a work so sacred that nobody was allowed to copy it. Mozart went home and wrote it out from memory, then returned once to listen again and correct his few mistakes. Instead of punishing him, the Pope awarded him the Order of the Golden Spur; and for a while, Wolfgang playfully signed his letters *Chevalier de Mozart.*

In his 15th year, Mozart appeared in Mantua in a typical program. The announcement of that program listed the following attractions: "A clavier concerto, which will be handed to him, and which he will immediately play at sight; a sonata handed to him in the same manner, which he will provide with variations and then repeat in another key; an aria, the words of which will be handed to him, which he will set to music and then sing himself, to his own accompaniment on the clavier; a strict fugue on a theme to be selected, which he will improvise on the clavier; a trio in which he will improvise the violin part. . . ." It should be noted that the bulk of Mozart's public success came from his performances while a prodigy, rather than from his originality as a composer. As a matter of fact, most of the great composers were acclaimed primarily for their performing skill, a fact that has often been misinterpreted by those who like to think that earlier composers were more popular in their day than "modern" composers are in theirs.

While he was in Italy, Mozart won membership in the coveted Philharmonic Society of Bologna, after astonishing the judges by finishing a four-hour composition examination in one hour. In Milan his opera, *Mitridate, Rè di Ponto,* was a huge success and had no less than 20 performances in 1770-71 under his own direction. And, about that time, his voice changed. With manhood, he began to taste the bitterness and frustration of a musician's life, as well as some of its sweetest fruits.

Mozart's mature life was riddled with problems. The first that he recognized was the Archbishop Heironymus of Salzburg. When Mozart returned from Italy, aged 17, things there had changed. The previous Archbishop, who had been his friendly protector, was dead and Heironymus had been installed. Leopold was third capellmeister, and Mozart was employed for the time being as court concert master. Very soon it became clear that the new ruler had no respect for music. He allowed his 100-odd court musicians to develop slovenly musical habits, resented every sign of Mozart's success as a composer and frustrated his undisguised search for a more congenial position. Heironymus is said to have been impressed only by men of imposing physical stature. Mozart was short, slight and boyish, and the titled churchman frequently insulted him. Nevertheless, Mozart spent four years of constant composing and maturing in the Archbishop's services. During this time he shed many of the frivolous qualities of the Italian style and began to display some of the soberer beauties of Germanic counterpoint.

Meanwhile, when he was 18, Wolfgang received a commission from Maximilian, Elector of Bavaria, to write a comic opera *(opera buffa)* for Munich. This could have meant a chance to leave Salzburg forever, and Mozart set to work with a will. The opera was *La Finta Giardiniera,* a delightful score whose performance was interrupted time and again by thunderous applause and cries of *"Viva maestro!"* It also got high praise from the musical press: "If Mozart is not a forced hothouse plant, he must become one of the greatest composers that have ever lived," wrote the critic Christian Schubart after the performance. Nevertheless, the Elector failed to reward Mozart with the expected court appointment, or even with another commission for the next year. The young man gloomily returned to Salzburg, and to the Archbishop's chilly presence. There, he worked at his violin playing and amused himself by writing some 30 instrumental works, including his five violin concertos and the lovely *Haffner Serenade*. Every chance he got, he left town in search of a better position, until eventually the Archbishop flatly refused to let the composer go on "another begging expedition." Mozart lost his temper and resigned, forever, he thought, from the Archbishop's employ.

He was 21 when he started his last grand tour, heading for Paris with his mother. It was his first trip without the experienced presence of his father, but Leopold mailed advice with every post. The tour was, he pointed out, for the purpose of increasing Mozart's fame and money supply, and securing him a worthwhile position. Only the first of these objectives was realized to any degree. It is difficult to see what went wrong. Were Mozart's enemies really powerful enough to frustrate success at every crucial point —as he and Leopold firmly believed—or, as some scholars are forced to conclude, was Mozart simply fated to worldly failure?

In any event, the fault was not Leopold's; he contributed the very best advice. He was a fine musician and was capable of training the boy and displaying him to good advantage. For the first decade of his musical life, Wolfgang had been more than dutiful. His head was constantly full of music, and nothing could suit him better than to write it down—and then hear it, for no composition is truly born until it is performed in public. We cannot say it was Leopold's fault that his *wunderkind*'s appearances paid off less handsomely than he had hoped. Perhaps the older man's stiff-backed personality stood in the way of a court position for his son, or perhaps Wolfgang himself could not put on the frothy kind of show that noblemen liked to stage in their courts. He certainly could not flatter their ignorance or commend a mediocre performance, and such honesty was bound to make enemies.

The following are some characteristic words of advice from father to son.* Leopold warns Wolfgang on his easygoing nature: "You are too ready to answer jestingly on every occasion." He gives an order: "You will not lose sight of your main object, which is to make money." Some psychology: "Never play carelessly, or people will think you consider yourself a great performer." In loco parentis: "Be very careful of the paving stones in Paris in wet weather . . . extremely slippery." The jealous musician: "If [the famous composer] Gluck and Piccini are there you will avoid their company as much as possible, and you must not form a close friendship with [that other one,] Gretry." How to be successful: "When composing consider not only the musical [listeners] but also the unmusical . . . to every ten connoisseurs there are a hundred ignoramuses . . . do not neglect the so-called popular style, which tickles long ears." (Mozart's answer was that he wrote music "for all kinds of people, but not for the long-eared.") On keeping an orchestra happy: "Each performer, even the most inferior viola player, is deeply touched by personal praise and becomes much more zealous and attentive." Stern wisdom (trying to head off a poor marriage): "Now it depends solely on your good sense . . . whether you die as an ordinary musician, utterly forgotten by the world, or as a famous capellmeister . . . whether captured by some woman, you die bedded on straw in an attic surrounded by starving children [or] after a Christian life spent in contentment, honor and re-

* The Letters of Mozart and His Family, translated by Emily Anderson, London, 1938.

nown, you leave this world . . . your name respected by all."

During this tour Mozart dutifully made several tries for a permanent position. He challenged a Munich nobleman to gather every composer possible from any part of the world, and he would "dare compete with them all." In Augsburg he made a few florins by public concerts. In Mannheim he waited out half the winter for word from the Elector but failed to win an appointment. In Paris he was in great demand as clavier player and violinist but earned neither much money nor a position.

The tour had its compensations. In Augsburg, Mozart made friends with the piano maker, Andreas Stein. He was in one of his prankish moods on the day of the first encounter and introduced himself incognito, astonishing the craftsman with his playing. "I prefer Stein's pianofortes," he wrote to his father. "In whatever way I touch the keys, the tone is always even. . . . He guarantees the sounding board will neither break nor split. When he finishes one he places it in the open air, exposing it to the rain, snow, the heat of the sun and all the devils in order that it may crack. Then he inserts wedges and glues them in."

The next month (November, 1777), Mozart found himself in Mannheim, the birthplace of German opera, and was caught up in the general enthusiasm to produce German opera that could rival the melodious Italian opera of Pergolesi, Piccini, Salieri, and the dramatic French opera of Gluck and Gretry. He took delight in the Mannheim orchestra and especially in the orchestra's pair of clarinets ("You cannot imagine what a wonderful effect an orchestra with flutes, oboes and clarinets makes," he wrote to his father), and he became friends with most of the musicians and had fine success with his clavier playing. He heard quantities of music, besides his own, and made a comment that shows the musical vitality of those times: "I heard a Mass by Holzbauer," he wrote. "It is already 26 years old, but good." All the while, he was so anxious to compose that he wrote, "I would rather neglect the clavier than composition." He did not neglect either one, and neither did he slight his love life: one of the reasons for his long dalliance in Mannheim was a pretty young singer named Aloysia Weber.

Whenever possible Mozart played piano with local orchestras, and before he finished, turned out a total of 23 large concertos for his own use. Each one of them was not only a handsome vehicle for his astonishing, spirited and gracious keyboard technique but also a masterpiece. In his hands, the piano concerto grew into a form of major importance. Instead of its previous status as a diversion for the elite, it became vital and full of tension. Melodic contours began to assume extramusical, almost human meanings, and climaxes resembled man's crises of joy and anger; form seemed to grow in a natural manner.

Because of their length and complexity, concertos ordinarily contain only three movements. The first movement resembles the sonata form movement of the classical symphony and quartet, except that the solo instrument has its own opportunity to play the theme, usually after the orchestra has finished its whole exposition; there, as well, the soloist may have a new tune of his own to contribute. The contrasting colors and textures between piano and orchestra made it possible for Mozart to extend the sonata structure like a cantilevered bridge. The second movement is generally a tender and lyrical dialogue between piano and orchestra; the finale may find the soloist dashing about in fine bravura passages to storm up an impressive closing climax. Just before the final cadence, Mozart inserted a

cadenza, an extended showy solo which, for all its dazzle, is nothing more than a long-winded resolution of the suspenseful, tonic six-four chord. Cadenzas were usually improvised in Mozart's day, serving to impress the audience with the performer's technique and inventiveness. Later, as virtuosos developed technique at the expense of inventiveness, most cadenzas were written down and memorized along with the rest of the work.

When he was 29, Mozart completed his D minor piano concerto. This was his first concerto in the strong and portentous minor mode and the most daringly dramatic of all his concertos: it was the one that marks him as the forerunner of Beethoven. The following year, while working on *The Marriage of Figaro,* in a rush of creativity he completed two more: the serene and delightful A major, and less than a month later, the C minor, one of the great concertos of all time. In the richly colored C minor, the orchestra's wind section is more complete than in any other Mozart concerto, comprised of the usual single flute, and pairs of oboes, clarinets, bassoons and trumpets. Here, more than ever, Mozart combined his solo instrument and orchestra in a symphonic structure of imposing grandeur and permitted himself to wander as far as the key of F sharp major (in the first movement) without ever seeming to lose track of the basic tonality.

Mozart's playing of his own concertos was the marvel of professionals as well as amateurs. "Everyone is always amazed that I can always keep strict time," he wrote. In *tempo rubato* in an adagio, the left hand should go on playing in strict time, he explained, while the right at first languishes behind, then speeds up to come out even at the end of each phrase.

Mozart finally completed his meandering trip to Paris in March, 1778. The city was enthusiastic about music, and particularly about Mozart's ways of making music, but no Parisian offered him a job. However, it was in Paris that Mozart made the acquaintance of the French school of opera (headed by the great Gluck, about whom Leopold warned his son), which he absorbed effortlessly as usual, and which became the final element in his development as a well-rounded opera composer. He had already soaked up all he needed of the lyrical, frivolous Italian style and the more earthbound German opera. French opera was strongest in dramatic consistency and poetic freedom, with a fondness for forceful declamation and with a nice balance of serious and comic elements. Mozart had assimilated all three styles by the time he was ready to compose his greatest masterpieces, *Don Giovanni (Don Juan), Le Nozze di Figaro (The Marriage of Figaro), Così fan tutte, (Women Are Like That)* and *Die Zauberflöte (The Magic Flute).*

Paris had nothing more tangible to offer him. Indeed, discouragements mounted: his mother died while they were there, and his father never ceased his steady barrage of pleas for a return to Salzburg. Even discounting the Archbishop, Mozart found Salzburg barely bearable: its speech and manner of living were quite insufferable to him. But, at the end of summer, 1778, he was convinced that things would be better there—that the Archbishop would give him better pay and would eventually advance him to a position of rank in the court. With a heavy heart, he departed for home.

The degree of his reluctance may be gauged by the detours he made on the way. He stayed for another month at Mannheim, visiting his friends in the orchestra. Then he went to Munich to pursue his suit of Aloysia Weber, and there she rejected him, probably thinking he would never be able to keep up with her promising career as a cadenza, an extended showy solo which, for all its dazzle, is nothing more than a long-winded resolution of the suspenseful, tonic six-four chord. Cadenzas were usually improvised in Mozart's day, serving to impress the audience with the performer's technique and inventiveness. Later, as virtuosos developed technique at the expense of inventiveness, most cadenzas were written down and memorized along with the rest of the work.

When he was 29, Mozart completed his D minor piano concerto. This was his first concerto in the strong and portentous minor mode and the most daringly dramatic of all his concertos: it was the one that marks him as the forerunner of Beethoven. The following year, while working on *The Marriage of Figaro,* in a rush of creativity he completed two more: the serene and delightful A major, and less than a month later, the C minor, one of the great concertos of all time. In the richly colored C minor, the orchestra's wind section is more complete than in any other Mozart concerto, comprised of the usual single flute, and pairs of oboes, clarinets, bassoons and trumpets. Here, more than ever, Mozart combined his solo instrument and orchestra in a symphonic structure of imposing grandeur and permitted himself to wander as far as the key of F sharp major (in the first movement) without ever seeming to lose track of the basic tonality.

Mozart's playing of his own concertos was the marvel of professionals as well as amateurs. "Everyone is always amazed that I can always keep strict time," he wrote. In *tempo rubato* in an adagio, the left hand should go on playing in strict time, he explained, while the right at first languishes behind, then speeds up to come out even at the end of each phrase.

Mozart finally completed his meandering trip to Paris in March, 1778. The city was enthusiastic about music, and

particularly about Mozart's ways of making music, but
no Parisian offered him a job. However, it was in Paris
that Mozart made the acquaintance of the French school
of opera (headed by the great Gluck, about whom Leopold warned his son), which he absorbed effortlessly as
usual, and which became the final element in his development as a well-rounded opera composer. He had already
soaked up all he needed of the lyrical, frivolous Italian
style and the more earthbound German opera. French
opera was strongest in dramatic consistency and poetic
freedom, with a fondness for forceful declamation and
with a nice balance of serious and comic elements. Mozart
had assimilated all three styles by the time he was ready
to compose his greatest masterpieces, *Don Giovanni (Don
Juan), Le Nozze di Figaro (The Marriage of Figaro),
Così fan tutte, (Women Are Like That)* and *Die Zauber-
flote (The Magic Flute)*.

Paris had nothing more tangible to offer him. Indeed,
discouragements mounted: his mother died while they
were there, and his father never ceased his steady barrage
of pleas for a return to Salzburg. Even discounting the
Archbishop, Mozart found Salzburg barely bearable: its
speech and manner of living were quite insufferable to
him. But, at the end of summer, 1778, he was convinced
that things would be better there—that the Archbishop
would give him better pay and would eventually advance
him to a position of rank in the court. With a heavy heart,
he departed for home.

The degree of his reluctance may be gauged by the detours he made on the way. He stayed for another month
at Mannheim, visiting his friends in the orchestra. Then
he went to Munich to pursue his suit of Aloysia Weber,
and there she rejected him, probably thinking he would
never be able to keep up with her promising career as a

play a melody together—often supported harmonically by other instruments—the quartet is more like four separate soloists, none of them capable of playing chords for very long, none free enough of contrapuntal duties to support another by doubling his melody, none sufficiently distinct from the others in tone color or dynamic level to provide much variety of sound. Sensuous sound effects are rare in string quartets, and broadly dramatic music is almost unheard of. It is concentrated music, and it takes concentration for the listener to apprehend it.

Mozart had had little use for the form in the ten years previous to 1783: nobody wanted to commission quartets, and Mozart had no need to write any for his own use. Under the stimulus of his friendship with Haydn, however, he started to write them again. In them Mozart reaches a peak of classical perfection—establishing balance between voices and between formal divisions, introducing cool and fastidious colors and textures, and doing the expected thing but doing it so that it almost seems unexpected. The quartets are clearly something more than perfect objects of a craftsman's skill; theirs is the distinct but indefinable quality that music-lovers associate with spirituality.

These qualities are most clearly found in the slow introduction to the C major quartet, the passage that gives it its distinguishing nickname, *Dissonant*. This extraordinary passage begins with a pulsing repeated bass note that creates a sense of expectancy. Gradually the feeling swells as other parts enter. Twice it reaches a high point of anguished dissonance that continues to stretch and strain as it seeks resolution. Although other instances of this spiritual feeling abound in Mozart, none is so clear—or so controversial—as this one. It is one of the classical period's most remarkable movements. Even Haydn was perplexed about it; when somebody asked him if it could possibly be correct, he shrugged and said that Mozart must have had his own reasons for doing it that way.

Some time in 1785 a Venetian schoolmaster named Lorenzo da Ponte turned up in Vienna, where he later became poet laureate. He and Mozart soon found they saw eye to eye on that most recalcitrant of art forms, the operatic libretto, and between them created three of the finest: *The Marriage of Figaro, Don Giovanni* and *Così fan tutte*. Mozart's father thought the first was surely headed for disaster, because he could see nothing but trouble in the Beaumarchais political satire from which it was taken. As it happened, neither could Wolfgang, and he made sure politics were kept out of the text—a masterpiece of frothy humor and human pathos, set in a puzzle of mistaken identity, thwarted intrigue and unthwarted amour. Today, *Figaro* is Mozart's most popular opera, but it failed resoundingly everywhere it was played during his lifetime except in Prague.

The next year, Mozart and Da Ponte finished *Don Giovanni,* a great opera, full of thoroughly disagreeable characters. Tragedy, in the person of the superamorous Don is relieved by rustic buffo characters who are made all too credible through Mozart's profound ability to sketch human personalities in music. Mozart is supposed to have written the *Don Giovanni* overture in a stagecoach the night before its première. The story is probably true, but it does not mean that he sketched it hastily. On the contrary, he had the music completed to the last detail in his head, like everything he wrote, and the act of jotting the notes down was little more than a job of copying. Mozart said that *Don Giovanni* was not composed for Viennese people. "It is better suited to Prague," he wrote, "but to tell the truth, I wrote it for myself and my friends." The work was a failure wherever it was performed, although it had 15 command performances in Vienna, and to this day remains a bittersweet connoisseur's work.

In the summer of 1788, in a perfect frenzy of composition, Mozart wrote his three finest symphonies, No. 39 in E flat, No. 40 in G minor and No. 41 in C major (the *Jupiter*). These three last symphonies sum up all the best of Mozart's previous instrumental style, and even surpass it. They are still couched in the polite, graceful idiom of the late 18th century—there is still an aura of *galanterie* about them—and this has caused many a listener to hear nothing more than grace and charm. Today, in an age when music often favors the small ensemble over the giant orchestra, and musicians are again interested in the niceties of counterpoint, it is easier to perceive their depths of expression. The G minor symphony, in particular, has tragic undertones—in the sighing chromatics of the first theme; in the thin line of the slow movement as the violins soar up to an unbelievable dissonance and then resolve it with a bit of drawing-room lace; in the relentless, Beethovian surge of the minuet; and in the bold force of the finale.

The *Jupiter* (so named for unknown reasons by un-unknown persons) pushes still further into the dramatic future of musical composition but without the tragic undertones of the G minor. This is the work that a 19th-century conductor named Hans von Bülow liked to speak of as Beethoven's first symphony rather than Mozart's last, perhaps because of its slow movement, so deep and intimate that it already foreshadowed romanticism.

For all his mastery as a composer, Mozart was a slave to the mundane life about him. He was sinking deeper into debt because of too many luxuries and extraordinary medical expenses—for Constanze bore him child after child until her health failed (only two of their six children survived). Hoping to improve his fortunes by another concert tour, Mozart left for Berlin. On the way he played in Dresden and Leipzig and "learned something" from one of Bach's cantatas, even if he earned little money from his performances. In Berlin, King Frederick William II offered him a capellmeistership—and Mozart turned it down out of some misguided feeling of loyalty to the Austrian emperor. He returned to Vienna in worse financial condition than when he had left.

By the following summer he was reduced to writing pitiful letters begging for money, always with the promise to repay with interest, as he constantly hoped for financial improvement. Living on these borrowings, he wrote, again with Da Ponte, the little masterpiece *Così fan tutte,* a gem of a work that has never been a big hit but which is brimming with lovely tunes and good-natured comment on human failings.

When the Emperor Leopold II acceded to the throne, the court did not see fit to invite Mozart to the festivities at Frankfurt, so he went on his own funds, in hopes of finding patronage among the noble crowds. Success there was—in praise and friendliness; but as usual there was no extra money, and Mozart returned sadly to his Constanze, wanting to love her more than he did, hoping to provide for her better than he could. When finally he was made assistant capellmeister at St. Stephen's Cathedral, it was without pay but with the promise of succeeding to the senior position—which he never lived to accept.

In the summer of 1791, with Constanze in Baden for her health, Mozart found himself in a state of heightened sensibilities and frayed nerves, during which he composed because it "wearied him less than resting"; then did not dare to compose because it affected him too much. Nevertheless, he completed his last and most successful opera, *The Magic Flute,* a mysterious allegory on the beauties of free-masonry, in a fanciful Egyptian setting. The libretto, which he put together with a talented fellow named Schickaneider, is a wispy thing that must be taken with every concession from the listener but is nevertheless full of charm, and it inspired some of Mozart's most spiritual music. It is in the German form known as *singspiel,* which has arias connected by spoken dialogue, and consequently has none of the delightful, melodious recitative of Mozart's Italian operas. Before he finished it, he was commissioned to write another opera for the coronation of the King of Bohemia in Prague. In 18 days, partly in carriages and inns, he wrote *La Clemenza di Tito* and returned to Vienna to finish *The Magic Flute.*

Meanwhile, he had been approached by a mysterious stranger, all dressed in gray, with a commission to write a requiem Mass for an anonymous patron. In his super-normal state, Mozart became obsessed with the strange assignment and it is not altogether surprising that he felt the patron was God Himself and that the *Requiem* was for his own funeral. Before he finished it, he became suspicious that he was being poisoned by a less talented but more successful composer of the court (Antonio Salieri), and he finally took to his bed to wait for the end.

He died on December 5, 1791 of, in the best *post-facto* judgment, Bright's disease, which had made him weak and swollen. His pupil Sussmayr was present with the unfinished manuscript for the *Requiem* and Mozart gave him last-minute instructions on how to finish the work. His sister-in-law reported that he knew he was dying, for he said to her the same afternoon, "You must stay here tonight and see me die." A third-class funeral was held, and the body was buried in a pauper's grave, its exact location quickly forgotten because the funeral party turned back in a violent rainstorm before the actual interment. Constanze later married a Danish diplomat, Georg Nikolaus Nissen, who became Mozart's first biographer.

Mozart's music was rarely published with opus number, and what numbers there were usually gave erroneous clues to the true musical chronology. To set the record straight, an Austrian naturalist, Ludwig von Köchel, got to work and examined Mozart's letters, contemporary newspaper stories and the quality of paper and ink used in the original manuscripts. Finally, in 1862, he published the 551-page *Köchel Chronological Thematic Catalogue,* and each Mozart composition has been listed with a "K-number" ever since. In 1937, the late musicologist, Alfred Einstein (some of whose writings have been used as an authority for *A Popular History of Music*) revised the catalogue, integrating the entire voluminous body of post-Köchel Mozart research with his own original scholarship. The scholarly process may never end, for our curiosity about genius is limitless. Surely, the popularity of Mozart's music has never reached a higher level. In 1956, the bicentennial of his birth, his music received more concentrated attention than that of any other composer who ever lived, a lavish tribute from a world that still does not fully understand him.

THE COMPOSER BECOMES AN INDIVIDUAL

BEETHOVEN

LUDWIG VAN BEETHOVEN was born in Bonn, Germany, on December 17, 1770, at a time when Mozart was 14 and probably engaged in rehearsal for his first big opera in Milan, and Haydn was at last beginning to master the delicate balances and tensions of his sonata form movements. With Beethoven, the story of music turns away from the search for forms and how to use them toward an exhaustive search for musical individuality. For the first time, that barely definable concept, "originality," becomes a goal to be sought, and for the first time the composer begins to think of himself as a hero.

Our picture of Beethoven is unlike that of his predecessors. He is not an artisan but an artist, a champion of human freedom, a brooding, overbearing personality, whose private legend it is tempting to force into a parallel with his artistic one. He is claimed by the romantics as one of their number because they thought he had abandoned the strict and orderly forms of classicism. Actually, he opened form, spread it thin, even freed it, but he never, never destroyed it.

Part of the stunning—if not always attractive—vitality and richness of his music lies in his use of thematic "development." This development, as it matured under Beethoven's talents, became a mysteriously evolutionary process. By some magic of concentration, Beethoven was able to give an air of significance, of momentousness, even to the smallest details. These he nourished and permitted to unfold to the limits of possibility and showed, as it were, the themes maturing and becoming adult. The process of thematic development has become so much a part of the musical scheme of things that it is practically a requirement for great music; music that does not develop thematically seems static to us, and sometimes we feel it is sentimental. There are people who object to development on principle, such as the mythical Frenchmen who heard the beginning of a Beethoven quartet. "Wasn't that a lovely theme," exclaimed one. "Indeed yes," said the other. "Let's leave quickly, before he starts developing it." (It should be noted that the French are among the finest interpreters of Beethoven in the world.)

Beethoven did not invent development, but he did develop the scherzo, a movement he substituted for the more delicate minuet and used as an outlet for his robust humor and sarcasm. Also, he was the first to use hammering repetition as a dramatic device and was roundly criticized for it. With him, composition became such an intense matter ("Music," he said, "must strike fire from a man's mind") that he was markedly less polite than his predecessors.

Beethoven's father was a singer in the Elector's court. His ancestry was Flemish (*van* is no indication of noble ancestry as *von* is). His mother was a silent, conscientious woman whose life was spent trying to make ends meet and to keep her husband out of the taverns. The father crammed music—chiefly the violin—into the youngster as soon as he saw signs of talent and had him play piano in public before he was eight (his age was advertised as six). But young Ludwig had none of Mozart's childhood flair, and his early appearance was not followed up. He seemed a normal child, who had his moments of moroseness, when he would retire to the attic and think what he called "beautiful thoughts." He learned instrumental and operatic music from a teacher who fortunately based his instructions on Bach's *Well-Tempered Clavier*. Beethoven quickly displayed a talent for improvisation, with special interest in daring modulations, and soon impressed most of the cognoscenti in Bonn.

When he was 16, Beethoven was sent to Vienna to study with Mozart. The project came to nothing, although Mozart is supposed to have admired the boy's imaginative improvisations and said, "Keep your eye on him; some day people will talk about him." Ludwig returned home to find his mother dying and his father declining into drink. After his mother's death, Ludwig took charge of his father and his two brothers and found time to devote to Bonn's opera company. He played in the theater orchestra and had a cantata to show Haydn when that famous personage passed through town on his way from London in 1792. By the time he was 22, Beethoven was the darling of the countryside, and that year the Elector footed the bills for a trip to Vienna to study with Haydn. In Beethoven's notebook, before he left, Count Waldstein wrote a prescient inscription: "Mozart's muse still mourns and weeps for her protégé. In Haydn the inexhaustible, she found a house but not a home; through him she seeks someone she may again inspire. Work unceasingly, and from Haydn's hands you will receive Mozart's spirit."

In Vienna, Beethoven began intensive study of counterpoint, at which he was no better than any other beginner, and he produced his three trios, Op. 1, to bolster his already substantial reputation with the nobility. He had, too, a reputation as an uncouth fellow, but this was at least partly his conscious playing of a character role. Men who go far in the world, especially in the world of music, still know the value of presenting a distinctive public personality. Beethoven early learned the value of impressing on his noble friends, Lobkowitz, Lichnowsky, Esterhazy, Kinsky, et al., that he would stand for no nonsense from them about his being in their debt. He simply ignored the wishes of the men who still thought of music as a social grace, like fine table linen, to be ordered when it was needed. He was one of the earliest composers who insisted on deciding for himself what he was going to compose next. Socially, his rough manners were fearsome enough to get him what he wanted. Once, at a formal dinner early in his Vienna days, he was sent to eat with the servants, as Haydn and Mozart had done before him, and immediately walked out on the assemblage, leaving no doubt that he considered his talent as noble as their blood. This particular episode had its reward, for Prince Ferdinand of Prussia witnessed it and later invited Beethoven to sit at his left with the offending hostess on his right. But one reason for his violent temperament, his moroseness, his contentiousness was physical: Beethoven was disease-prone. He apparently fell prey to asthma, typhoid fever and smallpox as a boy, and was so far gone with some unidentified disease at the age of 17 that he said he "knew how to die." A painful stomach ailment never entirely left him, but that was nothing compared to his knowledge, when he was still in his 20's, that he was growing deaf. Nevertheless, he was quite capable of sweet thoughtfulness—if not always of understanding—for those near him or for those rare souls he felt to be talented and honest.

Although the young man brought a fabulous talent for improvisation ("It is easy to get along with nobility, so long as you have something to impress them with," he said) and a bulky collection of compositions to Vienna, it was not until 1795 that he published his Opus 1. His following was already considerable: the publisher's subscription list numbered 250. In 1800 he organized a concert of music by Haydn, Mozart and himself; but Vienna was more interested in opera, and to a man, the press ignored the wild young talent, Beethoven.

But this young talent was already ending his "first period," with his first symphony behind him and a second on the way. It is time we looked at this matter of "periods." These rather arbitrary, but useful, divisions of Beethoven's creative life were invented by a later biographer named William von Lenz, who noted that Beethoven said he was "starting on a new path" with his third symphony (the *Eroica*). Since there seemed to be a definite change in approach from then on, Von Lenz made it the beginning of the second period. The first period, then, includes two symphonies, three piano concertos and the first nine piano sonatas, all written in fairly submissive classical form, but with a brusque and daring style; the second contains symphonies three through eight, the opera *Fidelio*, the last two concertos for piano and the one for violin, fourteen sonatas, and three quartets, and is described as a period of vast and heroic proportions; the third contains the five last quartets, five piano sonatas, the ninth symphony and the *Missa Solemnis*, and has qualities of consummate artistry, deep introspection, tragedy and a strange blurring of the edges, as if all the music were part of a single vast composition. At this time, say his more poetical admirers, the iron had entered Beethoven's soul.

Beethoven started work on his *Eroica* Symphony (No. 3 in E flat, Op. 55) almost immediately after finishing the second. This is the work about which a wealth of legend has grown because Beethoven first dedicated the work to

Napoleon Bonaparte, whom he saw as a kind of super-human figure, "riding through history." Then, on hearing that Napoleon had made himself Emperor, he erased the dedication and replaced it with the words "to the memory of a great man," as if the hero were already dead. This inscription has been the subject of much scholarship, including plenty of speculation about the second movement (the funeral march) and the apparently significant fact that in the finale Beethoven uses a theme from his earlier ballet, *Prometheus*.

The first movement itself is of superhuman proportions, even by today's standards, and certainly by standards of Haydn and Mozart; it quite literally frightened its early listeners. It begins with two crashing chords. In good classical tradition, its first tune is less a melody than a state-ment of the tonic triad, played by the cellos in a sweeping triple rhythm, for nine of its ten notes. At the final note it falls into an alien tone that seems to open out into a totally new universe. It is that final note that is charac-teristically Beethoven, and the note that propels the move-ment along. The note is startling and ambiguous, with a strong feeling of incompleteness, and the ambiguity is in-creased by the hesitant-sounding syncopation of the high strings: is it really as secure as we first thought, or is the movement in an entirely different key, and, indeed, a dif-ferent rhythm? Beethoven soon resolves the questions in a fairly routine cadence in the original key and rhythm, but the seed is sown: one had better stay on the alert while listening to this piece. At one point during its first per-formance, the orchestra, faced with such unique demands, broke down.

In terms of melody, this is all that happens for the whole opening theme, for Beethoven immediately begins to throw different harmonic lights on his idea, to point out that it is charged with meaning (in case we missed it), to surround it with wisps of secondary thoughts and climactic modulations and to twist its triple rhythm until it sounds like double, until it finally emerges into the "bridge passage." This section consolidates the new key, but it contains several distinct new musical ideas, and from then on it is clear this is no ordinary sonata form movement. Nevertheless, the spirit and the harmonic progress are consistently within the sonata form scheme of things, but enormously complex and enriched. Beethoven did not name this symphony the *Eroica* (his publishers probably did, several years after it was finished), but he certainly knew he had hold of a heroic idea.

Six months after he finished the *Eroica,* in 1805, Beethoven's most important experience with the theater began —and would have ended, except for his fierce determination—with a disastrous performance of his opera, *Fidelio.* The plot, of French origin, is about a political prisoner whose life is saved by the courage and cunning of his wife. Beethoven filled the score with the warmth of his feeling for the subject and also with his feeling for symphonic structure. This made the musical numbers too long for good dramatic effect and may have been one cause of the opera's failure. After that lugubrious première, several of Beethoven's knowing friends sat him down, played the score again and again on the piano for seven hours, until he saw that it was musically top-heavy and agreed to make some cuts. The following year, the new version also failed; *Fidelio* was not a success until 1814, after further revisions. It is still rarely played in U.S. opera houses, but its repeated failures, and Beethoven's extreme fondness for it, had one happy result: he wrote two more overtures, *Leonora No. 2* and *Leonora No. 3.* The first took its form from the dramatic action and led up to the thrilling fanfare that climaxes the plot; the second was more symphonic and less literal in structure.

The year 1805-6 was a time of great productivity for Beethoven. In addition to such renowned piano sonatas as the *Waldstein* and *Appassionata* and the three handsome *Rasoumovsky* quartets, Op. 59, he was at work on his fourth and fifth symphonies. The fifth, is, of course, the familiar one with the rhythmic pattern that goes *dot-dot-dot-dash*—a pattern which has often been described as fate knocking on the door and which became an Allied victory symbol (the rhythm is Morse code for the letter "V") during World War II. It is a work of striking profile and surging power, a work which contrasts daring use of dissonance with unusually warm (for Beethoven) melody. When it is all over, we sit back with a feeling that, of course, it had to be that way.

That Beethoven knew just what he was writing into his masterpieces is beyond question. He did his preliminary work in sketchbooks, many of which have been saved. They show that his compositions came to him first as basic structures with all the fundamental harmonies and counterpoint complete—often before he had even thought of the tunes. The tunes themselves, even the most ingenuous, fresh-sounding of them, are the products of a vast amount of patient honing and polishing. The lovely, limpid melody of the fifth symphony's slow movement is a case in point. When it first occurred to Beethoven, it was a trite, bouncy little thing. As he put it through version after version, it became more and more refined. "Simplify! Simplify!" he wrote in the margin of his notebook.

"Once I know exactly what I want," he said to a young musician, "the underlying idea never leaves me. It rises and grows upward, and I see and hear the image in all its dimensions, complete in itself. . . . You may ask me where the ideas come from. I cannot tell you with any confidence, for they come unbidden, direct or indirect. I can almost feel them when I am walking in the open country or in a wood, inspired by the moods that a poet translates into words and that I translate into music. They echo in my ears, they ring out tempestuously, until at last they stand before me in notes."

Beethoven worked on his sixth symphony at the same time as his fifth, and the two were first performed in the same concert. Two more contrasting symphonies by one man would be hard to find. The sixth is the famous *Pastoral,* a name that Beethoven appended to the concert master's part with the subtitle "a recollection of country life (more an expression of feeling than a painting)." The first movement is headed, "Cheerful impressions on arriving in the country"; the second, "By the brook" (near its ending are woodwind figures labeled "nightingale," "quail," and "cuckoo"); the third, "Peasants' merry-making"; the fourth, "Tempest and storm"; the fifth "Shepherd's hymn—thanksgiving after the storm."

This music is in a very real sense an expression of Beethoven's love of the outdoors. He went to the country at every opportunity, where he walked in the woods or through the fields, and it was there that he was happiest. It would be a mistake to think of him as a dilettante nature-lover, however; his excitement was the raw material of creative power rather than mere pleasure. "Oh, God," he wrote in a notebook, "what splendor! In such a forest, on the heights is peace—peace to serve Him." The *Pastoral* Symphony is undeniably program music, a forerunner of the tone-poem which we will hear more about later on, but its poetic contents do not lack formal design; each movement is as thoroughly disciplined as the fifth symphony, despite the loose, airy and untroubled mood.

In 1812, Beethoven completed his seventh and eighth symphonies; the former is one of his most popular, the latter is unjustly regarded as lacking stature. It was Wagner who called the seventh the "apotheosis of the dance" —and one night actually danced it through while Liszt played it on the piano!—undoubtedly because of its extraordinary rhythmical insistence. But it is more than a glorified dance, for those imperious repetitions opened the door to new dramatic techniques of composition, moving music closer to a sense of human life and further from mere elegant embroidery. The seventh was played at the same performance as Beethoven's all but forgotten, and unlamented, *Battle* Symphony, written to celebrate Wellington's victory at Vittoria; although the seventh symphony's celebrated slow movement was so well liked that it had to be repeated on that occasion, it was far outshone by the noisy battle piece.

Beethoven was, by 1814, the year that a second revision of *Fidelio* succeeded, a figure of international fame. He gave a concert for his own benefit at which two empresses, the King of Prussia and numerous other royal personages were present. His financial position was secure, no matter how much he might worry over it, and he enjoyed a profitable relationship with his publisher. But he began to write less and less music. With 13 years left to live, he had reached number 100 in his 135 opus numbers, including eight of his nine symphonies, twenty-eight of his thirty-two piano sonatas, ten of his sixteen quartets, all five piano concertos. What happened? His deafness could hardly be the only cause, for like all practiced composers before and since, he heard the notes in his head and had no need to play them on the piano. But his affliction certainly contributed to his melancholia. Also, perversely, he took on many social obligations, despite the fact that they always irritated him. Most of his slowing down, though, must be attributed to the fact that his music was simply harder to write, for he felt compelled to build into it ever deepening qualities of human expression.

The death of his brother Karl, in 1815, left the bachelor Beethoven with the unpleasant task of caring for his nephew, also named Karl. He was a weak-willed and thoughtless fellow who strenuously resisted his uncle's compulsive caretaking. Beethoven disapproved of the boy's mother and tried to keep him from her. He fought law suits, kept in close touch with the boy's school and tried to inspire Karl with his own lofty ideals. The only apparent result was that Karl tried to commit suicide in 1826. This unhealthy relationship has been the subject of speculation for decades; one current theory is that Beethoven's obsession was based on a homosexual attachment.

After subjecting himself to a final fruitless bout with his ear doctors, Beethoven gave up conducting and went into seclusion. He quarreled with his servants, convinced that they cheated him, double-crossed his publishers and patrons (he sold several compositions, including the ninth symphony, twice), maligned the Viennese when they took a fancy to the gay operas of Rossini, and was even suspicious of his noble friends when they suspended his allowance temporarily because of a currency collapse. One of his admirers wrote a description that was apparently typical of Beethoven's life in 1819:

"Toward the end of August I went . . . to the master's house at Mödling. It was four in the afternoon. As soon as we went in, we heard that the two maids had left that morning. After midnight there had been a scene that had disturbed everyone in the house; apparently after waiting a long time, both of them had fallen asleep, and the food they had prepared had spoiled. In one of the living-rooms, behind a locked door, we could hear the maestro working on the fugue of the *Credo* [of the *Missa Solemnis*], stamping, singing and shouting. We listened for a while to this appalling noise and were about to leave when the door opened and Beethoven stood before us with a wild expression on his face. He caused us the greatest anxiety. He looked as though he had been through a life and death struggle with the whole tribe of contrapuntists, his sworn enemies. His first remarks were confused, as though he were surprised and displeased at being overheard. But soon he began to speak and said with remarkable calmness: 'A nice business! They have all run away and I haven't eaten since yesterday noon!'"

Creatively, Beethoven spent the years 1818-23 almost entirely on his two crowning concert works, the *Missa Solemnis* and the ninth symphony, although he turned out also a series of potboilers such as settings of Scottish songs, overtures and the last of those remarkable little enigmas for piano he called *Bagatelles*. Both of the big works use a chorus in addition to full symphony orchestra as a means of obtaining the broadest possible expression. (Originally Beethoven did not plan to use voices in the last movement of his symphony—he actually sketched the theme for another, purely instrumental finale.) When he completed the movement that stands as the finale, it was an overpowering structure in length, volume and tension, but there have always been doubts about its artistic success. For one thing, Beethoven was never quite at home with the human voice and wrote the movement in a tessitura so near the top of the vocal range that it all but vanquishes its performers, both chorus and solo, and it rarely gets a capable performance. The text is Schiller's "Ode to Joy," which Beethoven had long admired, and this paean to mankind soars in a magnificent mass of sound. Nevertheless, it is the other movements, such as the outsized scherzo, with its battering rub-a-dub rhythm on the kettle drums, that contain the ninth's best music. Beethoven was working on a tenth symphony when he died, but the number nine has for many years stood as a goal not to be exceeded by any superstitious symphonist. The *Missa Solemnis,* with its huge choruses, suffers from the same problems as the finale of the ninth symphony; in addition, it has a certain uncompromising cragginess that makes it difficult listening, even for the best-disposed listener. The *Missa* is truly a connoisseur's work.

Although these huge compositions make the most noise of all and occupied an inordinate amount of the composer's waning decade, the real crown of his musical achievements was his chamber and piano music: his "last quartets"—each one the equal of a symphony in everything except the number of players—and the last of his piano sonatas. All of these he conceived with a spaciousness and fullness that was rarely present in his early works, and with a robust wit and flow of ideas that continued to the end of his life.

Far from growing decrepit and repetitive, Beethoven continued to experiment; he occasionally used ancient modes instead of modern major and minor scales (e.g., in the "Thanksgiving of a Convalescent" movement of his A minor Quartet, Op. 132) to induce a strange, bodiless flickering from one key to another. This use of modes throws an important sidelight on tonality itself; that device, despite its comparatively recent perfection, was already losing its powerful grip on composers' imaginations. In his last works, Beethoven already found it more interesting to soften the harmonic outlines and undermine the sense of key. Beethoven, in fact, felt constricted by the rational bonds of tonal laws; his followers had even less interest in maintaining key-feeling. This easily demonstrable fact is not usually emphasized in history books, partly because they are written in support of academic harmony, which still considers tonality the foundation of music. Beethoven's first steps away from tonality foreshadow the development of the much maligned atonality and dissonance of 20th-century music.

Beethoven probably wrote all his sonatas with the piano rather than the harpsichord in mind, but only one has the word, *Hammerklavier* (Beethoven's own German word for the pianoforte), in its title: the Op. 106 in B flat, his longest and most demanding sonata, a work that some critics feel could not possibly be adequately performed by anybody under 40 years of age! Like the final sonatas, Ops. 109, 110 and 111, it appears to have very little respect for the solid formal virtues of the traditional sonata. The divisions between its sections, for instance, are often obscure or disguised. Its dimensions are outsized, and some say there is no piano capable of the thunder it requires. Its entire finale is a fugue, either because no other form would suffice to balance the huge weight of earlier movements, or because Beethoven wanted to prove he could write one. Despite the fugue's monothematic counterpoint, there is no diminishing of surging, dramatic flow.

For all their otherworldly qualities, suggested by attenuated trills and misty harmonic changes, the last sonatas are overshadowed by the string quartets of Beethoven's final years. He wrote all five during the years 1824-26, and these pieces are unique in Beethoven's career for the fact that they bear strong similarities to each other, thematically and expressively. It is as if his growing spirit had broken down the boundaries between one work and the next.

The principle of strong contrast or surprise, which had always been such a dynamic thing with Beethoven, and the flowing quality that made his surprises so surprising, seem to fuse here, with changes of mood taking place in every bar, sometimes even two opposing ones happening simultaneously. Form and content (those philosophical zombies of music appreciators) are finally brought together, to the point where some call these works a series of visions. As late as the beginning of this century, the "last quartets" were still being derided as the works of a deaf man who was also probably insane. Although there are wonders upon wonders to be found in these quartets, the most haunting are the first movements of the beautiful Op. 127 and Op. 131. The finale of Op. 130 was so huge it became a separate quartet in itself, called the *Great Fugue (Grosse Fuge,* Op. 133). In it Beethoven seems to have abandoned all his most effective devices; there is hardly even a crescendo or a splash of contrast. Here he starts off with a burst of energy and sustains it for one-seventh of the whole movement, followed by an equally uncontrasted pianissimo section of equal length. Walter Riezler, whose *Beethoven* is one of the finest books for the layman about music, writes about the *Great Fugue,* "This tumult is a different kind from that of the finale of the seventh symphony; the music does not storm forward, rather does it stamp about in wild ecstasy, like a savage as he performs some orgiastic dance."

Beethoven achieved a tremendous reputation with his music in his lifetime, and toward the end pilgrims began to stop in for visits with the man who was venerated by the entire world of music. Those fortunate persons who were admitted were often treated with great kindness and respect. Beethoven was by then totally deaf. But he talked with his visitors, and they jotted their exchange of words in "conversation books," many of which were preserved. The master continued to enjoy drinking bouts with his favorite companions, and the alcohol undoubtedly contributed to his death from cirrhosis of the liver. In his last years, he mellowed enough to become interested in other composers; he expressed unreserved admiration for Cherubini and praised Rossini's opera *The Barber of Seville*. He examined Schubert's songs for hours and remarked that the young composer was "gifted with the divine spark."

In 1826, ill and unhappy, he gave up life in the country, spent the whole summer in Vienna and then moved in with his brother and sister-in-law, apparently swallowing his contempt for their narrow lives. But there were numerous quarrels, and at the end of November he departed, chilled and grippy. For three months he was under medical care. Two days before he died, his mind began to fail but he made a few memorable statements: *"Plaudite, amici, comoedia finita est!"* (Applaud, friends, for the comedy is over!); and finally, when a case of fine wine arrived from a publisher, "What a pity, too late." He died on March 26, in, according to romantic legend, a raging snowstorm reinforced by thunder and lightning. During one flash, Beethoven is said to have opened his eyes, raised a fist, and gazed upward with "a grave and threatening expression." When he fell back, he was dead. Twenty thousand people attended his funeral, schools were closed, and eight conductors acted as pallbearers. Despite these tokens of veneration, his possessions were thoughtlessly auctioned off, and a great many valuable objects of study were lost forever.

PART THREE

A POETIC REVOLUTION

A POETIC REVOLUTION

UNLIKE CLASSICAL COMPOSERS, the romantics were fully conscious of their esthetic attitudes; they themselves used the word "romantic." They called medieval troubadour ballads about heroic deeds "romances"; their own imaginations were filled with exotic places and distant times, which they re-created in deliciously vague phrases and evocative tunes. Simultaneously, the romantics were engaged in a fierce revolution against what they considered the artificial formalism of classical music. In the process they softened the contours of music, relaxed its rhythms, lengthened its melodies and loosened its structure. Their own music was tuneful rather than motival, for it originated in song; the finest compliment one could give a romantic composer or performer was to say his music "sang."

The romantics felt they were reaching to say something that could not be put into words—they were out to express the inexpressible. Nevertheless, what they so often succeeded in expressing was their own feelings. Romantic composers externalized their dreams, blew up their sentiments, shared their ecstasies, shouted their triumphs.

The historical explanation for all this lies buried in the great liberation of the common man that was taking place at the turn of the century. The American and French Revolutions had recently taken place, and all of Europe was stirring with self-realization. The common man was be-

coming aware of his individuality, and he began to emulate such pleasures and conceits of the vanishing nobility
as listening to music. No longer able to look up to those
who had convinced him they bore better blood, the bourgeois turned his admiration to those who had better
talents.

Romantic music was directed toward the fullest possible expression of literary ideas in musical form. Each composer along the way contributed what he could toward
the ultimate fusion of words and music. The first romantic composer, chronologically, was CARL MARIA VON WEBER,
who was a romanticist ahead of his time; we remember
him best as a melodist of genius, and a powerful, if premature, proponent of opera in German. But it was FRANZ
SCHUBERT who set romanticism on the right path, with his
affinity for German poetry which delved into chivalric
legends, fairy tales, folk songs, magic, superstition and
fantastic heroism. Schubert took the poetry and set it to
music which evoked the mood and even the action of the
words. HECTOR BERLIOZ and FRANZ LISZT ballooned the
microcosmic romantic song into huge instrumental works,
both with and without words. Liszt's programmatic works
were called "symphonic poems," Berlioz's were "dramatic
symphonies." RICHARD WAGNER finally synthesized words
and music on the largest possible scale and called the form
"music drama."

Thoroughly romantic in spirit, but with more taste for
the firmness of classical form, were three other men of
the period. ROBERT SCHUMANN wrote short piano pieces
with descriptive titles of a most subjective nature and
nostalgic longing. FELIX MENDELSSOHN had a still stronger
classical bent; although he gave names to his symphonies,
composed with formal balances and almost Mozartian
clarity of texture, his romanticism had led him to study

the past. So much later as to make him "postromantic" in the eyes of some scholars, came JOHANNES BRAHMS, who saw his chance to improve on Beethoven's concept of the symphony.

The 19th century was virtually a golden age for composers, at least so far as public acceptance and artistic freedom was concerned. If they were lucky, they could rise to world-wide fame practically overnight. The romantic era, with all its emphasis on selfexpression, developed two new musical heroes—the virtuoso pianist and the virtuoso conductor.

THE CONDUCTOR

WE HAVE WATCHED MUSIC GROW in the complexity of its forms, the subtlety of its colors and dynamic shadings, the refinement of the instruments that produced it. It is time now to step aside for a few pages to take a look at that spectacular figure, the one man in the orchestra who plays no instrument, the man who stands with his back to the audience waving a baton and gyrating in a veritable fury of motion, the conductor.

Conductors existed as long ago as the days of Greek choruses. All the way up to the time of Beethoven these men and their counterparts kept their forces together by noisily stamping or rapping out the beat. The medieval choral conductor commonly swatted it out with a roll of parchment. He could not be very precise about his beat until music developed bar lines; he probably contented himself with cueing entrances and indicating accents. When instruments were first combined into ensembles, the clavier player was usually the conductor, responsible also for filling in the harmony, as Bach himself did. He gave cues to his players with a free hand, a nod of the head or a glance. He was commonly assisted by the first violinist, who stood by his side slashing the air with his bow or jabbing it with the scroll-end of his fiddle to indicate an entrance, or simply playing so loudly that the others could follow by listening to him.

The French composer, Lully, rapped on the floor with

a pole to establish his tempo and is supposed to have died from an abscess that resulted when he clubbed his foot by mistake. Haydn, Mozart and, in his early years, Beethoven all conducted from the keyboard, as did Stamitz, and his successor Christian Cannabich, with the great Mannheim Orchestra. But by the time he was an established composer, Beethoven had begun to conduct with a baton.

The conductor's basic purpose is to hold the orchestra together, to let every musician know the "beat." The beats are strong pulses of rhythm, divided in basic groups of two, three or four, and indicated by the conductor with a semaphore system that is simpler than it looks. Before he starts a performance the conductor will rap on his music stand, wait with baton poised until he has everybody's attention, then raise the baton in the preparatory upbeat, in the tempo he intends to maintain. At that moment, wind players inhale, string players raise their bows to position, and percussionists lift their drumsticks in preparation for the downbeat, which follows smoothly and consistently. Because the upbeat is already in proper tempo everybody knows exactly when the baton will reach its nadir, and the orchestra starts playing together.

At the beginning of the sheet of music on each player's rack, there is a time signature and a description of the manner in which he is to play. The latter is ordinarily an Italian word such as *allegro* (happily), *presto* (fast), *prestissimo* (fast as possible), *andante* (going), *moderato* (moderately), *lento* (slowly), *largo* (broadly), *maestoso* (majestically), etc. The time signature is indicated by numbers, in the form of fractions, written directly on the five-line musical staff. The upper figure indicates the number of beats to be played within each measure. The lower number specifies the kind of note to be valued at one beat;

e.g., 3/4 time means there will be three quarter-notes, or their equivalent, in each measure. 2/4 and 4/4 are march rhythms; 3/4 is waltz rhythm; 6/8, if it goes fast enough, is divided into two strong beats of three subsidiary beats each, and is thus also a march rhythm with a bouncing triple beat.

The conductor's baton-signals are divided in identical fashion, making the following basic patterns (heavy arrow indicates downbeat):

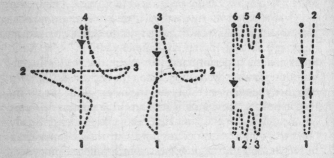

Composers of Beethoven's day also began to place expressive emphasis on the balance between separate kinds of instruments and explored the possibilities for subtle gradations in instrumental color. Since the noise-making potential of brass, wood and strings is in a ratio of approximately 4-2-1, it became the conductor's task to decide where the composer intended to place the emphasis— and then see to it that each instrument played just loud enough. This he learned to do with his left hand, while the baton-bearing right continued to tick off the tempo. His grab bag of left-hand signals ranged from a simple finger to the lips in a shushing gesture or a palm-down sweep for general quiet, to a clenched fist or a trembling handful of notes for noisy intensity. When composers began to write such vague but excitable words as *espressivo* (most expressively) over their notes, conductors learned to help out the performers by symbolically beating their breasts, clutching at their hearts or, more literally, turning to the string players and simulating the wobbling wrists of a fiddler's broad, emotional vibrato.

Once a man began to succeed at a career of conducting, he became the star, the headliner of any orchestral concert, and it was a fine, romantic position to be in: at the helm of a mighty body of men; steering them through the intricacies of an inspired symphony; urging them to superhuman efforts; discovering, it seemed, secrets in the music that nobody had suspected were there. By mid-19th century the conductor was regarded as a virtuoso in his own right, although sometimes he was not master of any instrument at all. He could be seen on the great podiums of Europe, hair and coattails flying, contorting his body in the agony of a symphonic climax, wagging his head in the trough of a tragic theme, sawing an imaginary violin in the ecstasy of an *espressivo* passage, going rigid with a fierce musical accent, whopping the drums and cymbals silently but ferociously as the finale roared in. He became a kind of middleman, in effect, not only making the orchestra play by the sheer impact of his will but also acting the music out for the audience, helping less informed listeners to see (or hear) what was going on, and at least helping them to understand what kind of emotions they should be feeling. It was what we call "good theater," and it helped to spread interest in music, right down to the present day.

Such a display may seem excessive, and it often is. The conductor's real work is all done before the concert ever begins, in rehearsals. If he is worth his pay, he learns

the music by heart before he ever faces the orchestra, studies it silently, hears it in his head, understands where and
why its various elements divide to form the larger structure, sees how to make the divisions distinct without seeming to separate them and how to underline subtleties to
increase the sense of musical coherence. In rehearsal, he
simply tells his men what he intends to do and how he
wishes them to play their important passages; in effect,
he lectures them on what this music means to him.

If he is competent and his manner is modest, the musicians will give him what he asks for. But orchestras
have always been touchy about taking orders from a non-
playing fellow and regard a new conductor with everything from mild suspicion to open hostility until he proves
himself. If a young man tries to take the podium by storm
at his first rehearsal and seems to be bluffing ("You, there,
seventh violin—that's a G sharp, not a G natural"), the
musicians know how to take him for a ride. One of today's famous orchestras has been known to play the whole
first theme of Beethoven's *Eroica* a half step too high, to
test the conductor's ear. When things get to such a point,
the whole ensemble has become demoralized and plays as
sloppily as it pleases. One novice conductor, so the story
goes, went through a terrible ordeal, his confusion increasing with every cacophonic moment until, in the middle of a pianissimo string passage, the bass drummer wal-
loped out a thundering note that was totally uncalled for.
"Now," demanded the conductor, near tears, "who did
that?"

"Interpretation" has become an ambiguous word in the
annals of concert music, for it implies that the conductor
is not reproducing the composer's work but only a fac-
simile, either overrich, overlean or distorted to suit his
own temperament. The job of interpretation, however, is

a necessary one so long as concert-goers demand music by composers of a century and more ago; until recently, composers left vast opportunities for interpretation in the performance of their scores, even after they adopted the use of metronome marks for setting tempos. Changing tastes also affect interpretation; 20th-century performances of Beethoven's fast movements are almost always slower than Beethoven indicated. Modern listeners, conditioned by a century of romantic hero worship, think of Beethoven as a titan and give his music more scope and spaciousness than he ever intended. On the other hand, the tempo of concert music in general has increased during the past century, as wind instruments have been mechanically improved.

Through the years, some conductors have made themselves almost as famous as the composers whose music they led. Louis Spohr was one of the first to use a baton. When he introduced the practice to London in 1820, he met strong resistance, but the effectiveness of his performance won everybody over. Mendelssohn commonly beat time for the first few bars, then stood quietly and listened, except during a particularly difficult passage of changing tempo; when the music was ended, he applauded with the audience. Hans von Bülow was a man who knew how to whip his orchestras into a storm of excitement, as did the French composer Hector Berlioz. Wagner and Strauss were noted conductors of their own works. In modern times, there are several men who have already become legends through their phenomenal abilities on the podium: Karl Muck, with the Boston Symphony; Wilhelm Mengelberg, with the famous Amsterdam Concertgebouw orchestra; Felix Weingartner and Bruno Walter, with the Vienna Philharmonic; Arturo Toscanini and Dimitri Mitropoulos with the New York Philharmonic-Symphony; Leopold Stokowski, with the Philadelphia Symphony; Serge Koussevitzky, with the Boston Symphony. The few modern attempts to establish conductorless orchestras have required excessive rehearsal time. The conductor is here to stay.

A ROMANTICIST BEFORE HIS TIME

WEBER

Carl Maria von Weber was born on November 18, 1786, in Eutin, Oldenberg. The German *von* indicates a noble ancestry, as distinct from the meaningless *van* in Beethoven's name, and Weber believed in his nobility all his life —without, it seems, any valid claim to it. Although he was born before his spiritual brothers, the romantics—Haydn was still writing his *Seven Last Words,* Mozart was just having his first success with *The Marriage of Figaro,* Beethoven was a teen-aged organist at Bonn—Weber's innovations of style, his free hand with form, his use of extramusical devices, establish his claim as the first romantic composer.

Weber's most important contribution was to German opera. His tremendous flair for dramatic effect and showy display undermine serious acceptance of his concert works, appealing as they are. His three best operas are *Der Freischütz, Euryanthe* and *Oberon,* all based on brooding, shadowy, medieval stories, all filled with magic and the heavy hand of fate. Their musical value lies in the fact that they are distinct entities rather than patchwork operettas; they possess unity of style and spirit, and are woven together by an imposing network of themes and motifs. Their nationalistic approach for the first time put German opera on a level with Italian and provided a link between Mozart's *Magic Flute* and the giant music dramas of Richard Wagner. For all his importance as an operatic composer, Weber is better known today for one piece of concert music: the grand waltz called *Invitation to the Dance*.

It was inevitable that something special should come from Weber. His father was Mozart's wife's uncle, and he himself was Mozart's godchild. Already his father had started two older sons on the path to music and hoped to make a profitable prodigy out of Carl Maria, like cousin Wolfgang. He was a restless, even nomadic fellow, vain and ambitious, both musician and theatrical impresario, and his second wife, Carl's mother, was a singing actress. When Carl was less than a year old, the *Weberschen Schauspielergesellschaft* (family theatrical troupe) went on the road, and Carl practically grew up in the wings of German theaters.

The boy apparently had neither the talent nor temperament to become a prodigy. While taking violin lessons from an older brother, he was told flatly: "Musician you'll never be!" When he was six, his parents decided that music was not his greatest gift, after all, and set him to painting in oils and learning to etch. By the time he was eleven, the family had moved to Salzburg, and Carl was put in the choir school, studying with Michael Haydn, from whom he said he "learned little . . . and that little with great effort." The next year the family was off again, this time to Munich, where he had teachers in both voice and composition—and almost gave up music entirely because his father had come across one Aloys Senefelder, the inventor of lithography, and decided to go into that profession. Young Carl lithographed his own *Six Variations,* for piano, Op. 2.

Fortunately, the impressionable youngster met up with

an opera impresario who had written a libretto—*The Forest Maiden*—and was perfectly willing to have the 14-year-old composer try setting it to music. It was performed at Freiburg without any success at all, and hotheaded Carl wrote angry letters to the local paper, lashing out at the critics ("barking like puppies") and blaming "low and premeditated cabals" for his poor performance. Perhaps his anger was justified, but of course his protests did no good and ultimately father and son were obliged to leave town.

The experience left no doubt in Weber's mind that he must write operas. Back in Salzburg for a while, he wrote a comic opera, *Peter Schmoll and His Neighbors,* which old Michael Haydn said was "full of fire, great delicacy and appropriate feeling," but which was also a failure. Weber kept the music and reused fragments of it to the end of his life. Meanwhile he went to studying again, this time with the well-known Abbé Vogler in Vienna and from him picked up a remarkable sense of orchestral color. He also developed an interest in folk music. It was a quiescent period for the 18-year-old composer, at least as far as composing went. He occupied his time in carousing around town, for nobody enjoyed the high life better. Meanwhile, Vogler championed his brilliant pupil whenever possible and finally obtained for him a job as conductor of the theater at Breslau.

This position revealed hidden abilities in the young musician. From the beginning he was perfectly aware of the sound he wanted to hear from his orchestra and was not afraid of browbeating the musicians to get it. He held unprecedented numbers of rehearsals, both with the full orchestra and with separate groups of strings, woodwinds, brass. He soon proved that he was a remarkable opera conductor, but his drastic methods, especially coming from an 18-year-old, plus his highbrow choice of programs—his favorite opera was *Don Giovanni*—turned Breslau opera-lovers against him, and he abandoned his position after two seasons. "I only vaguely knew what I wanted," he explained later, "and knew scarcely at all what I had to do." The result was a desultory few years as private secretary to a nobleman, during which he lived in luxury. Eventually he quarreled with his king and later was accused of a theft, apparently committed by his father. He was jailed and then exiled. This brought him to his senses. "From now on," he said, "I shall live for my music."

Back with Vogler, now in Darmstadt, Weber, another composer named Jacob Meyerbeer and the Abbé's other pupils formed a society to promote their art. Included in Weber's credo, as in that of any genuine creative mind, was the conviction that art "has no fatherland . . . we ought to value whatever is beautiful, no matter what climate or what region produced it." That year (1810) saw the production of another Weber opera, *Silvana,* with his future wife, Caroline Brandt, in the leading role. It was a failure; Weber complained that a well-publicized balloon ascension took place the same day, and even the singers cut short their arias to go and watch.

That year he turned out a jolly one-act *singspiel, Abu Hassan,* based on a story from *The Arabian Nights.* More significant was a melodramatic cantata, *Der Erste Ton (The First Note),* about the creation of the world. Its importance to the development of music was its use of leitmotifs. The leitmotif (literally: leading motive) is a musical theme used to symbolize a nonmusical idea. In addition to reminding listeners of the idea, the leitmotif establishes a mechanical means of thematic unity. It reached its most advanced state in the hands of Wagner, who managed, in many cases, to weave it into the musical texture so deftly that it seemed to belong. *Der Erste Ton* was one of Weber's first big successes.

During that time, Weber's musical society invented a new game, which they called "melody hunting." The point was to choose a popular song or folk tune and convert it into a "master melody," suitable for use in a concert piece. This kind of toying with music had its usefulness—*Invitation to the Dance* and *Oberon* are both supposed to contain samples of converted folk tunes—but Weber during this period was simply marking time. He had no permanent position and, at the age of 24, still no libretto to work on. "I am waiting in anguish for a good libretto," he wrote. "I do not feel right when I have no opera in hand." He did manage to meet one of the outstanding clarinetists of the day, a man named Heinrich Bärmann, whose playing inspired him to compose two brilliant concertos, a concertino, a set of variations, a duo-concertante and a quintet with strings for the clarinet—that then-rare woodwind.

Finally, in 1813, he settled one half of his problem by becoming opera director of the city of Prague. His restless nature was hardly overjoyed at the prospect of sitting in one place but, he joked, "It is worth something to be ruling lord of the opera. . . . I almost believe I can have people hanged and broken on the wheel, which suits my bloodthirsty disposition perfectly." He had his hands full for he had to revise the company from top to bottom and probably wished he *could* do violence at times. "The orchestra . . . is in complete rebellion," he wrote. "I have to draw up contracts, straighten out the disorganized library . . . draw up a catalogue . . . correct scores . . . prepare scenarios of the operas . . . describe scenes to painters and costumes to designers. . . . I get up at six . . . and am often at work until midnight. . . ." The rebellious opera company bowed to what Weber called his "iron scepter," and he put on no less than eighteen different operas in his first six months, with a performance every other day. When he feared that one of his productions would fail with the Prague public, he invented a practice that survives today: he tried to presell the public by inserting favorable advance notices in the newspaper.

In spite of his heavy schedule, he also managed to compose voluminously, particularly during his vacations. When news of the Battle of Waterloo reached him, he composed a battle cantata, *Kampf und sieg,* which was considerably more popular than Beethoven's *Battle* Symphony on the same generic subject. During the next two years he also found time to carry on several romantic intrigues, one of which culminated later in his marriage to Caroline. But his health was suffering, and he went more and more frequently to the mineral baths.

By 1817, Weber's reputation had spread, and he received an invitation to become operatic director in Dresden. It was a challenge—Dresden was a stronghold of Italian opera and, as leader of the opposition company, Weber would not even have the court's sympathy in his crusade for German opera—but it was too flattering an invitation to decline. He greeted the company with a lecture about "implicit obedience" and warned of his own "pitiless severity." Despite the well-established success of the rival Italian opera, Weber forbade his singers to indulge in their favorite liberties of the Italian style—those gaudy cadenzas interpolated by stars whenever they felt like showing off. In the pit, he conducted with a baton, indicating that he would accept no nonsense. He rearranged the seating of the opera orchestra, moving the winds to one side and the strings to the other, leaving the orchestra in a state of shocked indignation and the listeners in the royal box (on the windy side) complaining they could not hear the strings.

That year Weber finally found an opera text that satisfied him. Called *Der Freischütz*, it had everything: a pact with the devil; a scene in a wolf's glen where seven magic bullets were cast, to the accompaniment of demoniacal noise; and a scene in which a maiden's life is saved by her apparently armor-plated bridal wreath. Weber gave the tale some fine dramatic music, notable for its soaring melodies but even more for its orchestration. This was unlike anything ever heard before: the strings were daringly divided and subdivided, their notes were sometimes separated by airy distances; sometimes they were muted; sometimes they shuddered in low tremolos while the clarinets sang forebodingly in woody, low registers; sometimes they swept up and down the entire gamut in the kind of passage-work favored 130 years later by such superexpressive orchestras as André Kostelanetz's. In other words, the score abounded in what Weber himself described as "exaggerations" for effect—extremes of expression that were made to order for melodrama. But most important of all, it was written with an unerring sense of balance: the music and the drama were equally important and supported each other throughout. It marked the beginning of the age when music tried to represent specific states of mind—and even actions.

Freischütz was first performed in Berlin, to immediate and enormous acclaim. Practically overnight, Weber became the most popular composer in Germany. Critics, understandably reluctant to expose themselves too soon, admitted that something new and radical had happened but felt obliged to agree with one critic who said that out of a small nothing, Weber had created a colossal nothing.

In 1819 Weber completed *Invitation to the Dance*. This was a simple concert waltz for piano solo. Except for the implications of the title, Weber indicated no story. Nevertheless, it was soon agreed that the music depicted a scene in a gay ballroom, where a young man approaches and requests a dance from a pretty young lady. She tremblingly accepts, and everybody starts to dance, gently, then more and more warmly up to the whirling climax. Finally the couple part, as gracefully as they have met, and the music ends. The piece brims with brilliant runs and flashy bravura passages, as well as pretty melodies. It immediately became a successful concert work as well as favorite with young piano students, and so it has remained ever since.

Weber was commissioned to compose another opera, this time a great tragedy, to be premièred in Vienna for the 1822-23 season. Faced with the old question, where to find a libretto, Weber turned in desperation to one Helmina von Chezy, the same misguided poetess who was Schubert's undoing as librettist for his *Rosamunde*. The result was *Euryanthe,* a thoroughly confused and illogical medieval tale. The music is lovely—the overture is one of the jewels of the symphonic repertoire—but it was too highly flavored for the Viennese, and the première was a failure. Schubert called the work "utterly unmusical" and said, "when [Weber] does contrive to snare a scrap of melody, he is sure to crush it to death, like a mouse in a trap, with his overwhelming orchestration...." Beethoven, who had been impressed with the *Freischütz* score ("devilish queer stuff," he called it), tried to console Weber with the opinion that German authors did not know how to write good opera plots. The historical judgment is that *Euryanthe* is unstageable but that it is a shining landmark as the first German *opera seria*. Its failure left Weber literally half sick and thoroughly discouraged, and it was a year and a half before he regained enthusiasm for composition.

During that time he received offers of commissions for new operas from several places and finally agreed to compose *Oberon* for London's Covent Garden opera. His new libretto was again incredible and confused beyond all possibility of order, but it was possible to do it as a *singspiel* in the manner of a Broadway musical comedy. Weber's spirits were improved by an unexpectedly successful performance of *Euryanthe* in Berlin, but his doctors had warned that he could hope to live six years only if he spent a year in complete rest. He and Caroline now had two small sons, and he was worried about the condition of his family finances; a new success seemed the only solution. He studied his English, packed up his libretto and sketches, and in February, 1826, left his family and headed for London.

On his way he stopped in Paris, where he was welcomed by the most celebrated musicians of the day—Rossini, Cherubini, everybody but, by ill luck, his ardent admirer, Berlioz, whom he never met—and in England he found himself lionized from the moment he entered customs. He conducted oratorio concerts while finishing *Oberon* and prepared its performance in a state of depression, caused both by London's "thick, dark, dank yellow fog" and by homesickness. The première took place on April 12, amid scenes of wildest enthusiasm. The restrained English fought for balcony seats and applauded the composer for fifteen minutes before the first curtain rose. Weber, who regarded the London version of *Oberon* as unfinished, found it all "simply unbelievable" and deeply exhausting. Two months later, still in London, he returned home one night feeling seriously ill. He wound his watch, shook hands with his host, said, "Now let me sleep," and barred his door. He died in his sleep, from an ulcer in his throat and tuberculosis. His body was buried in a London vault to the accompaniment of Mozart's *Requiem* and was later removed to the Catholic cemetery in Dresden. One of the speakers at his grave was the man who was to inherit his mantle as Germany's greatest opera composer, Richard Wagner.

THE SONG IS BORN

SCHUBERT

THE IMPULSE that led Weber to write vocal music was even more strongly felt by a group of younger men. Unlike Weber, they verbalized their theories. They were romanticists, and they knew it. Musically, their art took the form of a species of song, song that was less artificial than the operatic aria but more sophisticated than the folk song. This song is so individual that it has retained its German name to distinguish it from any other kind. It is called "lied" in the singular, "lieder" in the plural. Its influence was immediately felt, and eventually it became responsible for the whole romantic ideal of "singing melody" that was to affect the piano and the orchestra, as well as to establish the style for the human voice that is still considered "natural."

The first master of the lied was FRANZ PETER SCHUBERT, who was born in Vienna on January 31, 1797, the only one of all the famous Viennese master composers who was a true native of that city. He died a short 31 years later, poverty-stricken, barely recognized for his sublime gift of melody. He left an astonishing volume of lyrical music, including ten symphonies (the great C major, No. 9, ranks with Beethoven's *Eroica,* and the two-movement, misnamed *Unfinished,* No. 8, is as great), 16 string quartets, 22 piano sonatas and 600-odd lieder. His greatest contribution to the development of music was the evocative style of his songs.

Franz was the twelfth child in a middle-class family. His father, as a schoolteacher, was required to teach music, and by the time Franz was seven, his father recognized his generous talent and sent him to a professional teacher. When Franz was eleven he won a scholarship at the Imperial and Royal Seminary, known as "the Konvict," to become a choirboy. Student life at the Konvict was no picnic, but it was considerably better than Haydn's life at St. Stephen's Cathedral, and curly haired, snub-nosed Franz learned fast. For an hour or two every day he played in the student orchestra—usually reading an overture and a symphony by Haydn or Mozart. His piano teacher listened to his expressive playing and said, "This one has learned it from God."

Young Franz began to compose regularly and voluminously. His counterpoint teacher was Antonio Salieri, the man Mozart unjustly suspected was trying to poison him. Salieri was a champion of Italian opera and infused in the teen-age Franz both a burning determination to write opera (partly in the belief that it was the only way to success) and a temporary antipathy to Beethoven.

When he was 15, Schubert's voice broke, thus ending his usefulness as a choir singer, but he was given a scholarship for further study, which he pieced out with contributions from one of his brothers. That year, he completed his first symphony, started an opera patterned after Mozart's *Magic Flute,* wrote string quartets for performance by his family at home, a more ambitious quartet (he wrote one movement in four and a half hours, or about as fast as he could copy), a Mass and a number of songs.

In the fall of 1814, Franz Schubert reluctantly became an assistant master in his father's school with the comforting knowledge that it would keep him out of the draft. That same fall he dashed out a song to a poem by Goethe: *Gretchen am Spinnrade (Gretchen at the Spinning Wheel)*. It was not his first fine song, but its musical content so magically complemented its poetic that it has come to be considered the first true lied.

Song was nothing new to high-born music-lovers at the turn of the 18th century. Europeans had a tradition of folk song that went back to the troubadours and minnesingers of the Middle Ages, and probably went back to the beginnings of music itself. Also they had tunes to hum from popular operas—at first Italian, then Mozartian—and from the light *singspiels*. But such song was a comparatively stiff and formal thing; it took Schubert's lied to soften its contours.

Schubert's inspiration was provided by the romantic verses of such poets as Friedrich Schiller (whose "Ode to Joy" was used by Beethoven in his ninth symphony), Goethe and a spate of lesser poets, many of whose words survive mostly because he set them to music. The kind of verses he liked best were melting, ecstatic descriptions of pastoral scenes and of rapturous romance. For example, from Schiller's *Laura und Clavier:* "Rapturous harmonies swarm in ecstatic profusion from the strings like new-born seraphim from their heavenly regions. The melody's magic power streams forth as suns, loosed from the giant arm of Chaos and aroused by the storm of creation, emerge, blazing, from the night." Or from Kosegarten's *Mondenacht:* "Embracing thee, by thee embraced, one with thee, closely united, spare me, spare me, sunk in bliss. Heaven and earth vanish before my love-intoxicated eyes."

Schubert found three ways to set such verses to music. (1) He wrote one verse of music and repeated it for each verse of poetry; this is called strophic treatment. (2) He followed the text as closely as he possibly could, setting each line with its own music, depending on the unity of mood, style and the interest of the words to make the song a coherent whole; the German word for this is *durchkomponiert,* which meant "through-composed." (3) He combined the two, most often by repeating his verse of music for two or more stanzas and then substituting entirely new music for the final lines to lend emphasis and surprise.

Nobody has been able to decide which of the three methods is most effective. It is hardly a burning issue now, but the argument ran hotly in Schubert's day. Schubert himself favored the freer, through-composed style, and sometimes made it so free as to begin a song in one key and end in another, because it seemed to him that was the best way to reveal the words' inner meanings. Goethe preferred to let the singer develop the expression by changing his inflections. Whatever the method, Schubert filled his songs with intense lyricism, which he set off by flowing patterns of harmonic change. Today the turns of phrase and harmonic devices he invented have become clichés through other composers' misuse of them. Nevertheless, in Schubert they can still sound fresh.

Schubert's vocal line, like his piano accompaniments, was designed with utmost care and insight to reflect, amplify and spiritualize the expression of the words.

Within each verse, Schubert followed the general pattern familiar in the popular songs of the 1950's, although his intentions were more serious, as a rule. Basically, this was the old tripartite song form that found its way into everything from a dance on the village green to Beethoven's symphonies. In such a song, the first melodic phrase is repeated, the second provides contrast, and the first returns as a conclusion. His *Ave Maria* is a free treatment of this form.

The year Schubert composed *Gretchen at the Spinning Wheel,* he also wrote music for three stage works of widely varying mood. No matter what the mood, their scores tended to ramble; it was soon clear, to everybody but Schubert himself, that the lyric stage was not his field. In 1815, he wrote his second and third symphonies, a piano sonata and "hurled down on paper," as he put it, one of his most famous songs, the dramatic and foreboding terror-tale, *Der Erlkönig,* published as Op. 1 several years later.

By this time, Schubert was a stocky young man of 18, with glasses covering his nearsighted and genial eyes, who loathed dressing up for social gatherings. A friend wrote that Franz hated as much as Beethoven to "bow and scrape." But where Beethoven intimidated his "betters," shy Schubert simply avoided them—and with them, the chance for financial security. Instead of influential noblemen, Schubert surrounded himself with a crowd of young Bohemians, poets and dilettantes. They provided the composer with some fine tavern companionship, excellent musical evenings and plenty of verses for setting to music, but with none of the prestige or money that he so often needed.

In 1816, he quit his teaching post in favor of the life of a Bohemian and, in effect, closed the door on respectability. His only predictable income was from his publishers, and it was small: not one of his large-scale, serious works was published before the year of his death. The publisher Breitkopf & Härtel returned his *Erlkönig* by mistake to an older composer named Schubert, and the man was furious that his name should be dishonored by such trash. Aside from two volumes of songs, subsidized by his friends, nearly every composition Schubert sent to a publisher resulted in rejection or underpayment. He made a few token applications for musical positions, but it is clear that he was happiest when he was free of such entanglements. With the exception of a few more months as a teacher in a noble household, he spent the rest of his life living off his poetic friends, bedding down wherever he was made welcome. He had sixteen different lodgings in the next eleven years.

Poets were not the only men who rallied around the Schubert talent. There was also, for instance, a famous and imposing tenor, Johann Michael Vogel, who was induced to spend an evening going over Schubert's songs. The singer was 30 years older than the composer, head and shoulders taller, and owner of a tenor's temperament. He remained frighteningly aloof for a while, but Schubert's melting melodies soon won him over. From then on, he sang them whenever he made an appearance. "You are too little an actor," he told Schubert, "and not enough of a charlatan." Schubert's productivity blossomed under such treatment. In his 20th year, he reached the halfway mark in his 600 songs—it was the time of such masterpieces as *Death and the Maiden, To Music* and *The Trout.*

By that time Schubert had learned something about his creative processes and tried to explain them to a friend: "Reading [a good poem] makes something happen to me at once," he said. "The melodies flow from me so that it is a real pleasure. When I read a bad poem, nothing goes right. I plague myself with it, and nothing but dry stuff comes out." He was accustomed to writing as many as eight or nine songs a day. They came out like snapshots: either they caught the spirit, the inner expression of the poem, or they did not. He rarely tried to rework a song, but he sometimes returned to a poem and tried it again in later years. As might be expected, he completely forgot that he had written some of them and once actually praised a song, completely unaware that it was his own. He usually worked from 6 a.m. until about 1 p.m., or joined his cronies at one of Vienna's cafés (the "Hungarian Crown," the "Black Cat," the "Green Anchor"), or walked the parks, attended a show or a concert, or went to musical gatherings that became known as "Schubertiads." Ever so gradually, his music penetrated Viennese society. *Erlkönig* became such a hit that it was the source of popular numbers: the *Erlkönig Galop* and *Erlkönig Waltzes*. He dedicated a set of variations to Beethoven ("from his worshiper and admirer"), who played them often, and he wrote music to two plays which were actually produced. One ran for six performances but the other, *Rosamunde,* failed after two.

In October, 1822, he began his B minor symphony, later called the *Unfinished,* which was destined to become one of the world's most famous compositions. This was his eighth symphony in order of composition; No. 7 was the C major; No. 9 was the lost, or at least mislaid, *Gastein* (1825); and the tenth was the great C major. The last is ordinarily listed as either No. 7 or No. 9, or both, the confusion arising from the fact that publication was delayed.

Schubert was consciously trying for concentration of form when he began his *Unfinished* Symphony, and he succeeded admirably. He wrote two movements, both of them growing out of emotional, songlike subjects, both of them nearly perfect. He sketched a scherzo as far as the trio, and even orchestrated a few bars, but it was soon clear to him that the makings of the third movement could not match the power and tension of the first two. He gave the score to a friend in gratitude for a favor, and the friend kept it for himself. It received its first performance 40 years later.

Schubert was headed for even worse luck. In 1823, he came down with a serious disease which biographers agree was syphilis, and which was practically incurable in those days. Schubert's love life is poorly documented except for a teen-age infatuation with a pretty soprano, which apparently haunted him most of his life. Otherwise, he seems to have found his loves where he could, often after a bout of drinking with his friends. At any rate, his disease left him with a rash and forced him to shave his head and wear a wig for a while; he also suffered severe headaches and (perhaps unrelated) excruciating pains in his left arm. He avoided company and wrote piteous letters to his friends: "I doubt if I shall ever be entirely well again" and "I feel myself to be the most unhappy, unfortunate creature in the world. . . . Every night, when I go to sleep I hope I will not wake again, and every morning reminds me only of yesterday's unhappiness."

Nevertheless, he continued to compose. He wrote one of his most famous song cycles, *Die Schöne Müllerin (The Fair Maid of the Mill)* consisting of 20 songs on a set of poems said to be taken from the posthumous papers of a traveling horn player. The song cycle had been invented, or at least introduced, by Beethoven seven years before in his *An die Ferne Geliebte (To the Distant Beloved)*, as an attempt to link short movements together—by subject matter or by musical devices—to make a more impressive whole. Such songs can be sung separately, of course, but heard in sequence, they become not only a coherent series of scenes but an emotional and musical entity. For Schubert, they represented a form of opera—but a distilled form that might be understood as the emotional highlights of a story—almost like arias taken out of context. Schubert wrote two other song cycles, *Die Winterreise* (*Winter's Journey*) and *Schwanengesang* (*Swan Song*).

In the next years, until he completed his *Winterreise* cycle, Schubert was more an instrumental than vocal composer—he wrote piano sonatas, three major string quartets and the "lost" symphony. The great C major symphony is the climax of his last years. This is the work that Robert Schumann discovered in Schubert's brother's house after the composer had died, and which he said half-seriously was of "heavenly length." The work is indeed enormous, starting out with ringing horn calls and extending just about as far as repetition could make it go. It is a work of ardent songfulness and powerful rhythmic vitality, truly a symphony in shape and scope—and one of the last to claim the name rightfully. Its outlines are actually simple; there are few daring modulations to distant keys, not a trace of the brilliant virtuosity that might have pleased easygoing Viennese, and little direct relation to folk music. It is, in fact, as classical as it is romantic.

Early in 1828, Schubert's friends persuaded him to give an all-Schubert concert to raise money and also to improve his prestige with publishers and the public. The Austrian Philharmonic Society loaned him its hall on the first anniversary of Beethoven's death, and it was filled to standing room. The program contained songs (sung by Vogel), a vocal octet, a string quartet movement, and a piano trio (his first to be published, Op. 100). The composer had many curtain calls. It would have been perfect except for the fact that the fabled violin virtuoso Paganini gave a concert about the same time, and none of the papers found space for Schubert.

Also, apparently, his finances were not much improved by this event. He could not even scratch up coach fare to

Budapest to give a concert. His health, too, kept him secluded in Vienna. "There is really nothing wrong with me," he wrote. "Only I am so weak I feel I am going to fall through the bed." By autumn, he was confined to his room, where he heard a private performance of a Beethoven quartet and got so excited his friends feared for his life. Shortly afterward he developed typhus, became delirious, singing almost continuously, and had to be held in bed by force. He died November 19, 1828, aged 31, leaving nothing but clothes and what his brother called "some old music." The Viennese buried him close to Beethoven and later erected a monument that cost many times his life earnings.

MUSICIAN AND JOURNALIST

SCHUMANN

ROBERT SCHUMANN was born in the town of Zwickau, Saxony, on June 18, 1810. He was the son of a book publisher, bookseller and sometime novelist—a man who prospered at the trade of selling prototypes of today's paperback reprints. He planned an intellectual life for his son Robert. At seven the boy started taking lessons in harmony and counterpoint from an organist. He was already composing, and local people claimed even then that he had a special gift for painting feelings in tone. But composing was of minor interest to young Robert, who preferred the career of piano virtuoso or journalist. Perhaps as a result, when he did turn to a composer's career, he attacked each musical form with self-conscious method: one year for songs and another for symphonies, before turning to chamber music. His mother was as proud of him and as indulgent as his father, but when his father died, she opposed an artistic career and sent Robert off to the university in Leipzig to study law.

Young Robert found Leipzig full of "everlasting noise and racket" and "cold jurisprudence" that crushed him with its "icy-cold definitions." Reading between the lines of his moody letters home (usually asking for money) we can be pretty sure Robert wasted little time on law. Instead he made friends with local musicians, who encouraged him to write songs and to study the piano seriously. His piano teacher was one Friedrich Wieck, a man who cultivated both an irascible manner and a sensitive keyboard touch—and whose daughter, Clara, at the age of nine was not only pretty but a talented pianist. Within a few years, Schumann was trying to decide which to pursue more ardently, his career or his teacher's daughter. Wieck showed Schumann the value of "pure, precise, equal, clear, rhythmical, and finally, elegant" playing.

The next year, Schumann was at Heidelberg, ostensibly to sit at the feet of legal luminaries, but actually to practice two hours a day on the piano, to give a concert and indulge in a giddy social whirl. He wrote immodestly to Wieck that he was "modestly aware of [his] superiority over all the Heidelberg pianists." He finally came to grips with the question of his future and wrote his mother a pleading letter: ". . . believe me, if I ever achieved anything in the world it was in music. . . . Jurisprudence so freezes me that no flower of my imagination will ever hope for springtime. . . . Now I stand at the crossroads, and am startled at the question—whither? My genius . . . directs me to art."

We may question whether Schumann knew what he did want. He was too well favored, intellectually and financially, for his own good; he left debts everywhere, knowing that his mother would pay them. But clearly the musical world was more to his taste than the juridical, and his poor mother, bedeviled by Wieck as well as by Robert, gave her reluctant permission for a musical career. As soon as he found a musical life within his grasp, Schumann lost some of his determination. "I am lounging around," he wrote. "It is the bane of all lively young souls that they would like to be a great many things all at once, and thus work becomes more complicated." He did work at the piano, but during the course of experimenting with a gadget for mechanically strengthening the always weak fourth finger, he crippled his own, and thus scuttled his hopes for a virtuoso's career.

When he was 23, Schumann turned his bubbling energy toward a peripheral project, the *Neue Zeitschrift für Musik (New Music Magazine)*. For him, it was a diversion, but its efforts to establish wider understanding of new music were important. Its editors were Schumann's friends, and most of them were musicians rather than amateur critics. This was a bold innovation, for most musical journalists, then as well as now, were nonmusicians. "We shall block up the worn-out ways," he wrote proudly, and he proceeded to do pretty much what he claimed.

The *Neue Zeitschrift* began with the announced purpose of honoring the poetry and significance of music, of supporting new music when it was valuable and fearlessly condemning it when it was bad. It published opinions that have become, whether or not because of Schumann's influence, the prevailing ones to this day. In order to present his arguments more easily, Schumann invented a small cast of characters which he called the "Davidite society of anti-Philistines": Florestan, impulsive, passionate and humorous; Eusebius, dreamy and reflective; and Master Raro, the reasoning, philosophical arbitrator between the two. One of the most famous paragraphs he ever wrote is the following: "Eusebius entered . . . with the words 'Hats off, gentlemen—a genius!' . . . laid down a piece of music. . . . I thought I recognized Mozart . . . wound through a hundred chords. . . . Florestan suggested that the variations might have been written by Beethoven or Schubert, had either of these men been a piano virtuoso. . . . How surprised he was when he read '*La Ci darem*

*la mano, Varie pour le pinoforte par Frédéric Chopin,
Oeuvre 2'!"*

Schumann revered Bach, who, he said, seemed to grow
more profound the oftener he heard him, and Beethoven:
in his listening, he said, he often found "beauty without
truth," and in Beethoven, "(though seldom) truth without beauty." The third member of his holy trinity was
Schubert. When Schumann visited the deceased composer's brother he discovered manuscripts gathering dust
on the shelves. One of them was the "great" C major symphony, of which he wrote: "This symphony leads us into
a region which we never before explored . . . over the
whole is thrown that glow of romanticism that accompanies Franz Schubert everywhere. . . . Except for some
of Beethoven's works, I have never observed such a
striking and deceptive resemblance to the voice. . . ."

Schumann's opinions were unfettered by tradition. He
objected to certain old fogies who lumped "schools" together, thus "throwing suspicion on the efforts of every
young composer, simply because there are weak and
objectionable points in the German-French school, as in
Berlioz, Liszt, etc." Late in life, he still found stimulus
in the discovery of young composers and put his powerful
stamp of approval on them: "There must inevitably appear a musician who can give ideal expression to his
times. . . . Such a musician has appeared; a young man
over whose cradle Graces and heroes have stood watch.
His name is Johannes Brahms."

Here are some quotations that show Schumann as a
penetrating aphorist—and reveal something of his musical times:

"I wish a race of monstrosities could arise in the world
of artists: players with six fingers on each hand. Then
the day of virtuosodom would come to an end!"

"One must listen to Italian music among the Italians; German music may be enjoyed anywhere. . . ."

"Much may be learned from singers . . . but don't believe everything they tell you. . . ."

"Listen carefully to all folk songs. They are mines of the most beautiful melodies, and will teach you the characteristics of different nations. . . ."

"There are people . . . who think they may reach the top by [practicing] mechanical exercises. That is as reasonable as trying to recite the alphabet faster and faster every day."

"The loftiest expression possible in music is attained by chorus and orchestra. . . ."

" 'Melody' is the amateur's war cry . . . certainly music without melody is not music. . . . But there are melodies of very different types; no matter where you open Bach, Mozart, Beethoven, etc., melodies will appear in a thousand different guises. . . ."

"It is characteristic of anything unusual that it cannot be easily understood; the majority is always tuned to the superficial. . . ."

"We cannot repeat the same forms for centuries, and should think about inventing some new ones. . . ."

"Men compose for many reasons: to become immortal; because the piano happens to be open; to become millionaires; because of the flattery of friends; because they have looked into a pair of beautiful eyes; or for no reason whatsoever."

"An occasional reminiscence is preferable to desperate independence."

Schumann also made one comment that should be etched in the minds of the music-loving public today, when the belief is all too common that musicians are unaware of the world around them: "Anything that hap-

pens in the world affects me: politics, literature, people
... I reflect about these things in my own way—and these
reflections eventually find an outlet in music."

The Schumann of these years was an engaging young
man. He could have developed into a thoroughly spoiled
brat and a dilettante. Instead he became a somewhat way-
ward but completely lovable prankster, sometimes a little
too fond of beer and cigars for the comfort of his friends,
utterly irresponsible in financial matters, inclined to little
discipline in musical matters but capable of inspired bursts
of enthusiasm. His musical criticisms reflect acute observa-
tion and an infectious love for good new music and musicians. He was no Pollyanna critic. He once said, in fact,
"The critic who does not dare attack something bad is a
halfhearted supporter of something good."

For the first nine years of his life as a composer, Schumann specialized in piano music, for he felt that instrumental music was the only way to "express the inexpressible"—words were too specific. His first published work
was a set of variations using the letters in the name of
the town Abegg as the notes of his theme. The second,
called *Papillons (Butterflies)* was a collection of little
pieces with no connection between them except the literary one that they were intended as impressions of a
masked ball. Schumann reveals his approach to the piano
—and all music—when writing about the romantic form
called the caprice. "In no other form do poetic liberties
sound so well," he wrote. "If, behind the lightness and
humor which characterize it, there also appears a sound-
ness and deeper insight, then there is genuine mastery."
Schumann himself approaches that mastery by fairly
sharp contrasts within a given work, between intimate,
dreamy expression and a brilliant but more superficial
quality comprised of stormy runs, big leaps, showy con-

trasts of staccato and legato.

Schumann's piano music encompasses his Op. 1 through Op. 23, and a good share of it is in the form of collections of little pieces, e.g. the famous *Carnaval* and the innocent *Scenes from Childhood*. Also from this period are four sonatas (the last is called a fantasy), all of them showing signs of poetic inspiration; and some perhaps self-conscious but original variations called *Symphonic Etudes*.

Schumann's gentle but feverish mind started to crack as early as 1837 when he was 27. Two of his relatives died that year, and Schumann was seized with fear: "Almost every draught brings attacks with it . . ." he wrote. "I do not even dare wash myself . . . violent rushes of blood, unspeakable fear, breathlessness alternate quickly." But by 1840, he seemed entirely recovered. His head was again filled with thoughts of marriage to Clara Wieck, and he had also overcome the obstacles, including a court trial, thrown in his path by old Wieck, who loved him as a son but could not see him as a son-in-law. His *Davidsbündler Dances,* Op. 6, were written in a spirit of happiness.

In 1840, the year he married Clara, Schumann discovered song: "What a bliss it is to write songs!" he wrote. "I have been a stranger to it for too long." Historians call Schumann Schubert's successor as Germany's great song composer. In his song year, he composed no less than 138 vocal pieces, many of them in cycles, in the manner of his piano cycles before them, few of them simply individual songs. As a master of keyboard technique, Schumann gave the accompaniment far greater importance than Schubert had, assigning to it transitions, explanations and summations, without which the whole song might have been meaningless. He developed a remarkable precision at catching poetic emotions in tone, evoking pages and pages of twilights, moonlit nights, exotic lands (Scotland among them) and a wide range of emotional tone in his song-stories, such as *Frauenliebe und leben* (*Woman's Love and Life*) and *Dichterliebe* (*Poet's Love*).

Robert and Clara were ecstatically happy with each other. But Robert's compositions, while they sold quite well, plus income from the music magazine, could not support them. When the Schumann income was pieced out with Clara's concertizing, it was adequate. There were other problems: Clara had to adjust her practicing schedule so as not to disturb Robert's composition. Often, she worked in the afternoons, while he was out with his friends at a local café.

In 1841, Schumann immersed himself in the first of his four symphonies (the *Spring*) which he sketched in four days, possessed by spring longing. He liked it very well indeed, although the public received it with less enthusiasm. By summer he was at work on another symphony. None of Schumann's symphonies is a masterpiece, for his orchestration was clumsy and intractable. Nevertheless, they have exuberant melodies and an abundance of that unmistakable softness of outline that we think of as romantic. At the end of a year of overwork, he suffered an attack of what he called "nerve exhaustion."

In 1843, he accepted a job from Mendelssohn, who was dominating Leipzig musical circles with his matchless command of musical instruments. The job was at the new Leipzig Conservatory, where, for a few months, Schumann taught piano and composition. He was not very good at it, for it seemed he could not bring himself to criticize or scold anybody at all. Next winter he and Clara set off on a money-making concert tour of Russia. The following fall, suffering from increasingly frequent delusions and terrors, he took his family off to Dresden, where he felt so much better he decided to make the move permanent, even though it meant resigning his editorship of the music magazine.

In Dresden he met Wagner, a decidedly incompatible personage: Schumann thought Wagner talked too much; Wagner said it was impossible to discuss anything with a man who did not open his mouth. Wagner thought Schumann's D minor symphony was banal, and Schumann thought Wagner incapable of writing four beautiful bars in succession. Nevertheless, he continued to follow Wagner's career and later changed his opinion somewhat: "Wagner," he wrote, "can be of great importance for the stage."

Until 1849, the Schumanns lived on the income from Clara's concert appearances, Robert's teaching, conducting (rarely successful) and royalties. That year he completed the C major symphony and his piano concerto (a colorful, bravura piece that pleased Clara immensely) and launched into the composition of large-scale vocal works: settings of scenes from Goethe's *Faust* and Byron's *Manfred,* which turned out to be better in concert form than it was on stage; and an opera, *Genoveva.* But Schumann's old affliction returned, now with the dismaying effect of "auricular delusions"—hearing music when there was none to be heard—more and more frequently until he could not escape from it.

Between attacks, his life seemed to be blessed. The Schumanns had five children who were beginning to listen to Mozart and Beethoven. Robert would compose in the mornings, walk with his beloved Clara, then work again until six, when he would go off to the tavern to read the papers over beer for two hours while Clara taught or practiced at home. In 1849, he wrote that it was "the most stimulating time for me; never have I been artistically more active or happier."

But trouble lay ahead. He accepted a conducting job at Düsseldorf, although he must have known that he was a poor conductor without the will to drive a chorus and orchestra through a long rehearsal; and he had some reservations about his new home when he read that the city held three convents and a lunatic asylum. "To the first I have no objection, if it must be so," he wrote, "... it was disagreeable to read the last; I must carefully avoid all melancholy impressions of the kind." Düsseldorfers received the Schumanns with gala festivities and a grand ball, which the newcomers were too tired to attend. Before many months, Schumann's ensemble rebelled, and he had to abandon conducting. He began to suffer severely with speech troubles, the inability to distinguish between actual sounds and the sounds in his head, and a feeling that all tempos were too fast.

The Schumanns' life was tense and indecisive in 1853; maybe they should move to Berlin or Vienna, maybe not. Then, once again came the most stimulating thing that could happen to Robert Schumann: the arrival of a new composer in need of a sponsor and a hero, the shabbily dressed Johannes Brahms. In a few weeks Schumann was calling him the "young eagle," began editing the young composer's music for publication, and wrote an article about him—his last—for the music magazine. Schumann almost forgot the impasse at home, so stimulated was he. When Brahms left Düsseldorf, the Schumanns left also, for a highly successful concert tour of Holland.

They were back home and Robert was busily compiling a book of his writings when insanity struck again, this time violently. In lucid moments, he asked to be placed in an asylum and even packed his clothes for the trip.

But the loving Clara put him to bed and mounted a close watch over him but not close enough; one rainy afternoon he slipped out and threw himself into the Rhine. After that, he was committed to the asylum he had feared. He lived two years more, functioning normally and even composing between bouts with his sickness. He died at the age of 46, on July 29, 1856. Clara lived on for 40 years, playing Schumann's music throughout Europe.

MASTER OF THE ORCHESTRA

BERLIOZ

WHEN HECTOR BERLIOZ burst on the musical scene, he presented a fine subject for caricature and raillery. He was a flamboyant personality who kept himself in the public eye by writing caustic reviews, composing music for the largest ensembles ever gathered together and conducting them with appropriate éclat. Such was his notoriety that almost nobody was surprised when he announced that his *Requiem* would require "a small orchestra" of 300-400 instruments and a choir of 4,000 voices; and few eyebrows were raised when he actually staged performances almost that big. Today, he is regarded as a master orchestrator—probably the first composer properly to consider orchestration as a separate technique—and his book codifying and explaining the various instrumental colors is still standard. He was also one of the great composers of all time, but this is not a universally accepted fact, even today. His critics point to his apparently willful treatment of harmony (some say it was ignorant treatment), his rather arbitrary use of leitmotifs, his loose treatment of form and what they consider an improper indulgence in dramatic devices.

Berlioz was born on December 11, 1803, at La Côte-Saint André, a very small town in southeastern France. Untroubled by false modesty, he later wrote that his birth was "unheralded by any of the events which . . . mark the advent of remarkable personages. . . . My mother never dreamed . . . that she was about to bring forth a laurel branch . . . [or] that she bore within her a fiery brand" (as Liszt's was said to have). It was the year that Napoleon Bonaparte reorganized the *Institut de France* and awarded the first musical *Grand Prix de Rome,* a prestige award that is still given annually to the outstanding composer at the Paris Conservatory.

Berlioz's father was a well-read, free-thinking country doctor who undertook to give his son some musical training, without, however, investing in a piano. Before he was twelve, Hector found a flageolet (a wooden whistle with a few keys) in a bureau drawer, learned how to play it and soon went on to learn the flute and how to read notes. His curiosity was stimulated by a group of amateur music-makers who gathered at his house Sunday afternoons, and he was soon composing "impossible" music with a freedom he might never have had if he had begun composing at the keyboard. Most of this early work he destroyed, but, with a thrift that never deserted him, he sometimes saved the melody for later use. Before long he was also a competent guitarist and a close, if somewhat mystified, student of harmony books.

When he was nearly 18, a blow fell: his father sent him to Paris to study medicine—with a splendid new flute as a bribe. Hector hated everything about his studies, particularly the dissecting room (he sang arias while cutting up cadavers), and one night he found his way to the opera where he was suddenly, irrevocably convinced he should become a composer. He sought out a music library and spent all the time he could there, studying scores.

Conceiving the idea that a musical success would make his illicit studies acceptable to his father, he found a teacher and began composing. An opera, he decided, was just the thing to make him famous; or, if not that, a church cantata. He completed the cantata and the first performance went down to defeat at the hands of unco-operative singers—or so he later said. But he borrowed money to pay his artists, and the cantata was performed again, with considerable success. When Berlioz *père* learned of this, he cut off Hector's allowance and ordered him home; later he relented, and the young man found himself, at the age of 23, ensconced in a Paris garret, living on dry bread and prunes, singing in the chorus of a second-rate light opera company, teaching, composing and, unknown to his family, studying at the Conservatory. He even bought a piano, just so he might have another musical instrument in his room. When he saw a pretty English actress named Henrietta Smithson playing in *Hamlet,* his composing was newly inspired; he determined to make a smashing success so he could impress her enough to ask her to marry him.

For the next three years, Berlioz composed furiously. He worked on his *Symphonie Fantastique,* published music at his own expense, wrote critical articles for whatever journal would buy them, brilliantly organized a concert of his own music and won the following strange critique: "M. Berlioz has genius . . . but . . . often wastes himself in combinations . . . which border on the wild and bizarre and are justified only by the fact that they succeed." For his future reputation, he kept entering the *Prix de Rome* competition, but each entry proved too radical for the academicians. His rhythms were too new, complained one; his music was not soothing, added another. He finally won the *Prix* in 1830, the first composer of lasting fame to achieve the honor. The winning work was a craftily conventional cantata called *Sardanapale (The Death of Sar-*

danapalus), whose big feature was a rousing conflagration scene. It was written, Berlioz recalled, during the Revolution of 1830, "to the tune of the dry thud of stray bullets ... over the roofs ... close to my window ... or on the walls of my room." He was a bit let down when he won and felt obliged to explain to another composer: "The score is not compatible with the state of modern music. ... [It is] full of commonplaces and ... instrumental vulgarities which I was forced to write in order to win the prize." The prize performance was a fiasco—a conductor's miscue quenched the conflagration—but Berlioz arranged another a few weeks later, at which he also introduced his *Symphonie Fantastique*.

This, as many a critic will say again, is a remarkable work for a first symphony. In it appear a number of Berlioz's most important musical characteristics, many of them his own inventions or extrapolations of existing theory. The work is in five movements—in itself a revolt against the classical four-movement tradition—each movement descriptively titled. (Originally the musical story was further explained in the program texts.) It is written with a distinct method of voicing that gives a spacious, ethereal effect, especially in the strings; a powerful use of crescendo that builds up smoothly into a stunning climax and relaxes just as easily; and a flexible treatment of rhythm that provides a pleasant surprise when an even number of beats is answered unexpectedly by an odd number.

The symphony is unified by still another typically romantic device. This is what Berlioz called the *idée fixe;* here it is a motif in the high winds or strings that turns up in all movements—as the misty image of a loved one might recur on the screen to obsess the bereft film hero. Berlioz introduces it simply, weaving it in neatly, altering it subtly for appearance in a pastoral setting, making it swirl grotesquely in the more macabre moments, fading and paling it as he blends it back into the fabric of the music that surrounds it.

Describing the symphony for the impressionable Parisian public, Berlioz wrote that it was autobiographical, and subtitled it "An Episode in an Artist's Life." The most titillating episode is a dope dream that apparently involves his beloved Henrietta and the roles she played. The work begins with "Dreams, Reveries," moves on to a ballroom waltz, a pastoral scene with shepherds, a rumble of thunder, then undergoes a change of mood with a "March to the Scaffold" and finally, a "Witches' Sabbath." Aside from the remarkable flexibility of its meter, the enchantment of its melodies, and the innovation of the recurring motif, there are some daring orchestral inventions in this symphony. Berlioz used a piccolo clarinet, for instance— the tiny relative of the usual orchestral clarinet—in addition to muted brasses and plucked strings; and, in the pastoral movement, he tried a shocker: a dialogue between reeds (oboe and English horn) and kettledrums. He was especially good to the brasses, freeing them from their routine block harmonies in climaxes and getting some melodic movement into them. His was an orchestra unfettered by custom; it was the first modern concert orchestra.

The *Fantastique* got a tremendous reaction from the Paris press and public. Leading musicians were equally interested; the great Franz Liszt made a piano transcription, and Schumann later wrote an understanding critique. He also voiced his disapproval of the programmatic approach, saying that "it smacks too much of the charlatan." Jacques Barzun, Berlioz's best biographer, points out that Berlioz inwardly agreed. The composer later said so in the program notes for the première, writing that he knew "quite well that music is not a substitute for speech nor for the art of drawing," and that he had never had "the absurd pretension of reproducing abstract ideas or moral qualities . . . only passions or impressions."

Berlioz left Paris in glory for the Villa Medici in Rome but had little use for the kind of Bohemian life that the *Prix de Rome* imposed on its winners. Even the café where he spent most of his time, along with the other prize-winners in the various arts, was "a miserable hole" to him. Besides, in a vain attempt to forget Henrietta, he had become engaged to marry a young pianist, and he had received no word from her. Then he learned that the girl had already married somebody else (the influential piano manufacturer Pleyel, in fact) and, in a frenzy of despair and jealousy, Berlioz determined to kill "two guilty women and an innocent man" (the girl, her mother and Pleyel) after which, of course, he would do away with himself. For this intrigue he disguised himself in a female servant's garb and, armed with a gun, headed for Paris, leaving directions that, should the dance movement from his *Fantastique* be played again, the low flutes should be doubled with clarinets and horns. On his way to Paris, he lost his disguise, and the whole scheme lost its appeal. Berlioz returned to Rome in a slough of despond. There he talked music with Mendelssohn and Michael Glinka (the "father of Russian music") but hardly found the heart to compose at all. Eventually, he sold his gun, smashed his guitar and left before his time was up. The memory of the dark Italian nights and the history-laden countryside was to provide him with inspiration for many compositions to come.

One of the few fruits of his visit to Italy was *Lelio,* a pastiche of melodies from earlier works, formed into a monologue with orchestral accompaniment. He said it was a sequel to the *Fantastique*—to provide a happy ending. The work was performed in Paris at the first opportunity and got fervid attention. Liszt and Chopin attended rehearsals, along with such literary romantics as Victor Hugo, Heinrich Heine, Alexandre Dumas and George Sand. At the concert itself Henrietta Smithson sat near the composer—at last!—and he braved an introduction. Berlioz thereupon canceled a trip to Germany in favor of courtship, and the marriage took place in October. To establish family life, the bridegroom borrowed 300 francs; despite numerous other debts and a fresh quarrel with his family, he was deliriously happy.

One of Berlioz's famous romantic admirers was the virtuoso violinist NICOLO PAGANINI (1782-1840). When the composer was 30, the violinist came with a request for a new concerto, preferably in the style of the *Fantastique*. Paganini wanted to play it on his Stradivarius viola. Berlioz obligingly turned out one movement for viola, chorus and orchestra called *The Last Moments of Mary Stuart*. Paganini, who wanted more opportunity to display his incredible virtuosity, was appalled at all the rests in the viola part, but he decided to leave the composer in peace, and the work proceeded uninterrupted. As it took form, its scene changed from Britain to Italy, its subject from the ill-fated Mary to Byron's superromantic *Childe Harold*. The work, Berlioz began to see, was to be "a series of scenes for orchestra, in which the viola would find itself involved . . . [as] a sort of melancholy dreamer. . . . Harold's melody is superimposed on the orchestral music, with which it contrasts both in movement and in character." This friendly interplay between soloist and orchestra was contrary to the romantic idea of the soloist pitting himself against the massed orchestra, and to the other romantic idea that a virtuoso piece could be played only by a fellow of heroic abilities.

When *Harold in Italy* had its première (without Paganini) in 1834, the audience applauded one movement so heavily it had to be repeated. As the luckless composer might have expected, a musician missed a cue, and the repeat performance ended in a shambles. Berlioz, whose common sense matched his flair for intrigue, decided the way to avoid such disasters in the future was to take up conducting himself. As for Paganini, he never played the piece, for he retired (suffering from cancer of the throat) before it was finished. He did hear it performed eventually and thereupon publicly bestowed 20,000 francs on Berlioz, "in homage." Since Paganini was reputed to be a devilishly tight-fisted man, the gift created a sensation, and the music world acclaimed its first "3 B's": Bach, Beethoven and Berlioz. Berlioz used the money to pay some debts and took time off from his onerous duties as a critic to compose his beautiful dramatic symphony, *Romeo et Juliet*.

Meanwhile, with masterly statesmanship, he wangled a government commission for one of his most famous and most vividly beautiful works, the *Requiem (Grande Messe des Morts),* for the seventh anniversary of the heroes of July 28, 1830. He composed even more rapidly than usual, inventing a kind of musical shorthand to jot down the fast-flowing ideas. In two months he had it finished. It demanded a full symphony orchestra, a large chorus and four brass bands (one for each corner of the cathedral), in order to fill the great cavern of *Les Invalides* with a glorious mass of sound. In the month remaining before the première Berlioz got the parts copied, proofread them and started to rehearse the performers—all 400 of them.

At the last minute the whole ceremony was canceled.

The commission was supposed to pay Berlioz 14,000 francs, but it was all he could do to talk the government out of enough to pay the singers' fees. Finally, in December, another performance of the *Requiem* was scheduled for *Les Invalides*. Berlioz scouted the domed interior for the best places to seat his musicians. At the performance, he prudently stationed himself back to back with the conductor, a man named Habeneck, where he could see the separate bands and the array of kettledrums. He tells the story in his own extraordinary autobiography: "There are, perhaps 1,000 bars in my *Requiem*. In . . . just *the* one bar where the conductor's direction is absolutely indispensable [between the *Dies Irae* and the full blast of the *Tuba Mirum*] Habeneck put down his baton, quietly took out his snuff box and proceeded to take a pinch of snuff. I turned rapidly on one heel . . . springing before him . . . stretched out my arm and marked the four great beats of the new movement. . . . When Habeneck saw that the *Tuba Mirum* was saved he said, 'Without you, we should have been lost.'" "Yes," answered Berlioz, "I know." This story may be partly the fruit of Berlioz's imagination, for autobiographies are not always accurate, and Berlioz, of all people, knew how to spin a good yarn. Nevertheless, it points up the lamentable state of musical performance at that time; even Paris was yet to acquire her first permanent orchestra.

Honors and successes followed at irregular intervals: Berlioz was made Librarian of the Conservatory, with a small but regular income, and a member of the Legion of Honor; later he was given the high honor of being elected to the *Institut des Arts,* parent body of the *Académie Française,* where he was pleased to vote an award to a youngster named Georges Bizet, two decades before he wrote his opera, *Carmen.* But even after his *Romeo et*

Juliet had three highly successful performances, Berlioz was forced to admit that "serious music does not keep its man."

At home, the once blissful Hector and Henrietta were estranged, and Hector had formed a liaison with a singer named Marie Recio ("she sang like a cat," he admitted). What was worse, his *Benvenuto Cellini* had been a miserable failure at the *Opéra*. It was withdrawn after four performances and effectively closed the doors of the *Opéra* to Berlioz from then on. Berlioz was forced to channel his dramatic gift into music dramas for concert performance.

In 1842, faced with financial failure in spite of his spectacular individual successes, Berlioz decided to make a concert tour of Germany, the first of many that were to fill the next years. He traveled with 500 pounds of music, which he sent ahead by mail coach, and carried a pair of sponge-headed sticks for kettledrums because of a shrewd suspicion that German players would have only wooden ones. He arranged his concerts from town to town on the basis of personal invitations. Both Mendelssohn, who disliked his music, and Schumann, who often loved it, helped him out. When he began rehearsing, usually he found that the orchestra in question had no ophicleide (an early form of the bass tuba) or English horn (the alto cousin of the oboe) or harp; or that the cymbals were damaged and unusable; or that the German musicians could not read the French directions on their music. It was, he wrote to Liszt, a task that was "never ending, still beginning and always unpleasant." Nevertheless, the orchestra of the moment gradually "walked, talked, became man"; as he put it, and the musicians, forced to strain their capabilities to do it right, became Berlioz's enthusiastic admirers. In the end, he often had the exhilarating experience of "playing on the orchestra," as if it were a giant instrument under his fingers.

Two years after his first tour, at Liszt's behest, he attended the unveiling of a Beethoven statue in Bonn; and in Vienna he conducted from the same podium that once supported Beethoven ("My legs trembled under me," he wrote, "when I stepped . . . on the platform . . . trodden by his mighty foot"). For an appearance in Pest, Hungary, he diplomatically wrote a grand march on a popular folk tune—the *Rakoczy March*. People said it would never succeed with the Hungarians because it began too softly, but Berlioz knew what he was about; his soft beginning built to the most air-splitting fortissimo the Hungarians had ever heard, and they burst into cheers. It was a good thing he programed the march last, he wrote, because "anything played afterward would have been utterly lost." Frugal Frenchman that he was, he incorporated it in his next big dramatic symphony, the *Damnation of Faust*, even though it meant taking Faust to Hungary. When somebody asked how it happened that his hero had traveled so far from home, Berlioz said: "I should not have hesitated in the least to take him anywhere else if it would have benefited my score."

Berlioz's *Faust*, a powerful work that overshadows the lackluster Gounod version and the Boïto *Mephistophele*, failed and remained in disrepute until 30 years after the composer's death, but the *Rakoczy March* became the most popular number of the symphony and is still often played even where the rest of the score is neglected. Disgusted by his failure, Berlioz took off on another concert tour, first to Russia, then to England. When he finally returned to Paris, on Bastille day, 1848, he found himself living on the same meager budget he had as a student, 25 years before.

"If only the music I have written might receive the same welcome here as in the rest of Europe, I might be forgiven for being alive and being French," he wrote. But despite despair, debt and concern for Henrietta, who was dying, he completed his *Te Deum,* a huge sequel to his *Requiem,* and his oratorio, *L'Enfance du Christ (The Childhood of Christ).* The latter work was performed with tremendous acclaim, a fact the embittered composer attributed to a misconception among Parisians that he had radically changed his style.

A few months later he attended a "Berlioz Week" in Weimar. That center was rife with Wagnerian fervor, and Berlioz was already annoyed by the growing influence of his German rival. "He wants to dethrone music and reduce it to mere expressive accents," wrote Berlioz. "I am for the kind of music that is so powerful that, in the proper places, it can conquer alone." Liszt wanted Berlioz to become a kind of Gallic elder statesman of the Wagner party, but Berlioz would have none of it. Nevertheless Liszt and his latest mistress encouraged Berlioz to start a new project, an opera based on Homer's *Aeneid.* This was to become a gigantic work, lasting six and a half hours, *The Trojans.* Berlioz wrote both text and music, taking his words from Virgil and Shakespeare, getting more excited each day. "I can hardly sleep," he said. "I think of nothing else." Finally, after three years, and with little chance of being performed, *The Trojans* was completed. People talked about it everywhere, but nobody wanted to produce it. Despite its lack of confidence in the composer, the *Opéra* accepted it but then never even attempted to stage the huge work. Berlioz was exhausted. He was content to let up for a while, to "live like an oyster, not thinking and not feeling." He was 56 and depressed at the deaths of many of his friends. But he could still be inspired, and soon he became enflamed about the idea of setting Cleopatra to music; "I think I could make an attractive creature out of that torpedo," he wrote. Nothing came of that, but he got busy again on his comic *Beatrice and Benedict,* his third real opera (based on *Much Ado about Nothing*), finished it and conducted it with huge success.

Eventually, after a series of musical intrigues, staged by his musical enemies, and after giving up his primary stipulation that the opera be presented uncut, he secured a performance for *The Trojans* in a Paris theater. The director, cast and stage manager tirelessly pestered the 60-year-old composer for cuts, changes, simplifications. In 1863 the première took place. The performance consisted of only two-thirds of the work, with the title *The Trojans at Carthage.* Berlioz hated every minute of it, but the piece ran for 22 performances, at boosted prices, and when he totted up his royalties and fees, the interest alone mounted to more than his annual salary as a reviewer. This was enough for Berlioz; he quit his reviewing jobs forthwith and forever.

There was scant happiness for him, however. His second wife had died the year before, and his son was to live only three more years. Berlioz tried to turn back to his childhood, made a pilgrimage to Provence and sought out his first love, now a woman over 60. In 1866, he conducted a performance of the *Damnation of Faust* in Vienna, and despite his suffering from a painful illness, he considered it the triumph of his career. He died in Paris in 1869, still curious about the younger generation of composers, still embattled against the "routineers, professors and the tone deaf."

THE PIANO

THE PIANO BEGAN TO OCCUPY BOURGEOIS PARLORS early in
the 19th century, a symbol of the common man's partici-
pation in the once-restricted art of music. It all began with
musicians' dissatisfaction with the limited expressiveness
of the keyboard instruments available in the early 18th
century. The tiny clavichord was fine for the intimacy of
the music room. The organ and the harpsichord were
quite adequate for spinning out lines of counterpoint, because sudden shifts of loudness and equally sudden
switches of tone color were perfectly acceptable. But as
counterpoint gave way to monody, keyboard players began to envy the subtle shadings of the violin and the
human voice.

Among the first attempts to make hammered strings
sing was a Hungarian instrument called the pantaleon
which looked something like a small grand piano with no
lid. It was the ancestor of the modern Hungarian cimba-
lom, which the performer plays with mallets, striking the
exposed strings in the manner of the xylophonist. Gradually, the idea of hammering the strings, rather than plucking them, won favor as the most likely way to convert the
harpsichord into a more sensitive instrument. But developing a foolproof keyboard mechanism proved to be an
imposing engineering problem: making a wedge-shaped
hammer strike the stretched string was easy, but making
the hammer drop back immediately, so it would not rest

against the vibrating string and cause an angry buzzing, was something else again. It was solved in 1709, though perhaps not for the very first time, by an Italian named BARTOLOMEO CRISTOFORI, who was employed to care for the harpsichords in the palaces of Ferdinand de Medici. Cristofori invented an ingenious escapement device, based on separate hinging or pivoting of the key and the hammer. It worked like this: depressing a key caused its butt or tail end (inside the box) to rise like a seesaw, and this tossed the hammer against the string. The movement of the butt caused it to slide out automatically from under the hammer—the process is called "escapement"—which was then free to fall back as soon as it struck the string.

This gave rise to another problem. The light, wooden hammer recoiled from the string with such force that it tended to bounce off its rest and strike again and again, causing a twangy, rapid-fire echo. Cristofori solved this by inventing a neat back-catch mechanism. Things still were not right, however, for, once struck, the strings would ring freely; when the performer finished playing a fast scale passage, the whole scale would continue to sound at once, in a dissonance that was highly offensive, at least to 18th-century listeners. To put a stop to the ringing, Cristofori arranged dampers of felt that rested on the strings, preventing any sound. When the key was depressed, it not only caused the hammer to strike but also pushed up the damper, freeing the string until the key was released again. The finished instrument was an oblong box slightly smaller than a harpsichord and capable of expressive effects; but, on the whole, it sounded weak and tinny, even by comparison with the harpsichord. In addition, the mechanism, with all its intricate wooden parts, was expensive. Nevertheless, the idea of an instrument of such subtlety was extremely appealing, and music for the *piano*

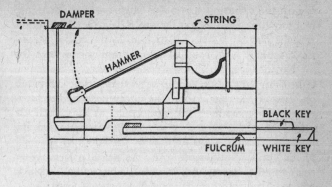

DAMPER STRING HAMMER BLACK KEY FULCRUM WHITE KEY

DIAGRAM OF PIANO ACTION

e forte was published as early as 1732.

But Cristofori's machine was only one—a very early one —of a crop of similar efforts. In Dresden, an organ-builder named GOTTFRIED SILBERMANN spent a lot of time puzzling out the problems, possibly with reference to descriptions of Cristofori's models, and came up with a workable affair that was played by the great Johann Sebastian Bach himself. As the years passed, other builders turned out their own designs, which appeared all through Germany. They were weak-voiced instruments with wooden frames that could not sustain much string tension and thus were neither as loud as a full-size harpsichord nor as flexible in shading as a good clavichord.

In the Bavarian city of Augsburg, a spiritual descendant of Silbermann, JOHANN ANDREAS STEIN, was building excellent claviers of all varieties and was particularly proud of his *forte-pianos*. Mozart spent a month in the city in 1777 and passed much of his time there with Stein, playing his latest models. "When I play vigorously," he wrote his father, "whether I leave the finger down or lift it up, the tone stops the moment I sound it . . . it will not block [i.e., the hammers will not stick against the strings and kill the tone]. . . . His instruments are made with an escapement. . . . When you strike the keys, his hammers fall back the instant they jump against the strings, whether you leave the keys down or up. . . . His claviers are really durable. He guarantees the soundboard will not break or crack." Mozart also praised another of Stein's improvements, a "machine you press with the knee" to raise all the dampers simultaneously. It was an early version of today's "loud" or sustaining pedal, which allows all the strings to ring until their tones die a natural death.

This, then, was the instrument that existed in the 1780's. Until that time, musicians thought of it as a kind of overgrown clavichord, except that where the clavichord was good for only a most intimate effect, piano tone could fill a medium-sized room. The piano sounded comparatively dull in timbre beside the harpsichord's dazzling, clangorous fortissimos, and it was regarded as difficult to play. This objection held validity: where a harpsichordist or organist could play with flatly extended fingers, simply depressing the keys to produce his music, the pianist had to vary the color, the loudness and the smoothness of his attack from a flowing legato to a pinpoint staccato, all with those same ten fingers. Opponents of the newfangled instrument pointed out that it could not possibly have the expressiveness of a clavichord, since, once the key was struck, the player had no further control over the hammer: it simply jumped against the string and fell back. In the clavichord, the wedge-shaped tangents rubbed against the string constantly and left it only when the player lifted his finger.

As a result, some fairly remarkable subspecies of keyboard instruments were concocted, all of them with the intention of producing music that was more subtly varied. There were examples of a combination harpsichord and piano; a three-manualed harpsichord and piano with the manuals facing each other across the box; a reed organ whose volume could be regulated by key pressure; and a remarkable contraption that was sounded by bringing spinning disks into contact with the strings, in an attempt to sustain the tone indefinitely. But German craftsman-ship, patiently whittling out the thousands of pieces of hardwood that went into the pianoforte, kept improving this instrument, and by the mid 1780's it was the most popular keyboard instrument in Europe.

This was the instrument that Mozart, then in his 20's, could be seen and heard playing on the stage of a con-verted flour mill, seated before an orchestra with his back to the audience, raising his right hand to signal the start of the music, occasionally nodding his head or singling out a musician with piercing eyes to warn the man that it was time for his entrance, at other times concentrating on his own flying fingers and allowing his concert master to do any necessary cueing. When it came time for his solo, the sounds he made were of subtle color and shading. In fortissimo passages, they resembled the metallic tones of a harpsichord, brittle and brilliant, edgy and quite loud. When he allowed a loud tone to fade away without inter-ruption, its quality changed subtly into the rounded sound we think of as typical of modern pianos. Similarly, when he struck the keys gently, the sounds he made were thick and quite heavy, almost exactly a duplicate of modern piano tone. Besides this duplicity of tonal character, Mo-zart's pianos had another kind of subtlety: the pitch itself seemed to change slightly with every note, sounding a fraction sharp at the impact, immediately dropping to true pitch. This happened because the strings could not be stretched very tightly: the wooden case and frame of the old instruments were simply not capable of supporting high tension without springing or buckling. Every blow of the tiny hammers tended to stretch the strings slightly, thus momentarily raising the pitch.

Mozart's dazzling dexterity on the keyboard was no accident. He was a thoughtful student of methods of producing legato runs and fingerings for the even more impressive broken chords that ranged up and down the keyboard. Since the duration of any tone on the piano could be controlled, within the limits of the dying string vibrations, by leaving the key depressed, Mozart had to learn a whole, extremely delicate series of muscular gradations aside from shading between loud and soft. To produce a flowing legato scale, he had to be sure to leave one finger down until the instant the next one activated the hammer mechanism; if he raised it too soon, there would be an empty instant between tones, and the effect would be one of a rattling staccato; if he held it down an instant too long, one tone would impinge on the next and create a blurred effect.

By the year 1824, there were at least one hundred piano builders in Europe and fifty in London alone (roughly the number in New York today), each turning out about twenty to fifty instruments a year if they were working in private workshops, or as many as 400 if they were using the industrial know-how of the new era.

The piano business was so good, in fact, that the music publishing business had to move fast to keep up. Fortunately, as so often happens when the demand for a product increases, new techniques made music more available. The invention of movable musical type spared the expensive and time-consuming process of engraving plates for the printing of scores, and a tidal wave of simple keyboard music hit the market. Austria and Germany bought up sonatas by C. P. E. Bach, Mozart, Haydn, Hiller, Salieri; keyboard reductions (with the voice singing the right hand melody) of songs from the operettas by Mozart, Salieri, Weigl, Muller; operatic arias by Mozart and Gluck; and something brand new and exciting—waltzes.

Most popular of all was a primitive kind of program music for which the piano was the perfect instrument: battle scenes and storm music. Battle pieces almost always consisted of a march-prologue, bugle calls, roaring cannon, charges with the pounding of horses' hoofs, cries of the wounded and a concluding national anthem or victory dance. The noisiest and most popular episodes in these warlike numbers were the cannon roars, accomplished, according to explicit direction in the printed scores, by pounding the piano's lowest notes with the flat of the hands. Mozart and Beethoven were among the composers who turned out such musical battle scenes. The storm music, of course, had thunder, which was indistinguishable from cannon roars, except in the program notes. It also included pattering of raindrops, rising winds, surging waves, and calms before, during and after. So popular were these works that pianos were build especially to perform them, with attachments to simulate cymbals, bells, drums, bassoons. They also had special soft pedals, one of which, the *una corda* device, which moves the entire action sideways and thus causes the hammer to strike only one or two of the strings allotted to each note, is still used on grands.

As the paying public grew larger, the demand for spectacular playing increased, and the misapprehension was born—which unfortunately, still exists today—that the more difficult a piece is to play, the better the performer who can negotiate it successfully. This idea gave rise to a whole series of "velocity" exercises, or "studies," written expressly to train fingers to a high degree of dexterity. Their composers were such men as KARL CZERNY, whose volumes of five-finger studies are still the bane of many a beginning pianist, and MUZIO CLEMENTI, who was the author of a famous method that he called *Gradus ad Parnassum* and later a dealer in pianos. A student who has been saddled with their endless scales and figure passages may find it hard to believe, but there is often real music in the pages of these unpretentious volumes. Many composers whose fame rests on broader foundations, e.g., Liszt, Chopin, Debussy and Bartók, have written studies—they called them "etudes"—that survive very nicely on musical value alone. Needless to say, conquering their intricacies ensures mastery of many of the instrument's technical hurdles.

Before the 19th century was half over, the piano underwent every major improvement it was to get to the present day, except for the powerful cast iron frame. Its structural strength was first improved in England, where the piano builder, Broadwood, added four or five longitudinal iron bars to take the strain of the stringing. In spite of a notion that this spoiled the tone, the bars became common, and metal was soon introduced into the frame itself. To increase power and vibrating time, three strings were tuned to a single note on the highest two-thirds of the instrument, while the lowest strings were wrapped along their length with copper wire to achieve the same result.

As piano frames acquired structural strength, strings were made of tougher stuff and pulled tighter, and after mid-century the piano could produce a thunderous amount of sound, and its soft tones seemed to sing. To improve the quality of this sound further, various substitutes were tried for the old pointed, leather-covered hammers, and finally the familiar round-headed felt hammers of today were developed. The Parisian manufacturer Erard improved the action with a complex double-escapement to permit more rapid repetitions of the same note and, in 1824, developed the first true upright (for apartment use), with its tail on the floor and hammers that struck downward from the front side of the strings. About the same time, Pleyel, another Parisian manufacturer, who was once a composition pupil of Haydn, took a successful step to stimulate trade by opening a concert hall off his factory premises, thus achieving valuable publicity and initiating a practice that continues to this day. The scene was now set for the entrance of that great romantic figure, the piano virtuoso, and for the composition that pitted him against a full symphony orchestra, the piano concerto.

THE PIANO GROWS UP

CHOPIN

FREDERICK CHOPIN casts the most delicately romantic aura of all the romantic composers. His birth date is shrouded in mystery; he seemed very frail while alive, and he died at the age of 39 of that most fashionable romantic disease, tuberculosis (Berlioz said he was dying all his life). During his lifetime he was fabled to be a sorcerer at the piano, but few except high-born and wealthy music-lovers ever actually heard him play. His music was emotional, even passionate, but his private feelings remained a secret. His love life, however, was a public scandal because of a seven-year-long affair with the novelist who called herself George Sand.

Chopin was to piano music what Beethoven was to the symphony. He wrote only a few more than 200 compositions, but piano music was never the same afterward. Schumann wrote of his music: "Imagine that an old Aeolian harp could play all the scales, and that an artist had blended them together in all kinds of fantastic decorations, but in such a way that you could always hear a deeper fundamental tone and a softly singing melody. . . ." And again: "One is mistaken if he thinks that Chopin would have every one of the little notes heard clearly; it was more of a surging of the . . . chord, emphasized here and there by the pedal. But one perceived wonderful, great-toned melody running through the harmonies, and in the middle there appeared . . . a tenor voice gradually taking shape."

The man who worked these unheard-of wonders on the pianoforte was the son of an immigrant French teacher in Zelazowa Wola, Poland. The generally accepted date of his birth is February 22, 1810, the same year as Schumann's, a year before Liszt's, three years before Verdi's and Wagner's, nine months after Haydn died. Chopin's birth was registered a year late, and his parents may have altered his real birth date because of fines or penalties that were attached to such tardiness. Nobody saw anything unusual about the boy, except to note his early (age six) talent for music. He got solid instruction from a local teacher, who introduced him to the same composers to-day's conscientious teachers would choose: Bach, Haydn, Mozart, Beethoven. From the start, Chopin's fingers adapted themselves with astonishing ease to the keyboard; when he was full grown, his hands were still rather small, but other pianists were astonished when they saw how far his fingers could stretch—like the jaws of a snake, some-body said. By the time he gave his first concert, at the age of eight, he was the darling of Warsaw society, and Poland cherished him from that time onward.

In the spring of his fifteenth year, he made his formal debut as a composer with his Rondo in C major, Op. 1. The next year, he became a fulltime student at the conservatory, where his talent was fortunately recognized and intelligently encouraged even though it did not conform to the rules. As a student he published his Op. 2, the variations on a Mozart aria that inspired Schumann's salute, "Hats off, gentlemen, a genius." When the young man finished his conservatory course, his father saw that he would have to go out into the world and sent him off to Vienna, the ex-capital of the music world (Paris had inherited that title). Everybody there who heard him play was astonished, and nothing would do but for him to give a public concert; it was a practical necessity anyhow, since his prospective publisher refused to touch the Op. 2 unless the composer introduced it himself. Somebody produced a fine piano, another "lent" the theater (and pocketed the receipts), an orchestra was rehearsed, and the fastidious Viennese were treated to an elegant performance. So favorable was his reception that Chopin was persuaded to give a second concert. When a third was suggested on the same terms (no fee), he declined and returned to Warsaw with a successful debut to his credit.

That winter, young Chopin found himself in the toils of hopeless love for a pretty and extremely popular singer. He never dared speak to her but secretly poured his feelings into his music. One result was the lyrical *Romance* of the first of his two concertos, in E minor. Before he left Warsaw again the next fall (1830) he completed the second concerto (F minor) and played it to an enraptured audience. In his 21st year, Chopin left Poland to face the world as a man.

In Vienna things were not the same at all. The "triumphal return" concert was postponed for months, and when it did take place, Chopin was simply one item on a group program. His publisher refused to look at his concertos. Worst of all, an anti-Russian revolution had broken out in Poland, causing Chopin great anguish and indecision: Should he return? Should he stay? Should he perhaps do away with himself? Under the circumstances, it would have been understandable if the handsome young man had buried himself in his heavy social life; but Chopin continued to compose. During this period he wrote his G minor ballade and the dramatic B minor scherzo, with its nostalgic reminiscence of home. He decided to seek his fortune in Paris but found the Russian Embassy would not let another of its nominal subjects go there to join the other Polish refugees. But, in one of those strange diplomatic niceties, it permitted him to go to "London via Paris." On the way he heard that revolutionary Warsaw had fallen to the Russians, and in a wild frenzy of despair he composed his famous *Revolutionary Etude*. In the autumn he reached the city that was to become his real home.

He was 21, a slight man with blondish hair, blue-gray eyes and irregular features dominated by a distinguished, aquiline nose. He made an impression of great refinement —some thought, effeminacy. Once, when someone asked what he looked like, the answer was "his music." Despite his delicate appearance, Chopin's inner life was a tumult. "He restrained himself," wrote Liszt, "without being able to tame himself. Every morning he again began the task of imposing silence on his raging anger, his white-hot haste, his boundless love, his throbbing pain and his feverish excitement, and managed to keep it in suspense by a sort of spiritual ecstasy. . . . He could not for a moment divert his attention from himself."

Chopin's style matured quickly. Although his melody is called "Polish," he never inserted a folk tune into his music. Instead, he transformed native tunes into something dreamlike and original. His were piano melodies; they can never be sung because of their wide leaps and lines that are far too long for human breath. Nevertheless, Chopin's music "sings" more lyrically than any ever written for the piano. By his time, of course, the instrument had been reinforced by iron frames, which permitted great string tension and a consequent sustaining power unheard of a few years before. Chopin found further ways to add to the illusion of singing by entwining the melodic line in a decorative filigree, enhancing it, supporting it and inflecting it with rolling arpeggios.

Since the lyrical quality of Chopin's music was so important, it was inevitable that the singer's device known as rubato should be heavily used—and abused—by Chopin interpreters. As we have seen, rubato was familiar to Mozart, fifty years before, but it is most closely associated with Chopin. The device takes the form of loosening the tempo, lingering, hesitating, edging forward in anticipation—all without destroying the fundamental pulse. Its effect is to increase the flexibility of the melodic curve and to give it more emphasis at the proper moments. This is known, for better or worse, as "expression," and when overdone it gives Chopin's music an insufferable air of faded languor that is not rightly a part of it. It is overused, of course, because musical notation is both inflexible and inexact; the result is, except for phonograph recordings, that no musical performance is ever exactly duplicated (not that it must be: there are certainly several correct ways of playing any composition). Chopin's own rule resembled Mozart's: left *("maître de chapelle")* hand steady; right ("singing") hand free to speed up or slow down.

The forms of Chopin's music were often of his own invention—the largest, he called "ballades"; the smallest, "etudes"; and not one of them has a descriptive program. Whatever its form, the music is of sweeping eloquence, its conciseness hidden under a semblance of improvisation. He wrote two sonatas which might as well have been given other names: the first, in B flat minor, contains the famous funeral march and a startling, fleeting finale written entirely in unison; the second, in B minor, is slightly less familiar. His four one-movement ballades might almost be considered heroic songs, although they use such architectural devices as the variation, the rondo or the sonata form whenever required. They are the finest of his large works.

His nocturnes are simpler, somewhat shorter forms, of a reflective nature, and as their name implies, evocative of moonlit landscapes. The form, if it is form, was invented by an Irish composer, JOHN FIELD (1782-1837), who filled it with practically every lyrical mannerism and expressive effect that Chopin himself used, but who lacked Chopin's subtlety and harmonic imagination. Chopin admired Field's music but thought the man coarse and vulgar. Field called Chopin's a "sick-room talent."

Chopin developed the etude while writing finger exercises for his own use. The result was a form that grew up with the piano. The etude is built on a single musical idea scanned from every angle until its emotional, as well as technical, resources are exhausted. Chopin wrote 27 of these studies, in two volumes, and there is no technical problem in his other music that is not dealt with among them. But even today, there are few pianists who can play them all up to speed and with the proper inflections.

Out of his idealized love for Poland, Chopin also wrote in the dance forms of his people: polonaises, waltzes, mazurkas. None of these closely resembled their prototypes, and certainly none of them was ever danced until the pieces were made into accompaniments for sophisticated ballets.

This then, was the music that Parisian aristocrats were about to hear from the composer who arrived there in 1831. "I don't know where there can be so many pianists as in Paris, so many asses and so many virtuosi," Chopin wrote. He was speaking of one of the world's most intense concentrations of intellect and creativity, for Paris was seething with the genius of writers (Hugo, Balzac, Musset) painters (Delacroix, Ingres) and composers (Berlioz, Liszt, Rossini, Cherubini). Chopin, who was a good bit shrewder and more worldly-wise than his gentle music and some of his biographers indicate, came fully armed with letters of introduction and quickly met all the right people. He was still concerned about his piano technique and diplomatically took a few lessons from the reigning virtuoso, Frederick Kalkbrenner. Then, with the backing of the wealthy colony of Polish exiles, he appeared in a "grand vocal and instrumental concert." He was a flashing success, playing his F minor concerto and his variations, Op. 2, as well as playing one of the six pianos in a set of Kalkbrenner variations. Liszt was present and became Chopin's admiring friend; Berlioz and Mendelssohn also became his frequent companions. But Chopin's second concert was a failure; he was quick to realize that his tone was too intimate to dazzle the blasé Parisians, and he never played again in a large hall. "The crowd intimidates me," he told Liszt. "I feel asphyxiated by its breath, paralyzed by its curious looks, dumb before the strange faces." He might have left Paris altogether had he not met the wealthy Rothschilds, of banking fame. Once they decided to patronize him, his success was assured. From then on, he made his living by teaching the daughters of the idle rich, and a handsome living it was. He charged a fee of 20 francs a lesson (roughly comparable to $20 today), which he requested his pupils to leave on the mantel in his fine, elegantly furnished flat. He played for his new acquaintances only in their private salons, thus helping to establish the legend of a remote and elusive personality. His admirers responded reverently. In Liszt's words, "It was not so much a question of the school of Chopin as the church of Chopin."

Already a legend at 27, Chopin had yet to get his love

life settled. He had managed to express his passion to one young lady and actually became secretly engaged to her. But his health was already beginning to break, and the girl's family, considering him a poor risk, intervened. At about this time he met the imposing figure of George Sand, a heavy-featured, dark-skinned woman of 32 who affected men's clothes and smoked cigars to express her feminine independence. She was in the midst of a divorce and simultaneously on the rebound from an affair with the poet Alfred de Musset. She and Chopin fell into each other's arms, and in 1838, the couple left for a winter "honeymoon" on the island of Majorca.

The scandal was intense—Sand was "that woman" to most of Chopin's acquaintances—and those who could think clearly at all about it predicted a tragic end to the affair. For a while it looked as if they were right: Chopin became violently sick during the wintry weather and was coughing blood when the couple returned to the mainland that spring. Then it looked as if they were wrong: Chopin had not received such loving care since leaving Poland. For eight years he and his beloved lived together, sometimes semi-incognito in Paris, sometimes at George Sand's summer estate, Nohant, where the intellectual world gathered often, and where Chopin was allowed to compose and live as he pleased while convalescing. But eventually the relationship broke down; Sand's grown children were jealous and undisciplined, and one of them apparently plotted a magnificent misunderstanding between the two. Chopin never returned to the comforts of Nohant, where he might have lived several more years; but he carried a lock of George's hair until his death.

It is easy—too easy—to think that Chopin left the spark of inspiration behind when he left George Sand. "I do my best to work," he wrote a friend, "but it just won't do. If

I go on like this, my new works will not remind you of warbling birds and not even of broken china. . . . I work a little. I scratch out a lot." It was certainly true that he was discouraged and slowing down. Whether this was the result of his broken love affair or of his increasing weakness from tuberculosis, it is hard to say. A most important factor was his own evolving attitude about composition, for he felt the need to develop his style further. His *Polonaise-Fantasie,* written during this period, shows signs of his preoccupation with new means of musical expression.

He returned to Paris in February, 1848, where he played for the last time to that elegant, sophisticated audience that was so characteristic of him and his time. Then, despite faltering health, he went to London, where he met Dickens, Emerson (there on a visit) and the great soprano, Jenny Lind; and from there, to Scotland to visit Jane Stirling, another lady pupil, who was undoubtedly in love with him.

Eventually, in the depths of despair, he returned to Paris. "I give myself the impression of . . . a violin's E string on a bass viol," he wrote. And, "Our best tuner has drowned himself . . . now I do not even have a piano tuned as I like it. . . . All that I have left is a big nose and an underdeveloped fourth finger." He died in a pretty Paris apartment, on October 17, 1849, in the presence of his sister. Mozart's *Requiem* was played at his funeral, and a huge cortege followed the bier to its resting place in a Paris cemetery. Before he was dead a year, a monument was raised to his memory.

VIRTUOSO IN SPITE OF HIMSELF

LISZT

IN THE WINTER OF 1840, Hans Christian Andersen went to a concert to hear a 29-year-old prodigy, FRANZ LISZT, play the piano. What he wrote about it was no fairy tale: "An electric shock seemed to thrill the hall as Liszt entered. Most of the women rose. A sunbeam flashed across each face, as though every eye were seeing a beloved friend. . . . As he played . . . I saw the pale face assume a nobler more beautiful expression . . . he grew handsome—handsome as vitality and inspiration can make one. . . . It did not sound like the strings of a piano. . . . The instrument appeared to be changed into a whole orchestra. . . . When Liszt had done playing, the flowers rained down on him."

Such a concert caused another writer to let himself go, perhaps with tongue in cheek: Liszt, he wrote, "treats his mistress—his piano—now tenderly, now tyranically, devours her with kisses, lacerates her with lustful bites, embraces her, caresses her, sulks with her, scolds her, rebukes her, grabs her by the hair, then clasps her all the more delicately, more affectionately, more passionately, more volatilely, more meltingly, exults with her to the heavens, soars with her through the skies and finally settles down with her in a vale of flowers covered by a canopy of stars."

This was the public face of one of the most remarkable in an age of remarkable figures—one who stands with

Byron as the incarnation of the romantic spirit and a true revolutionary. There is no doubt that Liszt was a consummate showman, with fingers of velvet as well as of steel; a flowing shoulder-length mane of hair; eagle eyes showing under beetling brows; and he always had an amorous scandal in the offing to titillate his public. Even the conflict with a rival pianist of equal renown, Sigmund Thalberg, who threatened to unthrone him, was grist for Liszt's mill. Thalberg was a mediocre composer but an excellent pianist, who made his impression by sitting quietly without smiling or frowning or dilating his nostrils while playing. His proponents, or Liszt's, arranged pianistic cock fights at the homes of popular hostesses, and the two played it out. Listz's compositions were distinctly the better, but the result was usually judged a draw. "Thalberg," said one wit, "is the first pianist in the world, but Liszt is the only one." Such was the musical humor of the day.

All of this folderol was, so Liszt believed, only the means to an end: he really wanted to be an immortal composer, not an ephemeral virtuoso. But to have time and money to compose, he had to work for a while as a prodigy, and there was little that he would not do to promote his reputation.

Liszt was born to the prodigy's life. His father was a music-struck man in the entourage of Prince Esterhazy. Though he dreamed of musical achievements, in the year 1811, he found himself in charge of peasants and sheep in the Hungarian village of Raiding. That was the year that a twin-tailed comet glared in the night sky for many months. It was still visible on October 22 when Franz was born.

Nine years later, Liszt's father noted his son's ability to improvise on the family pianoforte and took him to the

Esterhazy court. Franz so impressed the nobles there that they sponsored his public debut and arranged a subsidy for the next six years of his musical education. Father and son departed forthwith for Vienna where Franz studied with Czerny and Salieri. The boy's Vienna debut was greeted ecstatically ("God is among us!"), and eventually it was arranged for Beethoven himself to kiss his brow in public. Liszt's future was assured. A few months later, *"le petit Litz"* was the toast of Paris and wrote an opera (at age twelve) about everything he knew nothing about—unrequited love and gods and goddesses. It was performed four times and then—fortunately—shelved for good.

When his father died, in 1827, 16-year-old Franz found himself broke and unsettled. Taking advantage of his entré with the nobility, he started to teach. Then, when a love affair was thwarted by the young lady's father, he considered entering the priesthood. Finally, he decided to concentrate seriously on his piano playing, knowing all the while that he really wanted to be a composer. Within a few years he was the rage of the continent, both as a piano virtuoso and as a male—for he cut a wide swath through the feminine ranks, a fact that seems to have slowed him not at all in his touring. Ladies stole his handkerchiefs, his cigars, any memento they could lay hands on, and serious musicians (notably Schumann and Berlioz) were among his admirers. He settled down for a while in a liaison with an unhappily married countess, Marie D'Agoult, who lived five years with him and bore him three children.

As the flaming young prodigy made his way around Europe, he came through the German town of Weimar, the residence of Goethe and Schiller. There he made an advantageous arrangement with the reigning prince and prepared to make the place a kind of latter-day Athens. He contracted to live there three months of every year, playing, teaching and conducting. After a tour of Russia, where he won the affections of another unhappily married lady, the Princess Caroline of Sayn-Wittgenstein, he returned to remake the Weimar opera company. He produced no less than 20 contemporary operas, including Wagner's *Tannhäuser,* and became Wagner's heartiest promoter; Weimar became a famous musical center.

In Weimar, Liszt led a lovely life. He lived in a spacious villa, bedecked with trophies of his virtuoso career, including the Broadwood piano on which Beethoven had last played and a small clavichord once owned by Mozart. Among his pupils were the conductor Hans von Bülow and the pianists Anton Rubinstein and Carl Tausig. It was a gay, stimulating time, and Liszt and his princess gave many parties. But gradually he began to spend more time in his private apartment, at last composing as he had always wanted to. Caroline kept a protective eye on him. "He must be made to concentrate, otherwise he gets all mixed up," said she. "It is not genius he lacks, but the capacity to sit still." He wrote mostly for the symphony orchestra or the piano, and in both idioms was a master of far greater individuality than he gets credit for today. But to his contemporaries, he was a composer of virtuoso showpieces.

Virtuosity was demanded by romantics. Every great performer of the day was fascinated by the legend of Paganini, the man, so the story went, who could do things with his fiddle that only the devil himself should be able to do. He had been a technician of incredible skill who loved to excite his listeners with sizzling, popping combinations of pizzicato and bowed passages and then soothe them with legatos of velvety sweetness. The passage of years served only to enhance the legend. Schumann, Liszt and Brahms all were so fascinated, they used bits of Paganini's compositions as inspirations for their own dazzling music, translating fiddle wizardry into keyboard terms.

By the time he had settled into his life at Weimar, Liszt was reworking some of the Paganini compositions into grand pieces of his own. They are works of remarkable invention, erupting in scale passages of flashing octaves and tenths, slithering through chromatic chord changes, and sparkling with chains of trills, double arpeggios, hand-crossings, and feathery arabesques which accompany a cantilena melody—a whole literature of sounds nobody had ever heard from a piano before. They were put to use in a multitude of pieces, in free form, called "rhapsodies," "fantasias," "apparitions," "ballades," "elegies," "legends," "nocturnes"—anything to break away from the restrictions of classical sonata form. Most of them were one-movement works, even when they were of sonata size, and their unity, such as it was, was achieved by the use of a system of motifs. They seem loose and even sprawling today because of their improvisatory interludes that seem to have little formal function. Liszt and his contemporaries felt their form was justified by the poetic (rather than the strictly musical) content of the piece. He himself did not necessarily depend on poetic inspiration: a majority of his descriptive titles, such as *La Lugubre Gondola,* were appended after the music was finished. Liszt also wrote a sonata with all of its five motifs stated at the beginning. His other keyboard works, for which he is even more famous, are his transcriptions, called "reminiscences," "illustrations," "paraphrases." He reduced all of Beethoven's symphonies to piano score with remarkable imagination and furthered the cause of his beloved Wagner by composing imaginative pieces based on sections of the operas. Most popular of all his works are the 15 *Hungarian Rhapsodies,* built on gypsy themes from his native land, which he issued both in piano versions and in arrangements for numerous other instruments.

During his eleven years at Weimar, Liszt composed a large amount of orchestral music, also in nonclassical forms. Strangely enough, for a composer who was revolting against the restrictions of form, the best pieces of all were two with the formal name "symphony": the *Dante Symphony,* with female chorus, dedicated to Wagner; and *A Faust Symphony,* in three movements, with tenor solo and men's chorus, dedicated to Berlioz. While these are far from being literally descriptive, they represent Liszt's characteristic response to literary stimulus.

Liszt was the inventor of that popular form, the "symphonic poem." At Weimar he wrote a dozen of them. The most famous are *Tasso, Les Préludes,* and *Mazeppa;* they are a step farther along the romantic path that began with lieder, and they lead directly into the ultimate of all poetically inspired music, Wagner's music dramas. Today, Wagner far overshadows Liszt in the affections of the musical world, but Liszt's admirers point out, with only a little exaggeration, that Wagner could not have achieved his stature without Liszt and, indeed, got most of his musical ideas directly from the older man.

By 1857, Liszt was in trouble with the court at Weimar, which had become disenchanted with his propagandizing for the "music of the future." The break came after Liszt, against stiff opposition, championed an opera called *The Barber of Bagdad* by an actor-turned-composer, Peter Cornelius. The opera failed, and in 1859, after eleven years at Weimar, Liszt resigned, bringing to a close his most fruitful period of composition. He sought refuge in Rome, where the Pope had all but agreed to give permission for

Liszt to marry the already married Princess Caroline. A last-minute withdrawal of the papal dispensation put an end to that scheme, and Liszt entered into heavy studies and meditations that ended with his taking minor orders and becoming the Abbé Liszt.

He continued to compose and teach his "master classes," in which one pupil played while the rest listened. Gradually he emerged from his retirement to circulate between Rome, where Caroline was established, Weimar, where he became reconciled with the court, and Pest, where he was named president of Hungary's new Academy of Music in 1875. His compositions took on a more religious tone— he composed such huge oratorios as *Legend of St. Elisabeth, Christus,* and a Hungarian coronation Mass—but his music no longer had its youthful flair and achieved even less success than his earlier works. He became resigned, if not bitter. When he recognized one of his themes (from *A Faust Symphony*) in Wagner's *Ring,* he said, "Never mind, at least somebody will get to hear it."

But if the world refused to accept his music, it never forgot his playing. At the age of 75, after 45 years of retirement from concert playing, he set out on a "jubilee tour" and was received with open arms by Paris and the other capitals of Europe. That summer, the first year after Wagner's death, Liszt's daughter, Cosima Wagner, invited him to attend the Wagner festival at Bayreuth. He was suffering a chill when he arrived, and during the festivities a few days later he died. Wagnerites (including Cosima) felt that the news would disturb the worshipers at Wagner's shrine and kept it quiet. When a stranger asked who the funeral procession was for, another onlooker answered: "Wagner's father-in-law."

THE APOTHEOSIS OF ROMANTICISM

WAGNER

THE APPEARANCE OF RICHARD WAGNER on the musical scene brings our story in a full circle—or least into a tightening spiral—back to the point where music again depends on words. Wagner's music, so far as it is of interest today, consists of nine important operas, which he called "music dramas" in a wise move to distinguish them from the kind of opera being written in Italy. His contribution to the development of purely instrumental music stems from his confidence that the listener would understand his highly developed system of musical elisions and fragmentations so long as dramatic continuity was present, just as Bach assumed that his listeners could follow contrapuntal forms without benefit of words. Wagner's methods had a powerful effect on the composers who lived after him; there was hardly a composer who was not either for him, and adopted his techniques, or against him, and did all in his power to undermine them.

Wagner was not only a musician, but a poet, essayist and pamphleteer. As a poet, he successfully created the librettos he wanted, while his colleagues went begging. As a writer he poured out his ideas on life and art in a torrent of energy and conviction. With his diversity of interest, it is sometimes difficult to understand how he could have achieved such epoch-making results in music. He expanded the orchestra to unheard-of dimensions, even beyond those of Berlioz; he developed the system of leitmotifs to a pinnacle of smoothness and subtlety until they were practically themes, through which he could make his audience anticipate, recognize and revive a mood or idea at will. Above all, he was a super-romanticist; the process of merging poetry and music that came into being with Schubert's songs and that blossomed into Liszt's symphonic poems and Berlioz's dramatic symphonies bore its ultimate fruit in Wagner's music dramas.

Wagner was born on May 22, 1813, in Leipzig, the city where Bach spent his last years and where Schumann learned his trade. Berlioz, age ten, was experimenting with his guitar and flageolet; Schubert was 16, singing in the "Konvict" and getting ready to write his first symphony; Schumann was three; and Liszt, who was to become one of Wagner's patrons and eventually his father-in-law, was only two. Wagner's father was a police clerk who died when Wagner was six months old. His mother married a boarder, one Ludwig Geyer, a year later, giving rise to the speculation that he was the composer's real father. This became a *cause célèbre* just before World War II when Wagner turned out to be one of Hitler's heroes, since it was rumored that Geyer was a Jew. But today, the most authoritative sources solemnly agree that (a) Wagner looks too much like his uncle Adolph Wagner to leave any doubt, and anyway (b) Geyer's forefathers were Protestant Christian cantors.

Geyer was an actor by profession, and young Wagner spent many an hour on stage. The family was then in Dresden, and Wagner found his first hero in the flamboyant conductor Carl Maria von Weber. In such a theatrical atmosphere he soon fell into a habit of making up intense fantasies. His two older sisters became opera singers, and he himself began to compose and to write verses at a very early age. When he was 13, he translated three books of Homer's *Odyssey* from Greek into German. The same year, he wrote a full-scale tragedy called *Leubald und Adelaide*. While he was writing this gory epic (everybody died), he first heard Beethoven's music and determined to set his own book to music. To put himself on the right track, he borrowed a book on composition and began a study he found more difficult than he had imagined. He was remarkably sensitive to the effect of music. He felt, he wrote later, "a mysterious joy" on hearing an orchestra, and the sound of tuning violins gave him ghostly tremors. He took up the study of harmony with a member of the Leipzig orchestra for a while and fell under the spell of Beethoven's seventh symphony when he heard the popular rumor that it was a product of semi-madness. He stayed awake nights, ecstatically copying out Beethoven scores. His destiny was fixed when he heard Beethoven's *Fidelio* with a remarkable soprano named Wilhelmine Schröder-Devrient singing the title part. "From that moment, my life acquired its true significance," he wrote.

During his teens, Wagner wrote overtures, a symphony, an opera, which was destroyed in a fire, and another text, which he destroyed himself because it was too gory. Finally, at the age of 21, full of self-assurance and constantly undergoing new revelations of his destinies, he became conductor in the theater at the provincial town of Magdeburg. He thus became acquainted with the frothy, effective operas of the Italian school—Rossini, Donizetti, etc. "To produce anything fresh . . . in the realm of the symphony . . . according to Beethoven's methods," he later wrote, "was an impossibility." And so he composed another opera called *Liebesverbot (Forbidden Love),* an amorous romp based on Shakespeare's *Measure for Meas-*

ure that made professional use of every device for lively drama. The young conductor managed to wangle a performance at Magdeburg before the company collapsed from bankruptcy and internal dissension. Before the debacle, Wagner began a romance with the company's junior leading lady, Minna Planer, and in 1836 she became his first wife.

With a modicum of experience, he developed a firm conviction that he had a rare gift for helping singers, by means of "constant prompting ... vigorous directions as to necessary action" and his own loud singing. Nevertheless, he spent the next three years flitting from city to city, dodging bill collectors. In Riga, where he got a conducting job, he wrote the first act to a new opera, *Rienzi,* but it was not long before intrigue and debt caused him to leave hastily, with Minna and a large dog, on a small boat bound for London. It was a stormy passage and inspired Wagner's second important opera, *The Flying Dutchman.*

Eventually, the ménage reached that artistic nirvana, Paris, with the immediate object of scaring up a performance of *Liebesverbot.* It was hardly nirvana for the Wagners: the couple lived in a garret, scraping up pennies from Richard's odd writing jobs, concert reviewing for the papers, and hack music transcriptions. Debts piled so high that Wagner finally went to jail, where he finished *Rienzi* while Minna earned bread and butter by taking in a boarder. With pleas for a performance, Wagner sent *Rienzi* off to Dresden, and turned to the task of composing *The Flying Dutchman.* In 1842, Dresden sent its acceptance, and the Wagners left Paris as soon as they could save up coach fare.

In Dresden, *Rienzi* rehearsals went better than Wagner could have hoped. His teen-age idol, Mme. Schröder-Devrient, was to sing a leading role, and all the singers seemed to like the music. In fact one number so pleased them that they called it the "silver penny part" and jokingly tossed coins into a kitty every time they sang it—and the Wagners ate a little better. The première was a huge success, the audience remaining, so Wagner wrote, "in full muster," from curtain time at 6 p.m. until the last notes died away at midnight. Its success is not hard to understand, for it was nothing but an overblown Italianate opera, wordy, noisy and often crude, but impressive in its sheer size and appearance. *The Flying Dutchman,* which Dresden produced a few months later, received less acclaim, but it is clear that in the *Dutchman* Wagner was at last beginning to develop a musical personality. Out of his two big works came a job as court conductor in Dresden, filling the shoes of the deceased Weber. The result was a decent living for the first time: Wagner enjoyed a house, a dog and a parrot, besides his loving wife.

Wagner's love life is a fascinating story that has never been completely understood. He and his second wife, Cosima, collaborated on his autobiography *(My Life),* which is full of red herrings and self-justification; and it is understandable that he should take the opportunity to present himself in the best possible light. Ernest Newman did a major job of untangling; his two-volume history reveals Wagner as a voluptuary whose first wife was unable to stimulate his imagination or, apparently, even his libido for very long. While she lived, he had affairs with three other married women, including Cosima Liszt von Bülow. In the correspondence that has come to light over the years, Wagner addressed several other women in most intimate terms; it is abundantly clear that he never could be without love for long.

His sensuality also took other, more exotic forms. Whenever he could manage it, he lived in rooms magnificently draped in silks and satins and scented with delicate perfumes (his favorite was attar of roses, which he had shipped discreetly to his barber). His clothes, too, were of the softest and most luxurious fabrics; partly, it is believed, because his skin was painfully sensitive.

During his seven years in Dresden, Wagner wrote and composed his first truly characteristic works—and simultaneously exhausted his early style. The operas were *Tannhäuser,* which was produced in 1845, and *Lohengrin,* in 1850. "My real intention," Wagner wrote, "was . . . to force the listener, for the first time in the history of opera, to take an interest in a poetic idea, by making him follow all its developments." To do this he consciously tried to make music "assist in the understanding of the poetic lines," i.e., to describe the words and feelings in musical tone. The big difference between these works and the older opera of France and Italy is in Wagner's gradual, but not yet complete, assimilation of aria, recitative, duet and chorus into the continuous musical flow of the entire act. In his style there were still songs, some of them of great lyrical beauty, but the orchestra was beginning to assume greater responsibility for the expression.

In Dresden the 35-year-old Wagner got into political trouble. He had spoken out against the monarchy, and after backing an abortive uprising in 1849, he found himself a wanted man. He managed to escape to Zurich, where he devoted himself to a life of writing texts for his gigantic, four-opera cycle, *Der Ring des Nibelungen (The Ring of the Nibelungs)* and pamphlets, some of them explaining what he was trying to do in his music dramas. He wrote no music for another five years.

Wagner felt that music as it had been written (even by him) up to that time was inadequate for dramatic purposes. In a pamphlet called *Opera and Drama,* he explained what he meant: "The error in the art of opera consists in the fact that a means of expression (music) has been made the object, while the expression itself (the drama) has been made a means." This statement represents some clear thinking on the part of a man whose turbid, wordy "philosophy" was never as penetrating as he thought it was. Music has tried to make itself the dramatic focus, he said, and it has failed. Its only salvation must lie in a balanced collaboration with poetry, a merging of verbal and musical language. There should be no characters on stage just to swell volume, no matter how gorgeous the sound. There must be only characters essential to the plot. The chorus was *de trop*. It could be replaced by the orchestra, which was much better at subtle emphasis of the emotional situations on stage. Vocal melody would be conditioned as much by the sense of the words as by the demands of musical inspiration. This reasoning, once Wagner put it into effect, was responsible for another step in the process of making music more subtly expressive.

The *Ring* cycle is a magnificent, misty tale based on Nordic mythology. Its four operas—*Das Rheingold, Die Walküre, Siegfried* and *Gotterdämmerung (Twilight of the Gods)*—concern a magical ring fashioned of "Rhinegold" by a dwarfed inhabitant of the underworld (a Nibelung), who hopes to use its power to own the world. The gods seize the ring, and the giants who have built the gods' dwelling, Valhalla, seize it in turn. Both races become heir to the curse that the ring carries. At the risk of making things worse, the gods try to get it back. The old god Wotan goes to earth and establishes a race that will eventually produce a hero. (This is where Hitler got part of his "master-race" theory and is one reason that Wagner was the most venerated composer in Nazi Germany.) The hero's name is Siegfried, and he is the child of an incestuous love. He is destined to find Brünnhilde, one of the gods' warrior maidens (Valkyries), who is sleeping a timeless sleep surrounded by magic fire because she has disobeyed Wotan. Siegfried slays the dragon guarding the ring and wakes Brünnhilde. He gives her the ring as a love token and goes forth into the world to perform deeds of valor. Unfortunately, he falls into a trap, loses his love, his life and finally the ring, which sinks back to its rightful place with the Rhine maidens. But the curse does its work, and Valhalla goes up in flames as the fourth-night curtain falls.

Such imaginative scenes required some very advanced stagecraft, available only in the ideal theater of Wagner's dreams. There was no such theater; neither was there yet any music, but Wagner had no end of faith in his ability to get both things done—despite the fact that he was deeply in debt. He began composing again, late in 1853, under the stimulus of a visit from Liszt, who had been courageously staging Wagner weeks at Weimar. Inspired, Wagner left for Italy where, he says in *My Life,* he dreamed of falling into turbulent waters. "The rushing sound formed itself in my mind into a musical sound, the chord of E flat major, which continually re-echoed in broken forms." He woke up and realized that the prelude to *Das Rheingold* had been "revealed" to him. When he wrote the prelude, the persistence of that chord was in itself a daring innovation, but more audacious ones were to come.

One of these was the flowering of the leitmotif. By the time Wagner was ready to write his seven fully mature music dramas, he was able to spin a continuous web of music that lasted for an hour or so at a time. Even with words and situations to give it outline, and moods to underline it by harmonic and instrumental colors, this was an enormous amount of music to organize. With the leitmotif it became possible. Wagner had tried using leitmotifs merely as brief musical labels, but when he got to the *Ring* he realized they could be used to germinate a truly symphonic kind of music. They were, as a rule, terse, brief figures in the orchestra, figures that were sometimes literally descriptive, more often were not, but were always malleable enough to be developed and transformed in the manner of themes. All of Wagner's leitmotifs have been discovered, laid bare and labeled by Wagnerian scholars. Their names are "servitude," "smithing," "might of youth," "the ring," "twilight," "announcement of death," etc. Many of them, such as the "magic fire" motif, are true masterpieces of musical characterization; others are almost themes in their gracefulness; still others are mere figures without obvious portent.

The music that comes out of this method is rich but rarely lighthearted. The orchestra becomes the protagonist, the story teller, the generator of emotions and reactions, while the singers become more and more engulfed, less and less melodious. Nevertheless, the textures and colors of Wagner's huge orchestra were like nothing the world had ever heard before, and the world was stirred to depths it had not suspected music could touch.

The year he started to compose again, Wagner went visiting in Paris and met the 16-year-old Cosima Liszt. The meeting bore no earmarks of the fated relationship that was to develop; actually Wagner was in the toils of an affair with another lady, named Mathilde Wesendonck, and was writing one of his rare nonoperatic works, a piano sonata, which he dedicated to her. The Wagners had settled in a cottage on the Wesendonck estate in Switzerland. Wesendonck, a wealthy merchant, was proud to lend a hand to genius, and his young wife found the genius fascinating. During this period, Wagner completed the first two *Ring* operas and, perhaps inspired by his attachment for Mathilde, conceived the idea for his most popular opera, the passionate *Tristan und Isolde*. This is the medieval tale of the unhappy Princess Isolde. While a young courier, Tristan, is escorting her to her marriage with King Mark, she and Tristan inadvertently drink a magic love potion. Despite Isolde's marriage, their passion fatefully draws them together, and during a secret tryst they are betrayed. Tristan dies of sword wounds in Isolde's arms, and afterward she herself dies her famous "love-death."

Wagner had composed the music for the first act of this tragedy at the Wesendonck estate and had also made songs of some of Mathilde's poems (the one titled *Träume* closely resembles some of *Tristan und Isolde*'s most passionate moments) when Minna intercepted an incriminating love letter from her husband to Mathilde. She exploded in anger and frustration, then left. He himself departed for Venice in solitude, and then went on to Lucerne, where he finished the music for *Tristan*.

Meanwhile, the musical world was beginning to take account of his operas, and *Tannhäuser* was scheduled for a Paris performance in the fall of 1861. There was just one hitch: the Paris public would not accept any opera unless it had a ballet, and what was more, a ballet in the second act. Wagner rebelled at the first and then at the second condition but finally interpolated his famous "Venusberg music." *Tannhäuser* had been written much earlier and was harmonically pale and comparatively stiff. The Venusberg ballet was as flowing and sensual as anything in *Tristan* and stood out like a technicolor scene in a black and white movie. To add to his troubles, Wagner had scored for a dozen French horns, and he could not find that many in Paris. He finally had to compromise by substituting several saxophones borrowed from the inventor, "that terrible man," Adolphe Sax.

Things went passably well on the first night, but during the second performance sounds of shrill whistling arose from the audience. The opera manager paled, turned to Wagner and explained: "It's the Jockeys. We are lost." The rakehell members of the Jockey Club were indeed to blame. They had decided that *Tannhäuser* was not to succeed in Paris; it had to be withdrawn after one more disorderly performance. Wagner, who had been pardoned for his revolutionary activities, went back to Germany for the first time in twelve years. Then, after at last hearing a performance of his *Lohengrin* (in Vienna) he secluded himself with only one mistress in a cottage on the Rhine to work on a new inspiration: *Die Meistersinger von Nuremberg*.

This is a large work but, in some ways, the simplest of the grand operas of Wagner's mature life. Like all the others, its orchestra never pauses, but the music nevertheless is divided into quasi-separate numbers, in something like the traditional pattern of opera before Wagner. What is better, the voices sing the melodies rather than accompany a symphonic orchestra, and the melodies are lovely. The plot, too, is appealingly cheerful: it is about music. (Mozart's *Impresario*, Pergolesi's *Music Master* and Pfitzner's *Palestrina* stand out among the few operas about music.) The young knight, Walter, comes to Nuremberg and discovers he may win pretty Eva for his bride if he wins the mastersingers' songwriting contest. But the mastersingers' technique is so thoroughly bound with rules and conditions that no novice could hope to follow them. Walter's bid is based on his feeling that the rules stifle lyricism. His teachers, he says, are the older minnesingers

and the birds themselves. Before he invents the lovely song
that melts the judges' hearts and wins him the girl, there
is a humorous scene in which a stickler for the rules,
named Beckmesser, makes a fool of himself. This is Wagner's famous satire on his arch enemy, the critic Eduard
Hanslick, whose mistake it was to attack Wagner in print.
Hanslick was a perceptive writer, but he never would have
become immortal without the cruel Wagnerian parody.
Meistersinger also contains some mellow wisdom, dis-
pensed by an old character named Hans Sachs; and there
is a first-rate riot staged by the apprentices.

Wagner's idyl in the cottage on the Rhine was swamped
under a rising tide of debts. He had already spent the
money he expected to get from the Viennese première of
Tristan when the performance was abandoned as "unperformable," after no less than 77 rehearsals. Wagner
brought the ragged ends of his fiscal life closer together by
giving concerts of excerpts from his music, but by 1864 he
was in desperate financial straits. He was saved from debt-
ors' prison only by the intervention of the young King
Ludwig II of Bavaria, an ardent Wagnerite, who paid off
the heavier Wagnerian debts and appointed the composer
his adviser in Munich. Wagner settled down to finish the
Ring music and began, at the age of 52, to dictate his autobiography to Cosima von Bülow. By that time Minna was
dying in Paris, and Wagner's friendship with Cosima had
blossomed into an affair that was the scandal of Munich.
Von Bülow may have been glad to get rid of Cosima, or
he may have been just an all-out Wagnerian idolater; at
any rate, it was he who conducted the première of the no
longer unperformable *Tristan*. But King Ludwig, although he was an equally ardent admirer, bowed to popular disapproval of Wagner's way of life and reluctantly
asked him to leave town.

Wagner went to Switzerland again, and there Cosima joined him. This move angered her father, Liszt, and estranged him from Wagner. Before Cosima's marriage to von Bülow was annulled and she was able to marry Wagner, she bore him two daughters and a son, Siegfried. She outlived him 47 years, dying in 1930.

Meistersinger and *Rheingold* were performed in Munich, and the name of Wagner was becoming something of a legend all over the world. (Philadelphia went so far as to pay him $5,000 to compose a march for the exposition of 1876.) Eventually, in 1872, there were enough Wagner societies and wealthy donors to begin work on the composer's all-Wagner dream theater. This was the festival theater in the secluded city of Bayreuth. The city not only deeded Wagner the land for his theater but permitted him to establish (with assistance from loyal King Ludwig) his own home there, a villa which he named "Wahnfried."

On Wagner's 59th birthday, the *Festspielhaus* cornerstone was laid. Four years later the entire *Ring* cycle was given its first complete performance and was attacked resoundingly—and rather disgracefully—by the entire press. The next cycle drew small audiences, and the festival theater was closed temporarily with a deficit of some $35,000 while Wagner sought solace in travel. It was reopened in 1882 with Wagner's last opera, *Parsifal,* a pageantlike story of a search for the Holy Grail.

Wagner died in Venice the next year after a heart attack, but Cosima kept the festivals going until 1909, when Siegfried took over, and after him, his wife. Today, the annual Bayreuth Festival is organized by Wagner's two grandsons and is regarded as one of Europe's most desirable summertime musical events.

THE NATIONALISTS

So FAR, most of the development of Western music had taken place in and around Germany. By mid-19th century, non-German composers were fully, even painfully conscious of this concentration. They were, they believed, just as creative as the Germans; they simply had not managed to convince the public of that fact. Out of this competitive outlook came the phenomenon of musical nationalism, in which composers tried to give their music a character distinctive to a particular country. How could this be done? One way, thought composers of the day, was to use folk tunes as themes; if a composer loaded his symphony with Russian folk tunes, it was, they believed, bound to sound Russian.

In the early days of romanticism, this idea had already found expression in the folk song collecting of Schumann and, to some extent, in the operas of Weber, but it came to a climax much later. The Russians were the most active of all the early nationalists. They produced, in fact, some of the most important orchestral music of the '70's and '80's.

The first of the Russians was MICHAEL GLINKA, who is regarded as the "father" of Russian nationalistic music, although he never regarded himself as a musical reformer. He was born into a fairly wealthy family in Smolensk on June 1, 1804, a year after Berlioz. As a boy he showed small enthusiasm for anything musical, except bells, until he heard a clarinet quintet by an obscure Finnish composer when he was ten or eleven. It threw him "into a sort of fever," and a few days later he announced "music is my soul." The boy was able to practice music by making arrangements of Russian airs for a small orchestra that was in his uncle's employ, and he also took lessons on the piano and violin. When he was eleven, he was sent to a St. Petersburg school, where his musical studies were only incidental to a general education. There he developed a taste for the life of a playboy.

On graduation, he showed no inclination to go to work, nor, for that matter, even to study music seriously. He did take up singing and developed considerable ability as an interpreter of songs. This led him to compose songs which, however, nobody could sing as well as he, and to appear in Italian operas that were all the rage that year—he played such diverse roles as Donna Anna in *Don Giovanni* and Figaro in Rossini's *Barber of Seville*. When he was 27, he went to Italy for his health, immersed himself in Italian music and began composing. He found that he could not imitate the style very well, and he wrote, "We Northerners feel otherwise. . . . With us, love is inseparable from sorrow." A spell of homesickness turned his eyes toward St. Petersburg and made him long to compose in the Russian language. On his way home he dallied in Berlin, where he took some composition lessons and announced his determination to write an opera which "in every way [would] be absolutely national . . . not only the subject but the music." The opera was *A Life for the Czar* and the musical style was shot through with that particularly thick, dark, heavily lyrical quality that is unmistakably "Russian" even to listeners who recognize none of the folk melodies.

Glinka became thoroughly obsessed with his music and even took two acts of the uncompleted opera along on his honeymoon. He finally finished the opera in 1835, and it was presented a year later at the Imperial Opera. Its patriotic character and its ingratiating melodies were just what St. Petersburg had been waiting for; *A Life for the Czar* was a huge success. Glinka became famous overnight, got a good job as imperial capellmeister, and soon set to work on his other opera, *Russlan and Ludmilla*. Unhappiness with his married life delayed work; he finally left his wife, and apparently thereafter he felt better about composing than ever before. When *Russlan* was produced, in 1842, it was only moderately successful, but it turned out to be the work on which most of Glinka's fame rests.

In spite of his nationalist leanings, Glinka was not solely a Russian composer—he could write music characteristic of any country except Germany. Moved, like some of his followers, by the vivid colors of Spanish music, he went off to Spain to collect tunes for an orchestral work and then wandered from one capital to another—to Paris, where he gave a successful one-man concert and became friends with Berlioz; to Warsaw, where he settled for a while with a young girl; and back to St. Petersburg. Finally, he left for Berlin to hear a selection from *A Life for the Czar,* and he died there in 1857, at the age of 53.

THE FIVE

Before his death, Glinka met a young composer who so impressed him that he graciously called him a "second Glinka" and charged him with continuing the fight to set Russian music before the world. That man was MILI BALAKIREV, the most determined, if not the most prolific, composer Russia had yet produced, and the dominant member of the "Russian Five," sometimes called "the mighty handful": CESAR CUI, ALEXANDER BORODIN, MODESTE MUS-

SORGSKY and NICOLAI RIMSKY-KORSAKOV. Despite the lurking presence of PETER ILYTCH TCHAIKOVSKY on the sidelines, these men came to represent Russian music to the world.

Balakirev was born January 2, 1837, in ancient Nijni-Novgorod. Of his small output, Americans are familiar with just one tone-poem, *Thamar,* and a brilliant piano fantasy, *Islamey,* the latter best known in the orchestration by Alfredo Casella. His early training was in piano, and at 14 he was conductor of a private band near his home. A concert career seemed inevitable until he decided he did not like performing in public. He resorted to teaching piano, and then, as he gathered other men about him, to instructing, inspiring and even goading them to further efforts. His lessons consisted of a kind of post-graduate music appreciation course in which he analyzed the music—mostly German—and helped his associates achieve a sense of form and structure.

Rimsky left a description of Balakirev the teacher: he "knew a prodigious amount of music of all kinds . . . could remember . . . every bar he had ever heard or read [and was] incomparable as a critic of technicalities. . . . He was so despotic that he insisted that we remodel our music exactly according to his prescriptions. . . . Often whole sections of his pupils' compositions were not their work, but his. . . ."

In other ways, too, Balakirev carried out Glinka's assignment. He started the Free Music School, conducted the best music of his friends and, in 1866, prepared the first authentic collection of Russian folk songs. In spite of his zealous teaching, he suffered from poverty. Eventually he lost contact with reality, and between 1872 and 1876, he gave up anything to do with music. When he returned to the profession, everything had changed for him. He managed to estrange himself from his earlier friends and surrounded himself with an entirely different circle of musicians, whose names are forgotten today. He died in 1909, a strangely powerful figure in Russian musical society, a man whose own compositions were scarcely known even in his own country.

Borodin was a more prolific member of the Russian group. He is known to modern audiences for his darkly splendid opera, *Prince Igor,* and an orchestral tone-poem, *On the Steppes of Central Asia.* Borodin was born in St. Petersburg in 1834, the illegitimate son of a Georgian nobleman; as was the custom in such cases, he received the name of one of his father's serfs. By the time he went to medical school in St. Petersburg to become a research physician, he had already tried his unskilled hand at a concerto and a string trio.

He was a brilliant student and had already made his mark as a chemist when he fell under the spell of Balakirev and became convinced that composition was his real business. He sat down to write a symphony, with every bar "criticized and overhauled" by Balakirev, and spent the next five years at it. He labored equally hard over the libretto and score of *Prince Igor;* sometimes he was so discouraged that he raided the score for themes to use in a second symphony. His music glows with rich melody, set off by daring dissonances and by the exotic patterns of modal (rather than major-minor) harmony.

Some of Borodin's music found special favor with Debussy in later years, but Borodin hardly composed enough to become a major influence on the music world at large. He was more popular in Germany than at home, and he sadly commented that "Russian music is not the kind that makes for success." He died in 1887, leaving Rimsky-Korsakov and others to finish the orchestration and even some of the organization of *Prince Igor*. Two generations later his music underwent another revision when it became the basis for the Broadway show *Kismet*.

Mussorgsky was the most powerful and original of all the Russians, with a remarkable sense of musical characterization in his operas (among them, *Boris Godounov, Khovanchina*) and a matchless ability to capitalize on the melodic, harmonic and contrapuntal peculiarities of his country's folk music. He was born March 21, 1839, in Karevo, Government of Pskov, of a well-to-do landowner and a lady who wrote poetry. His nurse taught him Russian fairy tales and inspired him to improvise at the piano before he had any knowledge of composing technique. Although it was obvious that he had musical talent, Modeste was sent to military academy, where he learned hard drinking and fast living. He met Borodin and other musicians early in his career, went to Balakirev for lessons when he was 18, and made the thrilling discovery of his Russian musical heritage when he traveled to Moscow two years later.

It was not long before he determined on a musical career and resigned his army commission, but he suffered from a mental infirmity that kept him from sustained creativity. Also he wasted himself with too much drinking and finally had to retire to his brother's country estate, where he absorbed the spirit of the peasants' music and wrote some fine songs. When he was 28, he was able to concentrate sufficiently to write *A Night on Bare Mountain,* a tone-poem that describes one of his favorite imaginary scenes, a witches' sabbath. Also simmering in his mind was a wish to duplicate exactly in music the inflections of speech. To accomplish this, he spent long periods noting down and analyzing the changes of intonation that occurred in the course of conversations. Finally, after a couple of false starts, which resulted in scattered operatic scenes, he turned out a rough version of *Boris*.

This was too crude for the theater committee in Moscow, but Mussorgsky enthusiastically set about remodeling and polishing it, and the opera was finally performed in 1874. It had considerable popular success, but other musicians failed to see its virtues. Somewhat daunted, Mussorgsky started (but never finished) another full-scale opera, *Khovanchina,* and a lighter one, *The Fair at Sorochinsk*. He did complete his famous piano cycle, *Pictures at an Exhibition,* which is usually heard in an orchestral transcription by Ravel.

Mussorgsky died in 1881, probably of epilepsy, but also debilitated from over-indulgent living. His music fell into obscurity, then had a curious and undignified revival when Rimsky-Korsakov, with the best of intentions, put out his own corrected versions of *Boris* and *Khovanchina*. These comparatively insipid scores were for many years regarded as the best use that could be made of Mussorgsky's unskilled work. In recent years scholars have gone back to the original manuscripts and have revived the music in something like its original form—to discover that Mussorgsky was more a master than Rimsky had believed.

Rimsky-Korsakov was born into a family of naval officers in March, 1844, and his overwhelming ambition as a child was to become one himself. As an older man, he was fond of remembering the humbler side of his heritage; one of his ancestors was a serf girl. But his early musical influences come from an eccentric uncle who liked to sing folk songs, and from a monastery full of chanting and bell-ringing monks near his home in Tikhvin, Novgorod Government.

At the age of twelve he entered the Naval Academy at

St. Petersburg. While there he heard his first operas (*A Life for the Czar* was his favorite) and Beethoven symphonies. Off duty, he tried to orchestrate operas from piano scores, without knowing anything about the instruments he was writing for. Finally, he met Balakirev, who set him to work on a symphony, but his musical career was hardly started when it was interrupted by official orders to embark for a three years' cruise around the world on the Clipper *Almaz*.

Once back home, Rimsky took care of his naval duty in the mornings, studied Berlioz's *Treatise on Orchestration* and composed during his afternoons and evenings. Still ignorant of many of the methods of music, he brazenly accepted a position as Professor of Practical Composition and Instrumentation in the St. Petersburg Conservatory and managed to keep one step ahead of his pupils. With all the book learning entailed by this position and the experience gained in his job as Inspector of Naval Bands, he could hardly help absorbing a knowledge of music. Soon he became known as a master of practical instrumentation. He also became the most academic member of "The Five." In 1887 he composed a virtuoso orchestral poem called *Capriccio Espagnol,* in which, he said, the orchestral effect is the "very essence of the composition." It was a dazzling success, so Rimsky wrote two more like it, his *Easter Overture* and the most famous of all, *Scheherazade*.

For the next two or three years, Rimsky spent his time looking backward, nervously revising all of his earlier works. It was not until Tchaikovsky's death in 1893, that he felt secure about his own music and began work on an opera, *Sadko*. He was too busy to care about his appearance. The famed basso, Boris Chaliapin, described the Rimsky of those years as "unfashionably dressed [with] an unbarbered black beard . . . black frock coat that was hopelessly out of date . . . two pairs of spectacles on his nose, one in the front of the other."

Simultaneously with *Sadko,* Rimsky was working on another opera, *Christmas Eve,* "correcting" and rescoring Mussorgsky's *Boris,* and writing his own book on orchestration. His operas were of epic design and made use of fantastic plots and characters that permitted him to vary his music from crisp chromaticism (for supernatural scenes and people) to diatonic or modal lyricism (for earthbound humans).

For the next few years he concentrated on songs, attempting to develop his lyrical manner by first composing the melody alone, without the distractions of rich accompaniments. Then, in 1900, after the nationalistic school had lost most of its impetus—and its composers—he made efforts to become supranational with several operas on non-Russian subjects. As an elder statesman of music, faced with the enigmas posed by Debussy and Strauss, he made a pronouncement: "Music is now beginning to enter on a new and incomprehensible phase of development." He decided he was through composing and spent his hours on a musical autobiography, but at 62 he discovered he had still another opera in him, *Le Coq d'Or (The Golden Rooster).* It was, however, a satire on the stupidities of autocracy. The autocrats banned it, and he never lived to see it performed. He died in 1908 on his country estate.

TCHAIKOVSKY

TCHAIKOVSKY was the one major Russian composer of the period who was first and always a musician, and who was not a member of "The Five." His highstrung temperament kept him from such intimate relationships, but he did draw some encouragement from Balakirev. Despite the neurotic doubts and vapors that plagued his life, Tchaikovsky managed to be the equal of any of his contemporary Russians. He was born at Votkinsk, Government of Vyatka, in May, 1840, the son of a French immigrant. His governess recalled him as a porcelain child, upset by the slightest criticism, but sensitive and creative. Music was so stimulating to him that his parents finally canceled lessons because they seemed unhealthy.

Although his early studies were in the city of St. Petersburg, that citadel of "The Five," Tchaikovsky was sequestered at the Conservatory, which was an object of contempt to the wild and undisciplined nationalists. His master was the famed pianist Anton Rubinstein, who was Tchaikovsky's unresponsive idol for the rest of his life. The boy also studied conducting and adopted a peculiar stance, with his chin resting on his left hand while beating time with his right; for he suffered a terrifying delusion that his head would fall from his shoulders. When he was 26, he got a position at the new conservatory in Moscow, far from the disturbing influence of the nationalists, and settled down to teach and compose.

After a huge success with his first opera, *The Voyevoda*, taking no less than 15 personal curtain calls, he settled down to write *Undine*. At about the same time, he started work on a subject he could not quite spin into a complete opera; instead he made it into a "concert overture," *Romeo and Juliet*. *Undine* seemed destined for oblivion, so he used part of it for his second symphony, which turned out to be a great success in 1873. The next year he wrote the B flat minor piano concerto, the one that is so inordinately popular today. When it was first performed, it was considered unmusical, tuneless and unplayable.

When he was 36, after one unsuccessful fling at romance (he was jilted), Tchaikovsky got married, but one month after the wedding he developed a state of nerves that ended in fever and coma, and he left his wife forever. Fortunately, there was one woman who understood him thoroughly—a widow, Nadejda von Meck—who wrote of her "fantastic enthusiasm" for his music, and of her reluctance to meet him for fear of the "disillusionment . . . which generally follows every intimacy." Tchaikovsky responded, and the idyllic correspondence romance continued for 14 years, unsullied by the fact that Nadejda settled 6,000 rubles a year on the composer, which allowed him to give up teaching.

The year he found financial and emotional shelter under Nadejda's wing, Tchaikovsky completed his fourth symphony, his violin concerto and his most famous opera, *Eugen Onegin*. For a while, he hid from the world in Switzerland or any place where he could find peace. Then he gained confidence and made a highly successful tour as conductor of his own works—one engagement was at the opening of Carnegie Hall in New York, in 1891. Then, after he became financially independent through royalties and concert fees, he broke off his relationship—remote as it had been—with his benefactress. He started a new ballet, *Sleeping Beauty,* a new opera, *Pique Dame (Queen of Spades)* and another ballet, *The Nutcracker*. In the last, he used a new instrument with delicate chimes called the "celesta" which he discovered in Paris and kept secret lest Rimsky or Glazounov use it first. Finally, he decided to write a program symphony (his sixth) whose story would be known only to him. While composing it he was alternately tearful over its pathos and delighted that he still was able to compose. He wanted to call it simply "Program Symphony" but settled on the title *Pathétique*. In November, 1893, a few weeks after its première, Tchaikovsky caught cholera and died. Already renowned as a great melodist and a superb orchestrator, he was destined to become one of the most popular composers of all, but one whose sentimentality was to earn him the scorn of musical literates.

VERDI

GIUSEPPE VERDI, one of the staunchest of musical nationalists, never had to seek folk melodies for his operas; he composed them. He was born in the little town of Le Roncole, Italy, October 10, 1813. He was the son of an inn-keeper, and his early life was hard. It was the village gro-cer who heard the boy's sweet singing voice and raised enough money to send him to the conservatory at Milan. Unfortunately, the conservatory could not accept anybody as old as 19, especially if he were not a very good pianist. Instead, Verdi studied privately with a competent teacher. He was 23 when he married the grocer's daughter. By the time he was 27, both his wife and their children had died.

It is hard to say how much external events affect the course of a creative mind, but Verdi's personal tragedies, together with the failure of two of his early operas at Milan's La Scala, probably combined to mold his musi-cal character. He was ready to give up composition al-together after his second failure, but the wily and percep-tive impresario at La Scala got him interested in a new libretto, about Nebuchadnezzar. Verdi became fascinated, and composed his first big success, *Nabucco*.

After that, it seemed that Verdi could not fail, not only because of his fine, broad melodies and dramatic instincts, but also because of the powerful patriotic overtones of his operas. Some of the vigorous choruses from *I Lombardi* and *Macbeth* became identified with the national cause.

Later, the words *Viva Verdi* were scrawled on walls by daring revolutionaries (the acrostic: *V*ittorio *E*manuele *R*e *D'I*talia).

In his mid-40's, Verdi took a new and more tuneful path, with *Rigoletto, La Traviata* and *Il Trovatore,* operas which today are staples of any Italian opera company's repertory. In the middle of the 19th century, they were regarded as revolutionary. The first was a brutal story in which a father unwittingly murdered his own daughter; the second, in spite of its pretty waltzes, was a shocker, about the loves of a fallen woman (equally shocking was the fact that the characters wore modern clothes); the third was a woolly drama of gypsies and vengeance—and it had the "Anvil Chorus." Among Verdi's 27 operas, two from the late middle years stand out: *Don Carlos,* a powerful tale of the Inquisition, with some rich, affecting music for the two bassos; and *Aïda,* whose famous march and equally famous arias were no flash of inspiration but the result of years of refinement of Verdi's melodic gift and his matchless ability to turn music into a powerful dramatic instrument.

Verdi was born the same year as that contentious Northerner, Wagner, and the two were quickly set up as opposite poles of operatic composition. Wagner sneered at Verdi's music, and, so powerful was his influence, Italian opera was, until very recently, held in contempt by the world's intellectuals. Verdi never thought he was in competition with Wagner and was angered by the accusation that he tried to imitate the German composer. All he intended to do was write Italian opera as best he could, and that was often on a noble level indeed.

But musical and national politics, and Italy's defeat by the Austrians in 1870 soured the 60-year-old Verdi on musical life, and he went into semiretirement after *Aïda*. He was wealthy and venerated, and he enjoyed a quiet life at his big country estate. During his years of semiretirement, he did complete his *Requiem Mass,* in memory of the writer Manzoni; it remains one of his most affecting works, despite the fact that today it sounds more operatic than sacred.

It was not until he met Arrigo Boïto, a composer as well as a writer, that Verdi was moved to write another opera. He was in his mid-70's when the two men turned out one of the most dramatic and affecting operas of all, *Otello,* based on the Shakespeare play. Six years later they collaborated again, to create one of the finest operas of all time, the vivid, effervescent, incredibly complex, *Falstaff.* Verdi died in 1901, one of his country's most venerated musicians.

THE NEW CLASSICISM

BRAHMS

JOHANNES BRAHMS, somebody said, was a composer for
the middle-aged. His music is sane, solid; emotion recol-
lected in tranquillity rather than freshly experienced. This
makes a certain amount of sense as we try to understand
him, for apparently he turned from his early romanticism
—from his *sturm and drang* period—to become the staid
and well-balanced musician that is known to us. Although
Brahms may sound romantic to modern ears, neither he
nor his contemporaries thought he was romantic. If he
is romantic at all it is in the sense that he idealized the
past. For Brahms abandoned his early ideas of personalized
expression in favor of sturdy, classical architecture; but
the molds he used—the Beethovian symphony, sonata,
concerto—he filled with the warm sentiment that we
think of as romantic because of its softened contours, its
gentle melancholy. His enemies, the Wagnerians, thought
he was some kind of throwback; he himself said he was
born too late. Today, he is still the subject of animated
discussion between those who think he was Beethoven's
reincarnation and those who find him dull and verbose.

Brahms was born in a tenement in the red light district
of Hamburg, on May 7, 1833—the year that Schumann and
his talented friends went into the magazine publishing
business and Berlioz married Henrietta Smithson.

Brahms's father was a cheerful, precariously employed string bass player in the local bands who learned that his son, at the age of five, was the unmistakable possessor of that mysterious, often overrated quality known as "absolute pitch."

Absolute pitch is actually nothing more than a very good memory—a memory that specializes in musical levels. It means that the possessor of it can name any note that is played or sung to him. In Brahms's case, the ability was so obsessive that he could not overpower it. Once, so the story goes, he was touring with a violinist and had to play on a piano that was tuned a half tone flat. This posed no problems for the fiddler, who could simply tune his instrument to the piano, but it was torture for Brahms, who heard one note in his head when he looked at the score, another in his ears when he played it. He finally transposed all his music up a half step, a fairly prodigious feat. Absolute pitch is not necessarily a help to a composer; the ability that all composers must have is called "relative pitch," which means they can distinguish the intervals they hear between notes with unfailing accuracy.

Brahms's father, like the fathers of Mozart, Beethoven and Liszt before him, was bitten by the prodigy bug. He obtained piano lessons for his son at the age of seven and made him play a public concert at ten. To help out with family expenses, the lad began playing in the more respectable bawdy houses near the harbor, much as Negro pianists were soon to do across the Atlantic, in the honky-tonks of New Orleans. Some biographers see a connection between this early life and the fact that Brahms never married; he usually seemed more at home with rough women than with more respectable ones. By the time the boy was 15, he was composing popular potpourris and fantasies and had Op. 151 in print under various pseudonyms before Johannes Brahms had his Op. 1. When he was 20, he toured as accompanist to a violinist named Remenyi and made the acquaintance of one of the day's major violin virtuosos, Josef Joachim. Joachim was immediately impressed with Brahms's compositions, which included a violin sonata, and sent him off to meet Liszt and Schumann. Brahms found the giddy Liszt ménage at Weimar little to his liking; moreover he found himself out of sympathy with Liszt's loose style of composition. As for Schumann, he found in Brahms a new musical hero to praise.

Schumann gave the young composer a fine send-off with a dazzling article in the *New Music Magazine,* saw to it that Brahms's music was published, and gave him what amounted to a new home. It was only a few months later that Schumann entered the insane asylum. Pretty, 34-year-old Clara became Brahms's inspiration for the rest of his life—and possibly his mistress, if we are to extrapolate the feelings he expressed so warmly in his letters.

Brahms never really followed the "new paths" of romanticism laid out for him in Schumann's article but quickly turned his powerful intellect toward a new kind of classicism, firm in its rejection of extramusical references but full of romantic phraseology. His first three piano sonatas and a book of songs were badly received; his first orchestral work, his D minor piano concerto was, he wrote, "a brilliant and decided—failure." It was better liked in Hamburg than in Hanover and Leipzig. By the time he was 27, he was bursting with music in all forms and producing such chamber music as his first string sextet, which became a real success. For the next few years he rattled around between Hamburg, where he was disappointed to lose the conductorship of the orchestra, and Vienna, where he settled for conductorship of a choral group. In 1866 he completed one of his grandest and most important works, the *German Requiem,* a massive, serene, contrapuntal choral piece of intense seriousness. It was performed no less than twenty times in a single year all across Europe. Meanwhile, royalties were beginning to pile up from other works, particularly the popular *Hungarian Dances,* and Brahms was never again strapped for money. In 1869 he settled permanently in Vienna, and it remained his home for the rest of his life.

In 1873, aged 40, Brahms wrote one of his most enchanting works, the orchestral *Variations on a Theme by Haydn,* in a form that he found particularly workable. This was probably the most important study-piece for the work he had been building toward: his Symphony No. 1. But with Brahms it is hard to tell: he managed to conceal his preliminary steps completely, destroying his sketches and early versions with almost fanatical zeal, shyly presenting only the final, polished product for the world to see. All we know comes from a rather formal statement he once made to an American violinist. The composing process, he said, is "like a vivid dream." In a dreamlike state, "the ideas flow much more freely. . . . It is important to write them down immediately. . . . Sometimes I become so drowsy that I fall asleep, and then I lose the ideas. . . . To get best results . . . I have to be absolutely alone and undisturbed. . . . I let them germinate, sometimes for years, but I occasionally look at them again."

Brahms's first symphony fell like a thunderclap on the ears of the German public. The composer had kept it a secret even from his publisher, for by that time it was considered daring indeed to compose a symphony; it was a kind of affront to Beethoven. But von Bülow immediately dubbed Brahms's first symphony "the tenth," meaning, presumably, that it was good enough to follow Beethoven's ninth, and the music world seemed to agree.

The work begins with a slow introduction that is one of the grandest inspirations of all music. Over a portentous, throbbing beat its germinal ideas fan out sowing the seeds of all that is to follow. There is nothing in the four symphonies to equal this, no movement so closely organized, although other movements are more popular. The symphonies, like all of Brahms's works, are regarded in surprisingly divergent lights. One critic will call them "too intellectual," pointing to the clearly outlined contrapuntal devices (augmentation, diminution, etc.) and the carefully limned forms. "Too emotional," says another about the luscious melodies. "Too heavy," says a third, sizing up the thick, rather unvaried orchestration and the lack of anything resembling a scherzo or even an allegro. "Too square," says a fourth, as he points out that Brahms's accents are pedestrian and would be as thuddingly dull as a beerhall tune had Brahms not gone to such lengths to insert cross-rhythms and to throw accents on unaccented parts of the bar.

Like Schubert and Schumann, Brahms wrote songs during his whole creative life. His first love—and perhaps the most important single musical influence—was folk songs. Brahms liked to write accompaniments for these songs and to use the tunes as motifs for larger works. He also wrote a good many songs that might actually have been folk songs. His lieder rank with Schumann's, if not Schubert's.

By the time he was 50, Brahms was famous and even beloved—of everybody but the rabid Wagnerites—and his career hardly changed from that time on. His shabby figure, dressed in flannel shirt, patched alpaca jacket, and trousers that reached his boot tops, could be seen at various

watering places in the summers and touring the concert
circuits during the winters. He composed constantly. He
was honored by the Austrian emperor, received the "freedom of the city" of Hamburg and was offered honorary
degrees (he wrote the famous *Academic Festival Overture* for the University of Breslau). Common men everywhere tipped their hats to him on the street.

He died less than a year after his beloved Clara Schumann, leaving four symphonies, a violin concerto, two
piano concertos, a double concerto for violin and cello,
and a wealth of chamber music, piano pieces and songs.

IMPRESSIONISM

DEBUSSY

SOME EXTREMELY FINE MUSIC had come from nationalist composers by the last quarter of the 19th century, but the heavy emotional style of Wagner remained the dominant influence across the continent. Then there appeared a soft-spoken Frenchman of such enormous originality that Wagner almost immediately began to appear crude and old-fashioned. The Frenchman was ACHILLE-CLAUDE DEBUSSY. Whatever music he wrote was attacked; he was called a "destroyer of the art" because his slippery, phantasmic sonorities adhered so lightly to the bourgeois comforts of key-feeling. For better or worse, his style early won the epithet "impressionist," which was attached to the poets and particularly the painters who influenced him so strongly. As we shall see, his meager 130 compositions actually set music on a new course, a course that was to lead in two directions: straight back to Vienna and forward to the styles of the 20th century.

Debussy was born in a suburb of Paris on August 22, 1862, during a year when Europe was resounding to the passionate love cries of *Tristan und Isolde,* fortissimo. By the time he was 40, the musical world was hearing his own operatic lovers, Pelléas and Mélisande, whisper in a moment of tingling silence, *"Je t'aime"* and *"Je t'aime aussi."* In the 1860's, when Debussy was growing up, the musical idol of France was CHARLES GOUNOD (1818-93) whose opera *Faust* was already on the high road to the popularity it still, amazingly, enjoys. The Belgian organist and teacher CÉSAR FRANCK (1822-90) was reaching a peak of productivity; his lush counterpoint, as in the famous D minor symphony, was hailed as a new standard of French music. The academic AMBROISE THOMAS (1811-96) was soon to become director of the all-important Paris Conservatory, partly because of the success of his opera *Mignon*. JULES MASSENET (1842-1912) was about to turn out a string of immensely successful operas, including *Manon Lescaut* and *Thaïs*. GEORGES BIZET (1835-75) was at work on one of the world's finest and most popular operas, *Carmen*, only to die prematurely shortly after he finished it. JACQUES OFFENBACH (1819-80) was managing his own light opera theater and producing a string of 90 gay frolics (which featured the cancan) as well as the macabre *The Tales of Hoffmann*. CAMILLE SAINT-SAËNS (1835-1921), composer of *Samson et Dalila* and the ever-popular piece *Danse Macabre*, was becoming an important figure on the musical scene.

Almost to a man, these notable composers were influenced by the music and esthetic of Wagner—Paris richly deserved the nickname *"Le Petit Bayreuth"* in the 1880's. Wagner's leitmotifs—or something resembling them—were adapted to every purpose; replicas of his noble passions were held high for the world to admire; his massive, doughy orchestra was the rage among composers and the public alike. The maturing Debussy felt impelled to resist this influence, in his music, in his occasional newspaper articles and, most vehemently of all, in his private conversation. His judgment was that "Wagner was a beautiful sunset who was mistaken for a dawn." The dawn, as it turned out, was brightened by Debussy himself.

He was the son of a modest china-shop owner who wanted to send him to sea, but before the boy began to learn knots he started piano lessons with a one-time pupil of Chopin. This good lady quickly noted and encouraged his unusual talent and he, in turn, never lost his love of the piano, and particularly the music of Chopin. At the age of eleven, he entered the Conservatory to begin the only formal education he ever had.

The ultimate goal of all Paris Conservatory pupils is, as we have seen, the *Prix de Rome,* a prize that was designed to give the young musician a chance to write his first masterpiece, or at least give him three years of stimulating atmosphere living with a half dozen other creative young artists in the Eternal City. Debussy's eleven-year-long progress toward this prize was erratic. He preferred improvisation to practice, reading Haydn quartets on the piano to finger exercises, inventing his own brand of harmony to studying the established method. He angered the more conservative of his teachers and did poorly in their courses, questioned the more radical ones, and horrified his fellow students by impudent pranks, such as mimicking a professor an instant before he entered the classroom. As late as the age of 20, Debussy failed harmony courses because of his daring innovations.

Clearly, the Conservatory was not the best influence for a budding radical, but it hardly mattered, for Debussy found a patroness: Mme. Nadejda von Meck, the same wealthy widow who was subsidizing Tchaikovsky. Unlike Tchaikovsky, who never met the lady, Debussy became intimate with her, played piano in her family trio, tried his new compositions on her and traveled with her as far as Russia. She affectionately called him "Bussy" (he affected the spelling "de Bussy" at the time), and he proposed to her daughter Sonia, without success.

His next important social contact was a Mme. Vasnier, who quickly gave him the freedom of her home and, some say, her bed. As her daughter Marguerite remembered him, the 19-year-old Debussy was a big, beardless boy (he later sported a thick, black beard), who wore his curly hair flat on his forehead. He had, she later wrote in *Revue Musicale,* striking eyes, a strong personality, and strong, bony hands with square fingers that played the piano powerfully and sometimes very tenderly. He was a creature of moods who sometimes sulked when unexpected company arrived but who could be easily placated. He was, she said, never really polished.

Mme. Vasnier liked to sing Debussy's songs while he played the piano, and he wrote a number of them for her. He read in her library the most important poets of the day, Stéphane Mallarmé and Paul Verlaine. It was Verlaine who once summed up that generation's new antipathy to romanticism when he said that "one must wring the neck of eloquence."

During his last years at the Conservatory, Debussy buckled down to win the coveted *Prix.* His two first entries were cited for their originality, but it was only on the third year's try that he won, with his cantata, *L'Enfant Prodigue.* "I was standing on the *Pont des Arts* waiting for the result of the competition and watching with delight the scurrying of the little Seine steamers," wrote Debussy in his book, *Monsieur Croche.** "I was quite calm ... so seductive was the charm of the gay sunshine playing on the ripples. Suddenly somebody tapped me on the shoulder and said breathlessly: 'You've won the prize.'

---

* Claude Debussy, *Monsieur Croche.* New York, Viking Press, 1928.

Believe it or not, all my pleasure vanished. I saw in a flash the boredom, the vexations inevitably brought on by the smallest official recognition. I felt I was no longer free." It was also the end of his intimacy with the Mmes. von Meck and Vasnier, and the shadow of that sad eventuality may have passed through his mind.

Debussy went, reluctantly as Berlioz had before him, to live in the old Roman villa and in his frustration pored over the score of *Tristan*. He was required to send back a work every year to prove his value to the state which was supporting him but his composition went poorly. For two of the three years, he brooded and sulked, complained about the food, and buried himself in 16th-century polyphony. While in Italy, however, he was introduced to two aged musical giants, Giuseppe Verdi, who was then 72, and Franz Liszt, who was 74, but such contact with living legends was little stimulus to the youth. Debussy was, in fact, disconsolate in his cloak of new ideas, ideas that he was not at all sure he could bring to life successfully. Finally, after two of the three years were up, he abandoned the villa for Paris.

During his formative years, Debussy had developed a taste for exotic art objects of exquisite design and in 1889 he paralleled the visual experience with a heady taste of the clangorous gamelan and other oriental sounds when they were heard at the Paris Exposition. Some observers believe this to have been a significant influence on Debussy's style; probably more important were the six-note or whole-tone scale, and the presence of a brilliant, erratic composer named ERIK SATIE. Satie, it is true, had made independent harmonic discoveries, notably by building structures of thirds, one on top of the other, until the bottom and the top notes were eleven and thirteen notes apart. Satie even used these 11th and 13th chords in parallel motion, as Debussy did after him, but Satie was unable to organize his innovations into significant music. As a token of his friendship for Satie, Debussy orchestrated a couple of Satie's piano pieces, called "Gymnopedies"; little other Satie would be remembered except for their puckish titles and directions, such as *Three Pieces in the Form of a Pear,* and "play like a nightingale with a toothache."

The most important influences on Debussy were not musicians at all, but poetry and painting. The poets he admired most, unlike Schubert's poetic friends, were themselves convinced they were making music in words. Mallarmé stated that poetry "should evoke in a deliberate shadow the unmentioned object by illusive words," which is just what Debussy thought music should do in tone. He met frequently with these men—"symbolists," they were sometimes called—Mallarmé, Pierre Louÿs, Paul Verlaine, and formed his esthetic around them, so to speak. Seated at the piano during such a gathering, Debussy would angrily interrupt a eulogy of Wagner. "Even in Beethoven the process of development consists in repetition, in the identical restatement of identical themes," he would complain, and play part of a sonata. "And Wagner has exaggerated this procedure to the point of caricature. I would like to see the creation—I myself shall achieve it—of a kind of music without themes and motives, formed on a single continuous theme, which is uninterrupted and which never returns on itself." He was saying that he objected to the sturdy sonata, built on the repetition and development he scored as "professional rhetoric"—a mere "filling in." Actually, of course, his music had just as much form of its own, clouded and obscured though it was by his harmonic devices.

Debussy finished his first important work in 1894, a musical impression stimulated by a sensuous Mallarmé poem, *L'Après-midi d'un faune* (*The Afternoon of a Faun*). Debussy's music was to be a prelude, interlude and paraphrase finale, but only the prelude was completed. It turned out to be a brief piece, its ten minutes seemingly far too few to start a revolution. But that is what happened. When Debussy wrote *L'Après-midi,* nothing like it had ever been heard before. For him, it may have represented the turning toward a dead end, but it changed the entire course of music after Wagner. Its opening flute solo, written in the instrument's haunting, low register, sounds like a call to seduction; the lilting arabesque that follows, the stormy midsection, and the return of the flute theme, this time in the weighted harmonies of satiation, are clearly a response to the call. The harmonies are more mysterious, for Debussy has contrived them so cunningly that they actively develop the kind of textural qualities that had previously been created only by orchestration. The effect is nebulous and dreamy, but this music is superbly well formed, and the entire prelude blossoms from its single fundamental idea. Critics at its Paris première were puzzled, found its colors too rich, its outlines too vague, and in general gave it a poor reception. The public hissed. Nevertheless, it was far from a failure: *L'Après-midi* was soon repeated and quickly became an important concert item.

Debussy's harmonic innovations became the death rattle of tonality. The beginning of the end had been apparent even in the ambiguous, shifting centers of Beethoven's last works. It was more apparent in Liszt's chromaticisms, where the growing tendency to use all the notes in the scale weakened the purity of major and minor keys. It was still more apparent in Wagner's fluctuating interludes, which modulated from tonal center to tonal center so often that the listener's musical memory became clouded. In Debussy, the break away from tonality is systematically carried on. He used both the chromatic and the whole tone scales, both equally destructive to the old system. The second is an artificial scale that arbitrarily places each of its steps the same distance apart, i.e., each step covers two chromatic intervals. There are only six notes to the octave in such a scale, no note is more important than any other, and there are only two possible scales: the one containing C (C, D, E, F sharp, G sharp, A sharp) and the one containing C sharp (C sharp, D sharp, F, G, A, B). One reason for the lack of harmonic focus in the whole tone scale is that there is no true dominant. In the whole tone scale on C, for example, there is a G sharp but no G. Similarly, there is no "leading tone" whose tendency it would be to move toward the tonic, i.e., no B natural (or D flat) that wants to move to C.

Debussy did not bury himself in the whole tone scale, however. It was too limited a tool. He was able to obtain effects that undermined tonality just as surely by using ordinary chords and breaking one of the fundamental rules of harmony: the rule against parallel movement. The reason for the rule, Debussy knew as well as anybody, was to maintain a firm tonal foundation. Debussy liked to set up a solid foundation of, say, a big C triad, then move the whole thing over to D, then to E, perhaps to F sharp, until everything the listener knew and trusted about music had slipped out from under him. Other composers, once they realized that music had not returned to chaos when it evaded tonality, followed Debussy's trail and themselves set off in new directions.

While he was writing this brief masterpiece, Debussy was also working on his string quartet, some of his most famous songs, *Fêtes Galantes* and *Chansons de Bilitis,* and his opera, *Pelléas et Mélisande.* The quartet, for all its luminous sonorities and its typical Debussian melos, is not one of the works that best illustrates the composer's originality. Its form is actually quite conventional, as the forms of his three sonatas "for various instruments" were to be.

Much more to his taste were the nocturnes (*Nuages, Fêtes, Sirènes*) that he began the next year. He originally —and inexplicably—planned these as pieces for violin solo and orchestra, following one of the many false leads that came to his overactive mind. At some point it became clear to him that the fiddle solo was misplaced, and he substituted (with no particular thought of the difficulties this would make for performing organizations) a chorus of 16 women's wordless voices, in the last movement only. But he was sure from the beginning how he wanted to handle the orchestra: "I will employ groups of the orchestra separately," he wrote, "and discover nuances for those single groups; for people really are not daring enough in music, they fear a sort of divinity which they call common sense, which is indeed the most wretched thing I know."

He also broke a private rule and wrote some program notes. The pieces were not to be interpreted literally, he wrote, but rather in a "decorative" sense, especially in regard to the effects of light and shade. The first movement starts out with a slithering, shifting pattern in the bassoons and builds until it bursts into a prismatic climax. The second nocturne (*Fêtes*) has nothing to do with nocturnal events at all but alternates a busy triplet figure with a toylike march that starts in the distance (with muted brass), builds to a big climax as an imaginary procession moves into the foreground, and then fades away again. *Sirènes* is distinctly sensual; the women vocalize wordlessly, almost as if they were instruments, undulatingly, longingly. *Nocturnes* was first performed in 1900, to the despair of academicians and to the enchantment of others.

Favorable critics decided the work did not demand of music *all* it could give, but only what music *alone* could give; they said (happily) that it was an example of the very kind of form that Debussy disclaimed, that the composer was one of the most original artists of the day, possessed of refined and unerring taste. From then on, Debussy was a composer to be reckoned with.

These works were written during the 1890's, a decade which biographers agree was Debussy's most fruitful. Most of it he spent living in unmarried bliss with Gaby Dupont, and a good part of it was spent struggling with plans and music for stage works that he never finished. He was highly sensitive to words and colors, and none of the librettos he found could quite stimulate him to see them as operas. He was chronically impoverished and to make ends meet was desperate enough to give two-piano recitals of his despised Wagner, "that old poisoner" of musical wells. Apparently some Wagnerian poison rubbed off onto his own music, causing him to abandon at least one opera after he had started to compose it.

In a proper libretto, he said, the characters would not "argue" but would live their lives and work out their destinies. They would use words that would "only hint at things." "There is too much singing in musical dramas," he complained, without pressing the paradox. He would have singing only in lyrical moments; elsewhere, he would create a sort of low-keyed declamation. Music, he believed, should enhance, but not dominate, the poem.

Debussy knew he had found the libretto of his dreams in the summer of 1892, when he picked up a copy of the newly-published *Pelléas et Mélisande,* by the Belgian poet-playwright, Maurice Maeterlinck. The composer began work immediately, jotting down themes and even a few scenes before asking Maeterlinck's permission. He tore up one scene because it "smelled of Wagner" and said he was using "silence as a means of expression (it is perhaps the only way of bringing the emotional value of the phrase into relief)." He lived with his characters until he knew them as he knew real people and played and sang scenes to anybody who would listen and who was worth the trouble. Periodically he was full of doubts and misgivings and at one point feared the whole project would "end in smoke." Apparently it almost did several times. The first version was finished in 1895 and the second two years later, at which point the composer's friends had to beg him not to destroy it. Fortunately, there was a theater and a sympathetic conductor (André Messager) ready to produce it, but Debussy spent five more years in further revisions and orchestration before he decided it was ready for the world.

Unfortunately, Maeterlinck's wife expected to sing the lead but, through no fault of Debussy's, the part went to Mary Garden; Maeterlinck felt that he was betrayed and furiously wrote that he hoped for the opera's "immediate and emphatic failure." He almost had his wish. The public rehearsal was interrupted by laughter at some of the more sensitive moments, perhaps incited by a parody of the libretto that had been sold outside the door, and loud arguments accompanied the première the next night. But, to the amazement of practically everybody, the next performances were calm and *Pelléas* went through two dozen successful performances that spring and the next fall.

The story of *Pelléas* is as wispy as the music. Mélisande is discovered lost in a mysterious wood by Golaud, who brings her back to his father's castle. She and Golaud's young brother, Pelléas, fall helplessly, innocently in love. Murmuring with him at a fountain, she loses her ring in it; exploring a windswept grotto, she loses a golden ball;

mooning outside her tower window, Pelléas gets entangled in her long, golden hair. Golaud, desperately jealous, slays Pelléas, and the disconsolate Mélisande dies in childbirth, without telling her husband whether she has actually been unfaithful. Debussy set this fragile drama with utmost consideration for the discreet, narrow rise and fall of the French language, with never an exclamation and with little that sounds like song. He even went to the trouble of drawing out a plan of the syllabic accents before starting to compose. "The characters in this drama endeavor to sing like real persons," he said.

As in his songs, the music in *Pelléas* is even more vaporous than the words, so undramatic as to be static. The orchestra has been described as a "tonal envelope" surrounding the words, protecting them from the harsh glare of ordinary sounds. Strangely enough, considering Debussy's feelings about Wagner, *Pelléas* has its own system of leitmotifs. But *Pelléas*'s motifs are so subtly buried in the orchestral texture that they can rarely be noticed, and they are never sung.

Debussy was to write two more important orchestral works: the atmospheric, three-movement *Images,* of which only the languid movement titled *Iberia* has become familiar, and the magnificent, ever-popular tone-poem *La Mer (The Sea)*. It is typical that the critics of Debussy have never been able to agree on how to classify his music, even superficially. Of *La Mer,* some writers said it was a return to classical form, a return to tangibility after the ineffable dreaminess of *Nuages*. Others saw in it a continuation of the eloquent style of *Sirènes*. Still others point out that its three movements are sufficiently unified to be considered a sort of symphony: the first one undulates and then grows until it pitches and heaves, while what one writer called a "chorale of the depths" sounds below; the second depicts the waves' caprice in a kind of dream-frolic; the third builds up a wilder sea and climaxes in a ringing blast of brass that gives the lie to the idea of Debussy as a whisperer, an effeminate, ineffectual dreamer.

During his entire life Debussy played the piano, and played it very well, although he complained of nervously gathering fistfuls of wrong notes whenever he played for more than two people. Right to the end, he adored Chopin, the man who had turned the piano into a singer, and edited an edition of his music. But Debussy himself was to expand the instrument's capacities more than any other composer after Chopin. As had happened to Liszt and Chopin, Debussy's critics accused him of trying to make the piano not a piano. He himself spoke of "caressing his soul" with his delicate touch, and he certainly made listeners forget there were hammers and strings. In his piano music, the characteristic intimate, gliding, homeless qualities of his style are more apparent than anywhere else, for the sound of a piano has less tonality of its own than other instruments; it can slip, with no noticeable shift of color or emphasis, into any harmonic locus whatsoever, and its sustaining pedals can cloud the sound between one chord and the next.

Debussy wrote for the piano frequently, for when he was not writing solo piano pieces, he was writing songs with piano accompaniments. His major works for the piano were suites: *Suite Bergamasque, Pour le Piano, Estampes, Images, Children's Corner* (written for his beloved daughter, "Chou-Chou"), twenty-five *Préludes* and twelve *Etudes*. With the exception of some of the *Etudes,* all of these little pieces have poetic or pictorial names, but as always, they attempt to describe a reaction to a subject rather than the subject itself. Among them we find min-

strels, wind and waves, eccentric generals, veils and perfumes and, of course, the famous sunken cathedral, and
the demure girl with flaxen hair. Debussy said his *Etudes*
contained "a thousand ways of treating pianists according
to their just deserts"; each one is focused on some particular problem of what the critics call "digital dexterity," and
each one is a little masterpiece of musical invention and
often humor.

About the time that Debussy was finishing *Pelléas,* he
was in the process of losing his affection for his wife, "Lily-
Lilo." The cause was Emma Bardac, a much more worldly
lady, the wife of a wealthy banker whose son was one of
Debussy's piano pupils. The lady herself was a fine singer
and a brilliant conversationalist. She was thought to be
rich, and many of Debussy's acquaintances decided therefore that he was a cad; probably all he was was soft-
headed. At any rate he lost friends when he married her,
and he went through a rather sad period.

About the same time, there occurred *l'affaire Ravel,*
when that composer's admirers discovered what they believed to be suspicious resemblances between an earlier
piece of his and a later one of Debussy's. MAURICE RAVEL
was a fastidious composer of quite different inclinations;
he was 13 years younger than Debussy, the son of a civil
engineer and inventor. The resemblances between his harmonic idiom and Debussy's are obvious, but where Debussy sought for intimate, vaporous expression, Ravel was
a classicist at heart, a composer who neatly integrated his
impressionist details into the form of his compositions before he even thought of the themes, or so he said. There are
points of similarity between the two men: both wrote
Spanish-style orchestral pieces *(Iberia* and *Rhapsodie
Espagnole); erotic choreographic scenes *(L'Après-midi*
and parts of *Daphnis et Chloé);* and toccata-like piano

pieces *(Jardins dans la Pluie* and *Jeux d'eau)*. Both also wrote operas, but Ravel's little *L'Heure Espagnole* is warm, saucy and extroverted compared to *Pelléas*. Ravel himself credited the Spanish Emanuel Chabrier and Erik Satie (ten years his elder) as his real masters. Like Debussy, Ravel was a master orchestrator, but considerably more—a precision orchestrator, whose balances and acoustic effects are seldom hard to achieve in performance. His most famous orchestral tour de force is, of course, his *Boléro,* whose simple tunes and single, undeviating rhythm made it an immediate success; in Italy it stirred first-nighters to the point of riot. As a modern classicist, Ravel wrote more abstract music than Debussy—particularly chamber music—and gradually became a part of the age of modern dissonance. He lived long enough to develop a Gershwinesque feeling for jazz—it may be found in his remarkable *Piano Concerto for the Left Hand Alone* (written for a pianist friend who had lost an arm) and in his other piano concerto for two hands. Ravel died insane in 1937, already considered academic by the advance guard, a master who outlived his time. Debussy, on the other hand, fulfilled the romantic ideal by dying when he had exhausted the potentialities of his style.

From 1912, when he was again writing newspaper reviews to piece out his income, Debussy admitted indifference to new music—although he was familiar with at least two of Schönberg's quartets and his *Gurrelieder*. He was enthusiastic about Stravinsky's *Firebird* but said after the scandalous première of Stravinsky's *Le Sacre du Printemps* he was afraid the composer was going the more radical way of Schönberg. The relationship between Stravinsky and Debussy was, for the most part, a sympathetic one. Rimsky-Korsakov once advised Stravinsky not to listen to Debussy's music. "One runs the risk of getting accustomed to him," he warned, "and one could end by liking him." Nevertheless, the young Stravinsky brought his *Roi des étoiles* to Debussy's Paris flat, as student to master, and the two men played it over together on the piano. Debussy's own music never absorbed any characteristics of the new, balder dissonance.

In his later years, he completed other works for the stage, notably *The Martyrdom of St. Sebastian,* and the ballet, *Jeux* (about a lost tennis ball and an amorous triangle of players searching for it in the dusk). But as World War I closed in, Debussy realized death was upon him. He lost his driving urge to compose, spent more time conducting in public (at which he was not particularly good) and playing piano transcriptions (at which he was superb) for whatever money it would bring. He spent his last years working on his remarkable piano *Etudes* and the curiously formal sonatas, which he signed *"musicien de France."*

He was operated on for cancer in 1915 and became, as he described himself, "a walking corpse." Injections of morphine to kill his pain further stultified his will to compose. On March 25, 1918, with the shells of German Big Berthas falling around him, Debussy died, and a small cortege braved the bombardment to take him to his grave. He left no estate except his manuscripts. His daughter, Chou-Chou, died of influenza a year later, aged 14. His widow and his ex-wife both lived into the mid-30's, obscure and almost penniless.

A RADICAL TECHNICIAN

STRAUSS

In a review written in 1903, Debussy called Richard Strauss "very nearly a genius" after hearing his tone poem *Ein Heldenleben (A Hero's Life)*. Whenever he heard a Strauss tone-poem he was impressed, if not exactly delighted by its tremendous vitality. *Till Eulenspiegel,* he wrote with relish, "might almost be called 'an hour in a lunatic asylum.' Clarinets trace addled parabolas; trumpets are muted so that the horns, expecting a sneeze, hurry to utter the customary 'God bless you!' ... If the double basses were to blow their noses, if the trombones were to be stroked with imaginary bows ... I would not be surprised." For all his fun with the German composer, two years Debussy's junior but years ahead in fame, the Frenchman cheerfully credited Strauss with "amazing orchestral assurance" and admitted it was "impossible to withstand his irresistible domination." In 1912 Debussy heard *Death and Transfiguration* and called its composer "one of the dominant geniuses of our time." This, despite the fact that he was in complete disagreement with its literalness: "If people insist on wanting to understand what happens in symphonic poems, we may as well give up writing them."

Strauss was born in Munich on June 11, 1864, the son of a French horn player in the court opera orchestra. It is easy to imagine the aural atmosphere of his formative years: the golden, melancholy sounds of a French horn melody, its occasional brassy blasts—and in pianissimo contrast, the tiny splat of moisture dripping on the floor, as Papa Strauss drained the instrument during his daily practicing. Apparently the music he played was in the classical idiom. At any rate, young Richard took up composing at a tender age and turned out a series of abstract works in that style: a serenade for wind instruments, a symphony, a string quartet, two concertos, a cello sonata, all of them solidly in the Brahms-Schumann tradition. When he was 19, he quit school to become a full-time musician and the same winter became assistant conductor to Hans von Bülow at Meiningen. It was there that he discovered the music of Berlioz, Liszt and Wagner.

By that time Strauss was a thoroughly headstrong, even contentious man—a man who rarely felt the American's desire to be liked—and shouldered his way from one conducting position to another: from Italy to Munich to Weimar to Bayreuth (where Cosima Wagner was then in charge of the productions) to Berlin. Through his conducting, he became a masterful orchestral craftsman. Through his studies of Liszt and Wagner, he became interested in composing the tone-poems which were to ensure his success. From his 24th to his 34th years, Strauss felt the urge for realism—the same urge that in Italy was nurturing the *verismo* or "realistic" school which produced Mascagni's *Cavalleria Rusticana,* Leoncavallo's *Pagliacci* and most of the Puccini operas. Strauss completed his first tone-poems, *Macbeth, Don Juan* and *Death and Transfiguration,* and then came down with a severe case of pneumonia; during his convalescence, he wrote and composed an opera in the Wagnerian idiom. It was an utter failure, and the composer abandoned opera for six years. He wrote four more tone-poems—*Till Eulenspiegel's Merry Pranks,* taken from the tragic-comic medieval legend; *Thus Spake Zarathustra,* derived from the work by Nietzsche; *Don Quixote;* and *A Hero's Life,* which Strauss unabashedly declared was autobiographical. Each of these works, with the possible exception of *Till Eulenspiegel,* contains too much intricate musical activity for its own good. There is a high percentage of dross in the gold of this genius, giving some justification for the charge that Strauss wrote glorified beer hall music. Each work starts explosively but winds up in disillusionment after too much verbiage; Strauss, it seemed, was unable to express in music a truly noble tragedy or even a brave victory. Nevertheless, he developed an extraordinarily intricate contrapuntal technique, a technique that had several different lines of melody, often rushing about simultaneously, which gave a rich impression. To accomplish it, he used large orchestras of 24 winds and divided strings, about twice the number of parts used by Haydn.

Strauss composed one tone-poem too many, the *Sinfonia Domestica,* before he realized that the lode was mined out. Its realism is overdone, its jokes tired and heavily Teutonic. He was also to compose one more opera, *Feuersnot,* before he made his biggest success. The success was *Salome,* based on the Oscar Wilde play.

When Strauss saw the sordid play, which was already popular in Germany, it immediately suggested musical treatment to him. It is an elaboration of the brief, Biblical story of King Herod, his perverted step-daughter, Salome, and his captive, John the Baptist. In the opera, Herod has married Salome's mother, his own half-sister, but he casts lascivious eyes on Salome herself and asks her to dance for his pleasure. She may have anything she demands, up to half of his kingdom. Salome has other ideas, for she has become fascinated with John, who is confined in a covered cistern. She does her famous dance of the seven veils —an early form of strip tease, never made enticing by the big sopranos who sing the role—and, as her reward, demands John's head on a platter. Herod protests, but he has given his promise. The executioner descends into the cistern, the orchestra quiets to a terrifying rumble in the bass, punctuated by a sickly tweaking sound, and then the platter is handed to her with the severed head. The music then soars to its most sensual heights, while Salome triumphantly sings to the head and kisses the gory lips. Herod is revolted and orders her crushed beneath his soldiers' shields.

Across Europe and in America, opera-lovers were horrified at the idea of this plot, but they attended in hordes. The Kaiser banned it in Berlin, an act which only increased its appeal. The Metropolitan Opera withdrew it after one performance. Today, it still holds its sordid fascination, but it is no longer considered particularly sensational. Anybody who can tear his mind away from the happenings on stage can hear some remarkable orchestration, of the kind that irritated critics a half century ago: violas and cellos playing up in the fiddle range, clarinets shrieking in their highest register, and those uncanny bass tweaks during the beheading scene (Strauss said they did not represent John's cries of pain but the twinges of anguished impatience in Salome herself). The orchestra was Wagnerian in its symphonic texture, but its radical use of dissonant counterpoint was considered the ultimate of daring composition—until Strauss's next opera, *Elektra,* came along.

With *Salome* drawing nicely on two continents, opera houses outbid each other for the privilege of presenting *Elektra;* the publisher had some pages of the score in print before the rest of it was even composed. Hugo von Hofmannsthal, a German writer who wrote librettos for six of Strauss's operas, derived the plot from the classical plays of the Greeks, particularly Sophocles. The opera's single scene is the home of Clytemnestra, who has murdered her husband, Agamemnon, banished her son, Orestes, and degraded her daughter, Elektra. In the single scene of two-hours duration, Elektra, maddened and distraught, broods on the revenge she must take. Orestes eventually appears in disguise, and there is a "recognition scene" between brother and sister, which provides the only musical tenderness in the whole score. At the end of this meeting Orestes fulfills his destiny by murdering their mother, and Elektra falls dead after a grotesque dance of victory.

Strauss said in composing *Elektra* he had penetrated hitherto unexplored areas of contrapuntal writing: he achieved a texture of almost continuous dissonance by use of suspensions, appoggiaturas and altered notes. One of his techniques was to resolve his dissonances properly enough while causing the other voices to move on in the meantime. Thus his music became a constant flow of dissonances of varying intensity, as distinct from the alternation of dissonance and consonance common to earlier music. It was in *Elektra*, too, that he brought his orchestral technique to its highest point. Among his innovations: mutes for all the brasses (including tubas), giving a nervous, disembodied sound; flutter-tongue tones for brasses and flutes; trills for all winds, including brass; tremolos for strings playing in harmonics.

Critics found most of this music ugly, but nobody made the awful accusation of atonality. For Strauss at his most dissonant was still firmly rooted in the tonal tradition, and no matter how extreme his superimpositions, the basic tonality was available for reference. The real complaint was that his accompaniments, rich as they were, did not even attempt to depict the emotional content of a situation, but rather, described external action. Nevertheless, *Salome* and *Elektra* were epoch-making works. Unlike most new works of art, they were immediately and impressively profitable, and Strauss built himself a fine house in Garmisch.

Strauss's third great opera was *Der Rosenkavalier,* a piece that could hardly fail. He had asked Hofmannsthal for a libretto for "a Mozart opera." What he got was a period piece, spiced up with blunt suggestiveness and Viennese-style vulgarity. The first scene takes place during the overture, behind the curtain in the bedroom—or rather, the bed—of the Marschallin who, at 35, fears her charms are fading; with her is her 17-year-old lover, Octavian. Strauss's orchestra, graphic as ever, tells us exactly what is going on. Having had his sex joke, Strauss then settles down to the classic business of mistaken identity and mistaken love.

After the curtain goes up, old Baron Ochs interrupts the bedroom idyl, and Octavian (whose part is written for a woman's voice) thereupon disguises himself as a woman. The lecherous Baron makes advances to "her" while requesting the services of Octavian for the traditional task of delivering a silver rose to a young lady, as a sign of the Baron's intention to marry her. Of course, the young lady, Sophie, and Octavian fall in love, but it takes some fancy goings-on before the Baron is exposed for the fraud he is and young love has its way.

As usual, there is a mass of superfluous music in *Rosenkavalier,* but it comes as close as anything in Strauss to true sentiment; the final trio, in which the fading Marschallin blesses her lover and his new love, is nothing short of ravishing. The score is built around several waltzes, which inevitably leads to comparisons of Strauss with Vienna's beloved Johann of a few decades earlier. It is no match. *Rosenkavalier*'s melodies are simple, almost banal, and only their daring harmonies give them the rosy atmosphere that is all their own.

Having passed through three periods, Strauss had reached the age of 48 and had won financial security and the respect of the world. He was to write eight more operas, but none of them would ever match the big three, at least outside of Germany, and several were pale shadows of the others. But Strauss lived on while the world of music passed him by. By 1915, even history books began speaking of him in the past tense—a living legend. He continued to compose and wrote some songs of melting tenderness, some with piano and some with orchestral accompaniment, but no more major works. He died in 1949, at the age of 88.

———

Despite Strauss's important advances in orchestration and the counterpoint of dissonance, he is not the only link between the innovations of Wagner and the revolutions of 20th-century composers. Even more than Debussy, Strauss composed himself into a musical cul-de-sac. The missing link with the music of the future was provided by another Viennese contemporary, GUSTAV MAHLER.

Mahler was born in the Bohemian town of Kalischt, on July 7, 1860, and his early surroundings were a mixture of the romantic wooded countryside and the military barracks at the neighboring town of Iglau. At the age of four, he was playing soldiers' songs on the accordion, and soon he was astonishing his teachers with his quick ability to master musical problems. When he was still very young he imagined himself as a Wagnerian composer of music dramas, but it turned out that he was never to write a successful opera. Instead, he was to become one of the world's greatest operatic conductors. His narrow, ascetic figure and bespectacled face were to become hallmarks of the Vienna Court Opera, which he brought to its highest fame, and of the Metropolitan Opera, where musicians were astonished to see his baton descending on the downbeat without any preparatory "breath"—and were still more astonished to find that they started together nonetheless.

Mahler became a conductor because he had to earn a living, but he never earned enough to stop conducting. Constantly harassed by the need for security, he snatched precious weeks for composing when he could. His natural medium was the song, the romantic lied, but his mystical nature and his admiration for the symphonies of another Austrian, ANTON BRUCKNER, led him toward the super-symphony. On the way, he created a series of song cycles with orchestra that are symphonic in their size—notably his lovely, world-weary *Kindertotenlieder (Songs for Dead Children)* and his own premature farewell to the world, *Das Lied von der Erde (Song of the Earth)*—and nine enormous symphonies, some scored with voices. The eighth is called "Symphony of a Thousand" because of its huge chorus; some conductors say ironically it can be done with 500. Mahler's orchestra, for all its size, can sound as pure and limpid as a chamber ensemble, creating a counterpoint of arabesques that showed the way to a new conception of orchestral texture. "Mahler makes you feel naked," complained a musician in the Vienna Philharmonic. He was speaking of the exposed position in which he felt himself to be because so many of Mahler's instruments were treated like soloists. Mahler gets relatively little attention in the United States today, because he was unable to discriminate between original ideas and banalities—he had plenty of both—and his merciless lengths do not fit into the tempo of American living. Nevertheless, Mahler was important to the development of 20th-century music, both as a creative influence and because he was personally helpful to the radical group of composers that gathered around Arnold Schönberg.

PART FOUR

MODERN CHALLENGERS

MODERN CHALLENGERS

A LARGE AND GROWING MUSICAL PUBLIC in the first 15 years of the 20th century was being educated in terms of "eternal laws" of musical composition—even though they were forced to admit that the masters often broke them—when the dazzling music of IGOR STRAVINSKY burst on the scene with no apparent regard for laws at all; farther south, in Vienna, another musical lawbreaker, ARNOLD SCHÖNBERG, was starting riots with his fierce dissonances and the seemingly tortured convolutions of his twelve-tone techniques. These two men were to become the opposite poles of early 20th-century music, dividing the musical world between them, and making it impossible for music ever to return to the not-so-simple virtues of bygone years.

To Stravinsky, Schönberg and such important colleagues as BÉLA BARTÓK, SERGE PROKOFIEV and CHARLES IVES, it was abundantly clear that music had been at the service of poetry long enough and that the composer was more than ready to turn aside from voluptuous and sentimental preoccupation with his own heart and from heady speculation on the infinite. Music, they felt, needed to be purified, and that it had developed sufficient precision to make purification possible. This, of course, was a negative attitude (and some of the musical terms of the day showed their negative origin: viz., atonality, meaning a conscious denial of the principle of tonality). Under the more than talented pens of these men, the lush and massive symphony orchestra turned lean and contrapuntal or was pared down to become a new entity, the chamber orchestra. The new style seemed almost a parody of romantic poeticism, its sentimentality turned to grotesqueness, its exaltation to aggressiveness. The fractured motifs of Wagner became ends in themselves; the pastel impressionist colors of Debussy were darkened into garish expressionist hues; and the polyphony of the Middle Ages, and even of Bach, seemed to be reborn in the dissonant counterpoint of the modernists. Above all, the uncomplicated sounds of the romantics took on tensions and complexities. The tottering bulwark of tonality fell with a crash.

ATONAL MODERNIST

SCHÖNBERG

SCHÖNBERG WAS THE MOST CHALLENGING of the great 20th-century challengers of the romantic tradition. He was born on September 13, 1874, in Vienna, when that city was bubbling with the waltzes of Johann Strauss, basking in the symphonies of Bruckner—and still dreaming of the glories of Beethoven. By the time he was 16, Schönberg was a passable violinist and cellist, a close student of chamber music; and was convinced that he should lead a life of music. His father had died five years before, and the boy made a living by scoring other composers' operettas. He met and became friends with Alexander von Zemlinsky, who took him in hand and put him through a course in counterpoint.

Like most of the musicians around him, Schönberg found his deepest inspiration in Wagner, and his early works today sound very much like extrapolations of Wagnerian polyphony. At the time, however, Viennese found them strange and obtuse. His first major work was a string sextet, *Verklaerte Nacht (Transfigured Night),* one of the few tone-poems ever written for a chamber group. It is a long, lush and remarkably detailed work, rich in romantic emotionalism, and full of radical technical devices. Two years later, when he was 25, Schönberg completed the composition of *Gurrelieder,* which he decided to score for vocal soloists, three separate choirs and an orchestra of 155—a total of more than 400 performers participated in the première—and sent off to a music supply house for score paper with no less than 65 staves. He began the orchestration immediately, but this huge task was interrupted by his marriage, a teaching position in Berlin and work on other compositions; he did not complete the score until 1911. In final form, it bewildered even Richard Strauss and stunned the music world. Among its devices were two unusual ways to play the violin: *col legno,* tapping with the wooden part of the bow to create a sinister, almost pitchless, clicking sound; and *sul ponte cello,* in which the player lightly bows very close to the bridge to get a bodiless, buzzing effect.

Schönberg's other important early work was a symphonic poem, *Pelleas und Melisande,* which he completed a year after the appearance of Debussy's famous opera on the same text. Here, Schönberg was well along the path toward his controversial style. Already, a Viennese critic was calling him "a man either entirely devoid of sense or one who takes his listeners for fools. . . . Schönberg's opus is not only filled with wrong notes, as Strauss's *Don Quixote* is, but it is a fifty-minute-long wrong note. This is to be taken literally." Such was the temper of the musical times in Vienna, 1905, and such was to be the temper of critics wherever Schönberg was performed. *Pelleas* was also notable for its use of a trombone glissando, the now-familiar "smear" of circus and Dixieland jazz bands.

The massive orchestral apparatus, the dazzling complex of shifting colors, the emotional chromaticism, the brilliant contrapuntal detail all must have seemed to many inhabitants of that best of all possible musical worlds, the very end of musical development—and in some ways, it was. At any rate, *Pelleas* was Schönberg's last tone-poem and his last close association with the old style. There followed a series of radical little pieces with which he purposely turned his back on the threadbare comforts of tonality: the three piano pieces, Op. 11 and the suite of 15 settings of Stefan Georg's expressionist poems, *The Book of the Hanging Garden.* These were short, almost painfully self-conscious, unyieldingly dissonant works. No cliché of music literature is to be found in their few bars, no figure is ever literally repeated in their dense contrapuntal texture, and there is little or no sense of a home key.

"At the time," Schönberg said, "neither I nor my pupils were conscious of the reasons for [their intensity and brevity]. Later I discovered that our sense of form was right when it forced us to counterbalance extreme emotionality with extraordinary shortness. . . . Every innovation destroys while it produces." A new and fundamental problem nagged him; he had discarded the clarifying effects of tonal harmony—the restful cadences at the end of each important statement and the sense of tension and relaxation between dissonance and consonance—but he had no principle with which to replace them. A temporary solution to his problem came in an age-old device: writing songs and depending on the verbal texts to form and articulate the music. The most important of these songs are contained in that remarkable song cycle, *Pierrot Lunaire,* in which the soprano half-sings, half-speaks (in German the style is called *Sprechtstimme*) in an eerie, somnambulistic manner, while the chamber orchestra tweaks and twitches in a notably apt description of an inner psychological state. During the same period, Schönberg composed a vivid "monodrama" called *Erwartung (Expectation)* and another called *Die Glückliche Hand (The Lucky Hand).* Perhaps his still unformed musical expression was insufficient to satisfy him; at any rate, he turned to painting—in expressionist style—and also wrote a book, *The Theory of Harmony*.

But Schönberg became more and more convinced that musically he was on the right track—and that he and his pupils were probably the only composers on it. He founded a "Society for Private Musical Performances," that was to be, so the prospectus read, "free from the corrupting influence of publicity, with newspaper critics excluded, applause or hissing forbidden and members pledged to give no public report of the proceedings." Schönberg was president, and his powers were practically unlimited.

The years 1915-23 (during which Schönberg was twice drafted into the army and discharged again) were nearly empty of new compositions. The composer was busy conducting a composition seminar, which was attended by such renowned musicians as the pianists Rudolf Serkin and Eduard Steuermann and the violinist Rudolf Kolisch. It was not until 1923, when he finished his piano pieces, Op. 23, that he reached a theory to account for—and carry forward—the music he was writing. It is called, in various translations from the German, the twelve-tone system, twelve-note system, twelve-tone technique and dodecaphony, and has become the most controversial musical development in the 20th century.

This is how Schönberg had reached his theory. He studied his own music and that of his two most brilliant pupils, ALBAN BERG and ANTON WEBERN, until he saw its tendencies clearly. It was, he decided, continuously dissonant—so continuously dissonant that a common triad would be a jarring element; its melody was characterized by the appearance of tiny fragmented motifs and was rendered intense by the use of dissonant intervals, (i.e., augmented seconds, augmented fourths, major and minor sevenths and ninths) and the use of unrelieved chromaticism and wide skips; its harmony was so contrapuntal that he likened it to Bach, and so lacking in the common contrasts of tension and relaxation that it no longer bore much relation to any music that preceded it. Moreover, it weakened the important notes of a scale and strengthened the less important ones until all became equal and the listener's sense of key-feeling was set adrift. Schönberg realized that he was ignoring, if not actually negating, tonality, and that if his music was to be understood he must substitute another means of organization.

What he finally evolved was, in effect, a new system of tonality for each composition. It took the form of a "tone row" or "set," containing all twelve notes of the chromatic scale; a new row was devised for every work. The row was consciously set up (thus the anguished accusations that it was "cerebral," "abnormal," "chaotic," "mathematical" music, particularly from people who liked to believe that tonal music was somehow "natural"). One of the first rules of Schönberg's new system was that none of the twelve notes could be repeated until all had been heard, a rule that was designed to deny with finality any suspicion of tonal feeling.

The row appeared immediately in each work, although it was not necessarily the theme, or not necessarily recognizable at all. It could be used either horizontally, with all the tricks of the contrapuntalist's trade, or vertically, in the form of chords, or in a combination of both. There were other rules—the technique has evolved continuously in the years since 1923—all of which provided ammunition for Schönberg's enemies, despite the fact that there was a time when he denied there was such a thing as a twelve-tone system. Whatever the genesis, what Schönberg called "composition with twelve tones" is being used today by an ever-growing mass of composers, and they use it and study it for the same reasons other composers study and use the traditional disciplines.

In 1924, Vienna turned out to honor Schönberg on his 50th birthday. The mayor made a speech, and a huge chorus sang; his admirers published a volume of articles, critical abuse and testimonials; his publisher opened a Schönberg Library of Modern Music. Shortly after, he succeeded the renowned Busoni as head of the Prussian Academy of Fine Arts in Berlin, and he gained momentum in his composition, completing his third string quartet; his *Variations for Orchestra;* a one-act opera, *Von Heute auf Morgen (From Today to Tomorrow)* and a suite called *Accompaniment to a Cinema Scene.*

In the spring of 1933, Schönberg was dismissed from the Academy faculty for not meeting the requirements of the "Aryan paragraph." He went to Paris and there made a solemn profession of the Jewish faith and went through a period of composing music on Hebrew themes. The same year he emigrated to the United States, teaching first in Boston, then in Southern California, where the climate suited him better. His arrival in Los Angeles was a time for rejoicing among film composers, who flocked to study with him and pick up some of his masterful orchestral tricks. There was a short period when Schönberg benefited financially from this—he charged a rumored $100 a lesson—but the old Austrian put his pupils on a strict diet of fundamental harmony and counterpoint. The ranks of sound track composer pupils thinned precipitously, and from then until he died, in 1951, Schönberg taught music students and composed some of his most important works: a violin concerto, a piano concerto, his fourth string quartet. Periodically, he abandoned the rigors of the twelve-tone technique to indulge in the rigors of tonal composition. A concerto for string quartet and orchestra, loosely based on a Handel concerto grosso and an *Ode to Napoleon* for string quartet and voice brought down upon his head as much wrath for presuming to write in a traditional style as he had ever incurred by his most radical works. With a mere 50 opus numbers completed, he died— an enigmatic figure whose life seemed closely wrapped in musical thought; whose personal relationships, though occasionally intimate, left few anecdotes or revelations of his own personality, indeed, no clear impression of whether or not he was ever a happy man.

Schönberg warned his pupils against treating the twelve-tone system as dogma, and at least one of them who took his advice has won more popular favor than the master. ALBAN BERG was born in Vienna on February 9, 1885, eleven years after his teacher, into a comfortable family of business people. His brother and sister were both musical, and Alban began to compose seriously when he was 15. During his early years, he composed a number of songs, wrote volumes of fine letters, read extensively and apparently felt almost too deeply about things: at 18 he tried to commit suicide over an unhappy love affair. In 1904, after his father's death, when he was working as a government clerk, he met Schönberg.

The teacher kept him at fundamentals for four years. In 1908, he finished his piano sonata Op. 1—whose firm architecture bears traces of Brahms despite its debt to Schönberg—and began the seven tender songs that he completed over the years of apprenticeship. Berg developed into a pale, asthmatic figure of extreme sensitivity and with a capacity for self-criticism that limited his output to a few works. They include, however, major works. The biggest and most immediately successful was his opera, *Wozzeck,* based on an old play by Georg Büchner about the degradation and brutalization of a soldier.

The music is a miracle of richness and has, more than any music that preceded it, the extraordinary quality of seeming to emanate from the inner lives of its characters— not so much from their emotions as from their dark and twisted psyches. Strangely enough, Berg used traditional forms, along with twelve-tone techniques, in *Wozzeck*: a passacaglia, a near-rondo, a lullaby, a march, etc. Although it is next to impossible to detect these forms in a performance, they are there, underlining Berg's emotional ties with the past.

Wozzeck took six years to complete. It was first performed in Berlin, in 1925, and immediately established Berg as a major figure. His next important work was the *Lyric Suite* for string quartet, which again mixes past and future techniques and actually includes a literal quotation from the first bars of the ideal of all German music to that date, *Tristan und Isolde*. Berg's violin concerto, his last completed work—and one of his most remarkable—makes use of both a fully developed twelve-note technique and seemingly tonal harmonies. This neat trick Berg accomplished by dividing his twelve semitones into two groups that resembled diatonic scales and chords and thus gave the effect of shifting, but quite real, key-feeling. Berg died in 1935, already recognized as a powerful force in contemporary music.

Schönberg's other important disciple was ANTON WEBERN, who was born in Vienna on December 3, 1883. Stylistically, he was Berg's opposite, an inspired miniaturist who somehow managed to infuse every note with a tremendous significance and tension. Webern's orchestration is subtle and fragile, refined to the point where instrumental colors are as important as pitch in limning melodic outlines; his favorite dynamics marking is PPP (pianiss-*iss*imo). He presents his musical ideas discreetly surrounded by rests and scattered like a pointillist's specks over the extremes of instrumental ranges. Most of his music is correspondingly brief; one work lasts a grand total of 19 seconds. His compositions include music for string trio and quartet, a symphony, and songs accompanied by various instrumental combinations.

Webern's rarefied style has struck the fancy of younger composers more than either Schönberg's or Berg's. Its exquisite purity appeals, perhaps, to the same antiromantic instincts that have made neoclassical composers of so many young moderns. At any rate, it is Webern's developments that have stimulated the liveliest changes in twelve-tone dogma. At the close of World War II, he was shot by accident in Mittersill; his untimely death may have meant a restriction of twelve-tone growth.

Almost every important contemporary composer has dallied more or less seriously with the technique, and most countries have composers who are outstanding dodecaphonists. One of the finest is the Italian LUIGI DALLAPICCOLA, who often tempers his dodecaphonism with massive choral sonorities in the manner of Palestrina. In a more intimate vein, he writes warm-hearted counterpoint for small instrumental combinations, which he blends to perfection with the soprano voice. In America, the Vienna-born ERNST KŘENEK, who made his first hit in the '20's with his jazzy opera, *Jonny Spielt Auf (Johnny Speaks Up)*, has moved unpredictably into and out of the idiom. The most important native American, ROGER SESSIONS, has turned to it occasionally, despite a strong early antipathy.

NEOCLASSIC MODERNIST

STRAVINSKY

ANOTHER GREAT CHALLENGER of romantic musical tradition also began as a traditional composer. IGOR STRAVINSKY was born in Oranienbaum, near St. Petersburg, on June 17, 1882. His father was a basso of the Imperial Opera, and the boy grew up in a healthy musical atmosphere. Nevertheless, he was sent to law school, with music as merely a minor study. When he was 20, Igor met the greatest living Russian composer, Rimsky-Korsakov, and then and there abandoned the law career. By the time he was far enough advanced in harmony and orchestration for actual study with Rimsky, he was 25 and the composer of a firmly Brahms-like symphony. His Op. 2 was a song cycle whose style had advanced to the point where it resembled the impressionism of Debussy. The composer was becoming known as a rising talent. His future was secured when he was noticed by an expatriate dilettante named Serge Diaghilev, who was just starting his famous *Ballets Russes* in Paris. Diaghilev commissioned *Firebird,* which Stravinsky completed in 1910. Although it was recognizable as the best Russian style of his teacher, it was a fast step forward into his own blazingly primitive "first" style.

The following year in Rome, Stravinsky turned out a second ballet, *Petrouchka,* with a carnival story about a puppet who is brought to life. It had a startling mechanical kind of rhythm, appropriate to its subject, and a brilliantly colorful orchestration; but it was its harmonic innovations that made it so controversial. For Stravinsky boldly combined the chords of C and F sharp—the most distant possible keys—to make what quickly became known as the *"Petrouchka chord."* To theorists this was mayhem, for if one combined two keys what happened to tonality? As it happens, the key of C wins out in *Petrouchka,* and theorists later invented all kinds of theories to account for this triumph. The new technique was labeled "polytonality" (or bitonality), and it was decided that the foreign chords were actually decorations or elaborations of the fundamental ones, used as much for color as for harmony.

Stravinsky had other surprises up his sleeve. For several years he had been brooding about the idea of a pagan rite in which a girl is sacrificed by being made to dance herself to death. This became the famous *Sacre du Printemps.* It was used for a Diaghilev ballet presented in Paris in 1913, and tales are still being told about its première. Excitable Parisians were overcome by its eccentric, aggressive rhythms and its lawless melodies and harmonies. Before the performance was well under way, outraged customers were shouting sarcastic directions to the musicians as to how they should play it. Catcalls grew louder, until the dancers could not even hear the orchestra. Members of the audience began to strike their neighbors with fists and canes. Backstage, Diaghilev was shouting directions first to turn on, then to turn off the house lights, hoping to calm the pandemonium, while the choreographer was counting at the top of his lungs to keep the dancers in time. As for Stravinsky, he made his escape through a back window and rode through the cool night in wordless grief.

It was said, after that, that the *Sacre* was the destruction of music; it outraged all the laws, it had no melody, its shifting rhythm was chaos, its orchestra was nothing but noise, etc., etc. It is almost unnecessary to say that it went on to become one of the popular works of the symphonic repertoire, as so many radical works have done from Bach to Bartók. Stravinsky himself has called it a "romantic" work and only regrets it was published when he was a Russian citizen and thus is not subject to the international copyright laws which ensure payment of royalties.

It is strange that both the major innovators of the century should undergo a change of mind at about the same date, for Stravinsky and Schönberg, although they were aware of each other's music, were not close in any sense. Nevertheless, in 1918, Stravinsky abandoned his lush style, his color effects, his chromaticism. His next work was about as different as it could be: *L'Histoire du Soldat* was scored for seven instruments and narrator. Its music is lean and stark, its colors ascetic and its motifs concise, ironic, purposeful. It is the beginning of Stravinsky's return to classical forms, a change for which he himself is unable (or unwilling) to account. The fact is, probably, that the *Sacre* reached a pitch of development beyond which it was impossible for him to go. The works that followed were written in what is called "neoclassic" style, because of their symmetry and precision, their economical use of material, their quality of coolness and impersonalness: the remarkable octet for wind instruments (1923); the concerto for piano and wind orchestra, written for his first visit to the United States in 1924; the oratorio *Oedipus Rex,* for which he wrote the words in Latin so that listeners would not be bothered at his strange accentuations or distracted by verbal connotation; and the ballets *Baiser de la Fée,* in which he used selected passages of

Tchaikovsky—and used them pretty hard—and *Pulcinella,* in which he did the same with Pergolesi, perhaps because he felt some basic lack of melodic inventiveness.

In 1930, he completed the *Symphony of Psalms* for the 50th anniversary of the Boston Symphony, a highly successful return to his early love of splendid masses of sound. It is scored for large chorus and orchestra—without violins, in order to leave the most expressive vocal register uncluttered—and it is again a huge, gaudy, pagan work with skirling reeds offsetting the outcry of the chorus.

Although Stravinsky had become a French citizen after the first war, he no longer had reason to be a Frenchman after Diaghilev died, in 1929, and the *Ballets Russes* foundered. Stravinsky's wife and daughter died the same year, and when the second war loomed, he moved to the United States, settled near Schönberg in Hollywood, and became an American citizen. Like Schönberg, he continues to be controversial even when he is composing music that should offend nobody. He has been accused of commercialism because he has accepted commissions from the circus, from the bandleader Paul Whiteman and from the producer Billy Rose, as well as from Woody Herman for his fine jazz band (he wrote *Ebony Concerto* for this group). And he has lost favor with some of his admirers because of some of his latest compositions. His opera, *The Rake's Progress,* disturbed friend and foe alike for its bald imitation of Mozart and Tchaikovsky and its supercilious, super-effete libretto.

Whatever the ultimate judgment of Stravinsky will be, the world of music has inevitably been influenced by him, perhaps more than it knows. A whole French school sprang up after he first used polytonality, with men like Darius Milhaud and Arthur Honegger as its leaders and polytonality as its esthetic foundation. After Stravinsky became neoclassic, a second growth of followers sprang up, notably in America. AARON COPLAND and VIRGIL THOMSON are perhaps the leading figures of the neoclassical school, and a crowd of younger composers is following in their footsteps.

Only individualists like Bartók, whose remarkably convincing modernities grew directly out of his studies of asymmetrical Balkan folk music, and Prokofiev, whose position inside Communist Russia gave his music a national flavor, were able to resist the influence of either Stravinsky or Schönberg.

Strangely enough, these two men were neighbors in Hollywood for a dozen years but scarcely ever bothered to see each other—and the partisan fires around them blazed the brighter. But late in their lives both men allowed themselves an easing of stylistic tensions. Schönberg modified his twelve-tone techniques and occasionally abandoned them altogether; Stravinsky, shortly after his colleague's death, wrote a sextet and announced that it was composed in the twelve-tone system, and all of his subsequent music has been if not precisely "dodecaphonic" at least based on tone rows.

PART FIVE

VISTAS

VISTAS

BEFORE WE TAKE A SPECULATIVE LOOK at the future, let's look back at the past. We may conclude that, in general, composers wrote the way they did because of the instruments they had to write for. (Reciprocally, instruments were developed because composers needed them.) During the Middle Ages, the instrument was primarily the human voice used in groups; and the groups sang in unison, as in the Gregorian Chant, or were divided into two or more parts, resulting in the noble style we call "polyphony."

But some time during the Middle Ages imaginative men began to perfect another kind of wind instrument whose lungs were leather bellows and whose throat was wooden and metal pipes: the organ. By the middle of the 16th century, the organ had become the most important instrument of all, and composers were discovering ways of adapting their counterpoint to its instrumental singing.

Just as the organ was developed before voices lost their position of importance, so the orchestra had its beginnings long before the organ was relegated to a subordinate musical position. Like the organ, orchestral instruments were developed to accompany the human voice; first, wandering minstrels, then the more elaborate vocalizing of Italian opera. Gradually the orchestra attained independence as composers little by little found ways to make it speak coherently without the assistance of words: first by using variations over a figured bass, next by adopting repeated themes and then by the evolutionary process known as development. When separate orchestral instruments acquired recognizable personalities of their own, the classical orchestra was established. This was the instrument of Haydn, Mozart and Beethoven. It is still with us; it has undergone no fundamental development since the early 19th century.

A sociological change was responsible for the emergence of the next major instrument, the piano. It grew in popularity as music came out of the palace and into the apartment, out of the drawing room and into the concert hall, for it was the instrument that was adopted by the bourgeois. With its capacity for graduations of volume, it satisfied people's need for personal expression, and in virtuoso pianists, who pitted their strength against the combined strength of the orchestra, it satisfied their need for musical heroes. The romantic piano concertos of Beethoven, Schumann, Liszt and Brahms were the piano's major offspring; the piano sonata and other less clearly defined forms of Chopin fulfilled the more intimate qualities of the piano, in which the dreamer seemed to express his innermost feelings in solitude.

Since the middle of the last century, there has been no dominant new instrument. There was, of course, a busy period of consolidation and development. The organ was improved and enlarged until it became the versatile monster we can still hear in movie houses, sounding something like a symphony orchestra and a church organ combined, which is almost what it is. The orchestra evolved through the hands of such masters as Berlioz, Rimsky-Korsakov and Strauss until it now contains more than 100 members and commands a subtle but vivid spectrum of tonal colors. The piano was strengthened and refined and unexpectedly revealed new possibilities for sonorous effects in the hands of Debussy and the impressionists, and rattling, percussive conciseness in the hands of Stravinsky and Bartók. As for the human voice, its potentialities are no longer as fully exploited as they were in the golden days of Italian opera, for the microphone has made it possible for relatively untrained singers to attain Herculean volume. Without microphonic assistance, popular chorus masters have tried to make the voice imitate orchestral effects, and such serious composers as Milhaud and Schönberg have increased its flexibility through use of song-speech.

A great many 20th-century musicians have wished they could find a new instrument that would more accurately reflect the temper of our times, and some of the wishes have almost come true. The most ubiquitous instrument of the 20th century is the saxophone, the only orchestral instrument capable of rivaling brasses in volume. It was invented about 1840 by a Belgian instrument maker, Adolphe Sax, who got the idea for it while trying to play an ophicleide (of the tuba family) with a clarinet mouthpiece. The saxophone uses a single reed but differs from clarinets in its conical bore and the fact that all of its holes are covered with pads controlled by keys. It has been adopted by many jazzmen, but its real place is in the dance band, where its alto, tenor and baritone models are balanced by trumpets and trombones. Its raucous tones have been tamed to win it a place in some concert music, but it has never become a steady member of symphony orchestras.

In the early 30's a Russian inventor named Theremin invented the electronic marvel that bears his name. It is played by waving the hands in the air over a box full of electronic tubes. One hand moves vertically to control volume, the other horizontally to control pitch, and a single voice emerges from a loudspeaker. Its characteristic tone resembles a chorus of humming women or a musical saw. It has never become popular, partly because it is so difficult to control; it is hard enough simply to hit the right key on a piano, let alone a point in space. Several inventors have combined the same electronic principle with a mechanical keyboard; such instruments as the *Ondes Martenot* are sometimes heard in symphony concerts and as accompaniments for mystery films.

The growth of electronics has also permitted acoustical extensions of conventional instruments. Pianos have been invented whose strings are kept vibrating by magnetic coils, thus making it possible for a crescendo after the tone is struck; other kinds of electronic pianos have achieved a more limited but similar effect by picking up the tone via microphone and amplifying it through speakers. Every instrument from the violin to the harp has been adapted to electronic performance, which permits a peculiar inversion with fine expressive possibilities, such as a pianissimo violin tone, with all its buttery, hushed quality sounding at fortissimo volume. The only amplified instrument to reach a firm acceptance is the guitar, whose electronic descendant is practically a necessity in every modern dance and jazz band.

Periodically, some scientist comes up with a more radical instrument which is said to be able to synthesize any musical sound by artificially assembling the proper overtone characteristics and broadcasting them through a speaker. This is the principle of the electronic organ, familiar to listeners of daytime radio serials. Carried to extremes, it is also the principle behind the giant contraptions, occasionally announced by a big laboratory, that look more like typewriters combined with electronic computers than musical instruments. These are supposed to be able to synthesize the attack, timbre and quality of known instruments and of sounds never before heard by human ears. On such a device, a musician can theoretically play (and record) the sound of one instrument at a time, starting with the piccolo and ending with the double bass, until he has made, all by himself, and without payment of any union fees or hiring a hall, a recording of a full symphony. Usually it sounds more like a monstrous harpsichord.

Although musicians are not getting excited about new kinds of orchestral instruments, there are two related developments which seem likely to be the major influences on music of the future: jazz and the record player.

Jazz, like most of the lasting idioms of the past, has its roots in folk music. Jazz is primarily improvisation; its song is the blues, which grew out of ancient Negro work songs and religious laments; its form is related to the passacaglia and chaconne of Bach's day, except that its original theme (usually the whole of a 12-bar blues or a 32-bar popular song) is not necessarily played but is repeated only in the performers' imaginations, while they develop their group variations on it. In the 50-odd years that it is known to have existed, jazz has been thoroughly accepted as America's single great contribution to the art of music. Research on the beginnings of jazz is still incomplete, since new facts and old phonograph records are still coming to light.

Jazz was influenced by still another idiom: the ragtime of the minstrel shows that followed the Civil War. Ragtime was the white man's parody of the Negro music of the day, but it was also played (usually on the piano) by Negroes. It was accompanied by rhythmically twanging banjos and tapping feet, and its most famous expression is the strutting cakewalk. Characteristic of ragtime are uninhibited improvisation and syncopated rhythm, a steady pulse in which the weak beats (nos. 2 and 4) are unexpectedly accented. The rhythmic vitality of this music fascinated such European composers as Brahms, Debussy and Stravinsky.

The blues, on the other hand, was the legitimate descendant of African music, played and sung by Negroes themselves. It was a song of the slaves, along with spirituals, work songs, cornfield hollers and banjo tunes, and its name comes from the presence of "blue notes," the half-flatted third and seventh notes of the scale (E flat and B flat, in the key of C). The use of foreign notes makes the blues an unsophisticated relative of the polytonality introduced by Stravinsky a few years later, and its effect was equally piquant to its first listeners, who were both puzzled and moved by its haunting qualities. The blues was a vocal lament with undercurrents of humor, ordinarily (but not always) in slow, draggy tempo. The performer improvised three lines of verse: the first and second, identical in words and similar in melody; the third, a kind of answer in rhyme. The whole chorus was twelve bars long.

Sample (from W. C. Handy's *St. Louis Blues* *):

> *I hate to see that evenin' sun go down,*
> *I hate to see that evenin' sun go down,*
> *'Cause my baby done left this town.*

Between each phrase there was a long pause, which the singer used originally to dream up the next line. This pause began to be used by the accompanying pianist or banjoist to "take off" on an improvisation of his own, and it came to be called the "jass." There was commonly a throbbing, persistent rhythm to the blues—the element we

---

* Quotation by permission of the copyright owner, W. C. Handy.

still call "hot"—and it was characteristic of most Negro popular music from about the turn of the century; it stimulated its listeners to the point of intoxication. It was the musical equivalent of the Negroes' incredibly graceful dances on the levees—Virginia reels and quadrilles.

Another manifestation of jazz was the Negro wind bands that began to flourish in southern cities after the Civil War. These were the street bands that marched to and from graveyards in funeral processions—on the way, mournfully lamenting the departed, and on the return, "ragging" their defiance of death and poverty. Their other functions were of a happier nature, providing entertainment (and noisy advertisement) during Mardi Gras, weddings, mass picnics and boat trips, although it was not long before the purity of jazz's reputation became tarnished. This happened because jazz musicians found a home and a public in the parlors and bar rooms of New Orleans' Storyville, a section of town set off for the purposes of organized vice. Considering Storyville's easygoing atmosphere, it is not surprising that it played host to the Negro musicians—most of whom were not regularly employed elsewhere. It was probably there that the word "jazz" first became attached to hot music; originally it was a decidedly lewd verb.

The earliest jazz bands (in the 1890's) established the form of the "Dixieland" combos of today: a rhythm section, consisting of bass (tuba or bull fiddle), drums (bass drum, snare drum, suspended cymbals, woodblocks), banjo or guitar and, when the combo was not marching, piano; and a melody section, consisting usually of trumpet, trombone and clarinet (sometimes more than one of each). Probably the brightest stars of early jazz were the trumpeter Charles "Buddy" Bolden and his band, which included such names as Bunk Johnson and

Freddie Kepard. Bolden also fostered the careers of the clarinetist Sidney Bechet and the cornetist Joe "King" Oliver.

When Storyville was closed by government order in 1917, there was a melancholy exodus of jazzmen, mostly up the Mississippi to Chicago, Memphis and St. Louis. Jazz was underway. Younger musicians joined up with the old—a brilliant young trumpeter named Louis Armstrong joined the Oliver band in Chicago—and young white musicians began imitating their New Orleans style, creating an idiom of their own, known as "Dixieland."

Since most of these performers—some of them so brimming with talent they may even deserve to be called geniuses—did not know how to read music, it was either memorized or created on the spot. This made jazz almost exclusively a matter of improvisation; and even if the music was not newly improvised, it had the freshness of improvisation. The trouble was, it could not be written down; musical notation was (and is) simply too unsubtle to catch the nuances that are at the root of real jazz. As a result, most of the jazz created before 1920 was lost. After that, recording companies began to realize its commercial value; much of the inspired playing from the early days in Chicago has been recorded, and more and more is being reissued today on long-playing records.

When jazz established itself in Chicago, it acquired a patina of respectability, although it has never quite thrown off its bawdy-house reputation. White and colored musicians began to play together, and jazz spread farther. Its next major stopping place was New York, where it took on some of the affectations of more respectable music, and big bands of 17 or more pieces became the rage. Duke Ellington moved into the Cotton Club, and almost immediately his vivid melodies and throbbing rhythms made him famous. Paul Whiteman gave up his cello and started a large orchestra, playing something misnamed "symphonic jazz," and incidentally popularizing a jazz-inspired composition by a young tin-pan alley talent, George Gershwin. The piece was *Rhapsody in Blue*. Whiteman also included in his big orchestra a smaller unit of the best white jazzmen of the day (1927): Bix Beiderbecke, cornettist; Frank Trumbauer, saxophonist; Jack Teagarden, trombonist; and a hot vocalist named Bing Crosby.

It was not long before popular music, which previously had taken much of its style from operetta songs, began to adopt the mannerisms of jazz: a rhythmic lift, a 12- or 32-bar form and some of the jazzmen's lingo ("the blues," "hot time," etc.). In the mid-30's, that high flying and almost indefinable lilt known as the "jazz feeling," so typical of small combos, was injected into dance band arrangements, and the age of swing had arrived; among its heroes were Benny Goodman, Tommy Dorsey, Artie Shaw, Count Basie. The noun "swing" is no longer used, but a jazz group is still said to "swing" when it achieves that lilt.

As World War II approached, something happened to jazzmen. Perhaps the swing style had become too stereotyped for them, or perhaps they were tired of being cramped by band arrangements. At any rate, where even the most advanced orchestrations had reflected nothing more radical than a few impressionist harmonies of Debussy and Strauss, these malcontents began to experiment —at fortissimo volume—with the more dissonant flavors of Schönberg and Stravinsky, and particularly treasured the "devil's interval" of medieval music, the augmented fourth; and where the rhythm section had formerly confined itself to a strict two- or four-beat pulse, the experimenters tried spreading the pattern to cover two, three or more bars, breaking up the even beat with unexpected thuds on the bass drum. The unpredictable pattern of these drumbeats delighted the other players, and when they heard them they would shout an imitative reply: "bebop!" Leaders of the bebop (later called simply "bop") school were Negroes: trumpeter Dizzy Gillespie, alto saxophonist Charlie "Yardbird" Parker, pianist Thelonius Monk. Their music sounded hysterical and was much too wild for most kinds of dancing, but it displayed an incredible amount of imagination and instrumental technique. Concert musicians who might understandably have thought a solo was "faked" were then amazed to hear the whole ensemble play the same notes in a dazzling unison.

It was inevitable that bop should burn itself out with its excesses, both musical and personal (for it was more than a rumor that some of its stars were addicted to dope). Some of the performers died young, and the style itself settled into something milder and more musical, a nameless something that filtered through all levels of jazz and made much of it sound more like the concert music it paralleled.

The modern jazz flourishes in small groups, particularly on the West Coast. Its stars are as often as not one-time members of big bands (Stan Kenton's, Woody Herman's) who decided for one reason or another to strike out for themselves. They are about equally divided between Negroes (Oscar Peterson, pianist, the Modern Jazz Quartet) and whites (Dave Brubeck, pianist, Chet Baker, trumpeter). Their idiom is strongly contrapuntal; their beat, more persuasive than percussive. At their best they are free as the wind, so free that listeners may only fleetingly —or never—recognize the tune on which they are playing variations. Their style is, nevertheless, the style that has infected would-be jazzmen abroad, who are playing some worthy jazz and are even appearing on the American scene as jazz performers in their own right.

Whether this, or any jazz style, can (or should) infect "serious" music we have yet to see. The composers who have tried to incorporate jazz into their concert works have achieved nothing resembling the warmth or the peculiar relaxed motion that is the essence of real jazz; most jazz movements in serious music still tend to resemble ragtime. The fact that serious composers try to incorporate jazz may be more significant than the concert world is ready to admit—jazz may actually have more vitality than any other kind of music today and may very well turn out to be the major musical expression of the 20th century.

In any case, it is not likely that jazz and concert music will become one. They may come closer and closer, but the essence of jazz is the impression it gives of being born rough and makeshift, this instant; and the essence of concert music is its precision and, if you will, its thoughtfulness. The composer who is fortunate enough to experience some of jazz's own intimate activities must either abandon them when he writes his larger works, as has William Schuman, or capitulate to them, as has Vladimir Dukelsky (Vernon Duke).

It is my feeling, however, that the 20th-century instrument, the record player, is going to have a more important effect on the music of tomorrow than jazz. For one thing, it is the only means of preserving jazz. Second, it is placing concert music—or at least its technicolor shadow—within the living-rooms of a constantly growing public; concert music is not going to be lost in the shuffle, even if concert halls may be. Most significantly, it is creating a new attitude toward listening. The listener is not only at home—where he stays more and more—but he no longer has the mass reaction of the concert audience to help him respond to the musical activities on stage. He will not even have the visual help that he might get from watching a performer bring abstractions to life. The listener is becoming less and less a participant in music, even at the minimal level, and the record player is encouraging his laziness.

The record player began as inauspiciously as the piano, and it may provide the same kind of stimulus. It started in an area that seemed far from music. About the time that Debussy was inventing new tone colors through the spacing of harmonies on the piano and Stravinsky was daring the world to listen to music in two keys at once, inventors and gadgeteers were playing with what they called "talking machines." In the U.S.A., Thomas A. Edison had set a cylinder of soft metal foil spinning and embossed spiral grooves on it with a needle that vibrated at the end of a horn. He shouted down the horn "Mary had a little lamb!" Then he returned the needle to the groove he had made, put his ear to the big end of the horn and heard the tiny echo of his own words coming back to him. A few years later, musicians became interested in the contraption, but only as a documentary device, to preserve the echoes of their performances for posterity. Then canny businessmen glimpsed its commercial possibilities, and the industrial recording giants of today were born.

The latest major event in the history of the record player is the development of the tape recorder, which is both a recording and playback device, nearly foolproof and as compact as any living-room record player. Its significant advantage over disk recorders is that the tape may be cut with ordinary scissors and neatly patched together with plastic tape. In other words, it may be edited. As a result, a generation of amateur recordists has been born, the sons and daughters of parents who once upon a time gathered about the parlor piano, perhaps with their violins and cellos, to perform Beethoven trios, or at least to sing a round or two.

Some of the new amateurs content themselves with recording a symphony program from the radio or with copying a friend's recording of a favorite performance. Others have discovered a more creative possibility and are recording the sounds of life about them: car horns, church bells, crashing surf, water gurgling in a kitchen sink, the wind in pine trees—anything that catches their aural fancies. When they have a sufficient library, they experiment with the possibilities of casting them into compositions, by snipping out undesired episodes and cutting in others, or by blending and superimposing one sound over another, transmuting them by filtering and resonating devices into entirely alien sounds. A person interested in such tricks can remove every other note in a sonata and place it in front of the one which is supposed to precede it. But it is much more fun to snip off the clang, or ictus, of a tape-recorded steeple bell and preserve only the strange and lovely humming that remains, or to insert ten seconds of a 1,000-voice *a capella* chorus into the refrain of a nursery rhyme. Such compositions can never be adequately written down or played by any ensemble known to man. They can, in fact, be reproduced only on some sort of record player.

A number of composers in Europe and America are experimenting with tape and coming up with remarkable results. Perhaps the most advanced experiments come from

France in what the French call *musique concrète*. (Most of its sounds are natural, or at least everyday, sounds; musical sounds made by strings, winds and percussion are, on the other hand, abstract, far removed from nature.) The French subject their sounds to as many kinds of distortion as they can. By slowing a baby's cry, they lower the pitch, and out comes a baritone groaning in his beer. A carillon speeded up can sound like a doorbell. Playing sounds backwards results in effects that are surrealistic, sometimes mysterious and sometimes uproariously funny. Such sounds can be combined in any order, with or without themes and leitmotifs, to make compositions that are as convincing as a Chopin nocturne. *Musique concrète* is essentially a game. Composers who start from similar bases, such as the French-American EDGARD VARÈSE, turn the electronic techniques to more musical ends. Some experimenters prefer to use the sounds for an evocative effect: a steam locomotive produces nostalgia and a crashing surf a soporific or erotic effect; even the clunk of water dropping in a cave may arouse some as yet unclassified emotion rooted in eons-old racial memories.

The results, when they are made into successful compositions, may be just as potent as the experiments of Stamitz and Carl Philipp Emanuel Bach when they were discovering that melodies could describe emotions—and the creators of these new compositions may be subject to just as much scoffing.

However it turns out, the music of the future will probably bear little resemblance to the music of the past. We are unable to predict its shape because the forces of musical change—the modernist composers, the jazzmen—are made to appear disreputable by the forces of the status quo—the boards of directors of orchestras and opera companies. But even if the center of musical gravity shifts to jazz or tape-recorded sound, the concert music we know will certainly continue as an important musical force. As one modernist composer put it: "You do not kill your horse because you ride an airplane."

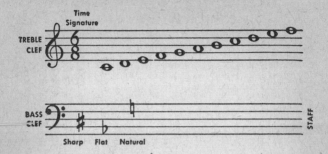

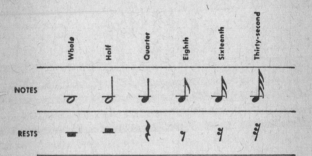

A dot beside a note or rest lengthens it by ½ its value.

A dot over or under a note (staccato) shortens it by ½ its value.

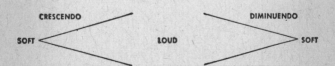

SYMBOLS USED IN MUSIC

COMPOSERS' LIFE CHART

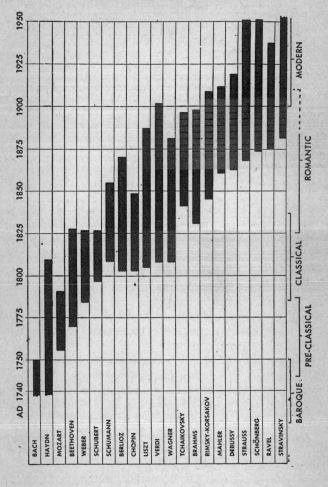

GLOSSARY

A CAPPELLA (Italian, *in church style*): A term used to describe choral music without instrumental accompaniment.

ABSOLUTE PITCH: A memory phenomenon which permits the possessor to identify any note he hears. Many orchestral musicians develop it through constant association with the tuning note A. See RELATIVE PITCH.

ACCIDENTAL: A note that has been raised (by a sharp sign) or lowered (by a flat sign) for a single measure during the course of a composition. See FLAT and SHARP.

AMEN CHORD: See SUBDOMINANT.

APPOGGIATURA: The use of an adjacent note to delay the appearance of a chordal note.

ARIA: A song; usually so called when it appears in an opera. The aria form (A-B-A) is the most fundamental form of all music.

ARPEGGIO: Serialization of a chord, i.e., the playing of its notes separately rather than simultaneously.

ATONALITY: The quality of not possessing tonality. Usually applied to certain 20th-century music of Schönberg and his followers but not approved by them because of its negative import. The prelude to Act III of *Parsifal* (which shifts key so often that it seems to have none) was one of the earliest atonal pieces.

AUGMENTED FOURTH: The interval outlined by three whole steps, sometimes called a "tritone," e.g., C-F sharp. The same interval as a DIMINISHED FIFTH.

CADENCE: The musical progression that leads to a pause or a moment of relaxation; it always appears at the end of a phrase.

CADENZA (Italian, *cadence*): The virtuoso interlude played or sung by a soloist just before his final cadence; used to delay the ending and to show off his technical ability. Originally improvised on the spot, but today usually written into the score by the composer.

CANON: A composition for two or more voices, in which each voice sings the same tune successively. *Three Blind Mice* is a canon.

CANTILENA: A term from the Italian word *canto,* "song," used to describe a flowing, songlike quality in instrumental music.

CASTRATO: A male singer who, because he has been castrated, has the pitch range of a female. Italian castrati of the 17th and 18th centuries were vocal technicians of the highest order but lost their appeal with the appearance of dramatic (rather than virtuosic) opera and with the appearance of women on stage.

CHAMBER MUSIC: Originally music which, because of the small number of musicians required, could be performed in a small room. In modern times, it is usually applied to solo and duo sonatas, trios, quartets, quintets, etc. The music, nevertheless, may be as long and complex as a symphony. A mid-20th century chamber orchestra is any orchestra smaller than a symphony orchestra.

CHORD: Three or more notes sounded simultaneously. Used extensively in concert music between the late 18th and early 20th centuries (and still used in popular music) but less applicable to important contemporary music, which moves contrapuntally. Chords include triads (the first, third and fifth notes of a scale), sevenths usually triads with the seventh scale note added), ninths (similarly), elevenths, etc.

CHROMATIC INTERVAL: The interval between two adjacent notes, a half step. See SCALE.

CLAVIER: The keyboard of any keyboard instrument, hence the instrument itself.

CLEF: The sign that appears at the beginning of each staff to indicate the pitch of notes appearing on it. The treble clef 𝄞 derives from the letter G, and the G above middle C is indicated by the second line, on which the clef centers. The bass clef 𝄢 is derived from the letter F, and F below middle C is the fourth line in the lower staff, on which *it* centers. A third clef, used today mostly by orchestra musicians, is the C clef 𝄡 which may be situated on any line of the staff; the line on which it rests is middle C.

CODA (Italian, *tail*): The episode, sometimes of large proportions (as in Beethoven), which brings a movement to a close.

COLOR: A nonmusical word used to describe luxuriant qualities of tone. A singer's voice that appears to have a different inflection for each note is said to be "colorful" or "well-colored," whereas one that seems to have no variety of tone is called "white." The richer instruments, e.g., English horns, cellos, give maximum orchestral color; and the middle note of a triad (the third) is called the "color tone."

COLORATURA: (Italian, *colored*): Applied to singing. A highly ornamental vocal line, whose execution requires long training and supreme control. A term originally used for all such singing, whether by male or female, but today usually understood to mean the soprano who can sing the style.

CONSONANCE or CONCORD (adj.: CONSONANT): The satisfying

sound produced by two or more notes whose effect is of being at rest. Octaves and fifths are the purest consonances. Thirds and sixths are accepted today as consonances which contain more "color." Complement of DISSONANCE.

COUNTERPOINT (adj.: CONTRAPUNTAL): Primarily, the technique of writing polyphony, but generally, the technique of combining any musical parts. Music is said to be contrapuntal when its several voices appear to be following separate courses simultaneously; if, on the other hand, they seem to be organized into chords, the music is called harmonic. The modern study of counterpoint is expected to create in the student a standard of values and to develop his musical judgment rather than to give him a set of rules by which to compose. In the U.S., the rules of counterpoint used are those outlined by the 18th-century composer and theorist, Johann Joseph Fux, in his famous *Gradus ad Parnassum*.

CRESCENDO (Italian, *increasing*): In music, a gradual increase of volume, indicated by this mark: ⟨ . Opposite of DIMINUENDO.

DESCANT or DISCANT: An early name for polyphonic writing. The descant is the second voice, which sings in harmony with the first.

DIATONIC: A scale pattern using whole steps as well as half steps, i.e., a major or minor scale. Today, meaning opposed to CHROMATIC.

DIMINISHED FIFTH: See AUGMENTED FOURTH.

DIMINUENDO (Italian, *diminishing*:) In music, a lessening of volume, indicated by ⟩ . Opposite of CRESCENDO.

DISSONANCE: The restless or clashing effect created by notes that are adjacent or (sometimes) whose overtones are adjacent. Seconds, sevenths and tritones (see AUGMENTED FOURTH) are dissonances. For practical purposes, a minor second, such as C-C sharp, is the most dissonant interval; a major second (C-D) is less so. Complement of CONSONANCE.

DO: In Europe, the name for the scale tone "C." In the U.S., usually the name for the TONIC of any scale.

DOMINANT: The fifth note of any key and after the tonic its most important note. Also, the chord built on that note. See TONIC, SUBDOMINANT.

DOT: Placed after a note, it increases its duration by half; placed over or under a note (staccato), it decreases its duration by half.

DYNAMICS: In music a general word for gradations of loudness.

ENHARMONIC: A shift of harmonic viewpoint without a change of sound. In an enharmonic change, C sharp is written as D flat. On keyed instruments this is the same note, but it is now related to all the flat keys instead of the sharp keys.

FALSETTO: False notes, such as a male may produce when he sings in the female range; the top notes of a yodel. The sound is sweet and without the color of a "real" tone.

FLAT: (1) The musical sign ♭ that lowers the pitch of a note by a half step; (2) inadvertently lowers the true pitch.

FORTE (Italian, *loud*): The louder half of the dynamic range, from mezzo-forte (*mf*) meaning fairly loud; to forte (*f*); to fortissimo (*ff*) meaning loudest. In later years, musicians and instruments improved, and the sign *fff* was written and played. See PIANO.

GAMUT: A contraction of the Greek words *gamma* and *ut*, meaning the whole musical scale.

GLISSANDO: An onomatopoeic mixture of French and Italian which means "sliding," used to indicate a trombone smear, a violin PORTAMENTO (q.v.) or a piano or harp cascade. Glissandos on the piano and harp are made by zipping a thumbnail up or down the notes.

HARMONIC SERIES: The acoustical phenomenon upon which all Western music is based, first discovered by Pythagoras: an ever-narrowing, ascending pattern of notes that can be heard or sensed whenever a tone is sounded. It results from a fundamental acoustical fact. A thick string, stretched to proper tautness and plucked, struck or bowed will vibrate, say, 32 times per second to produce a low C. When it is stopped at its midpoint, each division produces the C an octave higher ("first harmonic") at 64 vibrations a second. Divided in thirds, each produces the G a fifth higher, in sixths the E a sixth higher than that, then another G, an approximate B flat, C, D, E, F sharp (approximate), etc. Similarly with a column of air: a tin whistle (with all holes covered) can theoretically be made to sound the whole series by increasing the air pressure, as can flutes, French horns, trumpets and trombones. The woodwinds present a more complicated problem, since reeds and the shape of the bores also affect pitch. See OVERTONES.

HARMONY: The mixture of pitches heard at a given instant of a musical composition, often thought of as chords. Also the evolving patterns of chord progressions—actually, a function of COUNTERPOINT (q.v.). Usually accepted, with melody and rhythm, as a basic component of music, although the world produces plenty of music that has no harmony.

INTERVAL: The stepwise distance between two notes (e.g., C-G is the interval of a fifth). The addition of the word "perfect," "minor," "diminished," or "augmented" is necessary if the musician is to understand the exact interval. See STEP.

INVERSION: (1) Raising the bottom note of an interval or a chord by an octave, or vice versa, to produce the same harmony in a new form; (2) Playing a line of counterpoint upside down, as if in mirror fashion.

KEY: (1) The note about which a complex of tonal relationships gravitates to create TONALITY (q.v.). Most music for the past 200 years has been written "in" one or another key; i.e., it starts in the key, leaves it for contrast and returns to it at the end, leaving the listener with the feeling that the music has returned home. Since there are twelve different notes in Western music, there are twelve major and twelve minor keys. (2) The ivory or ebony mechanism on an instrumental fingerboard which produces a tone when depressed; also the metal lever on a wind instrument that controls pitch.

KEY SIGNATURE: From the 16th to the 20th century, the arrangement of sharps or flats at the beginning of a composition to designate what key it is in. All indicated sharps or flats are used throughout the piece unless temporarily negated by ACCIDENTALS (q.v.) or permanently changed by a new signature. See TIME SIGNATURE.

LEITMOTIF: A short, characteristic musical pattern symbolizing a person or idea. Most often used by Wagner.

LYRIC: (1) The words of a song. (2) A style of singing, more gentle than its complementary style, the dramatic. (3) Also used to indicate that a drama contains music, as in "the lyric drama."

MAJOR and MINOR: The two surviving modes or scales. On the white keys of a piano, the scale from C to C is major; from A to A, minor. The most apparent difference between the two is to be heard in their tonic triads, where the COLOR interval is a major third in the major scale and a minor third in the minor. Major keys are thought to have a bright, cheerful effect (most marches are written in the major); the minor is more melancholy and sometimes stronger.

MEASURE (also called BAR): The space on a musical score between two vertical lines called "bar lines" enclosing a specific number of beats. First used when music began to have definite meter, to help the musicians keep together.

MELODY: Melody is the most elusive—and the most fundamental musical concept. It must be defined broadly because of the changing style in musical taste and because nobody has yet been able to isolate the secret of a melody's appeal. Roughly, a melody is any pattern of single notes that can be comprehended by the ear. A poignant melody contains a higher percentage of dissonant intervals and more complex harmonic implications than a bland melody, whether it be in a popular tune, a symphonic theme or a fugue subject.

MELOS (Greek): Originally, the arrangement of notes in a melody (excluding rhythm), but now used to indicate a particular nature or style of melody.

METRONOME: A machine that ticks at specific tempos, used by musicians in practicing and by composers through "metronome marks" to indicate precisely the speed of their compositions.

MODE: A type of scale, or organization of notes within an octave from which melodies may be constructed. All scales except the chromatic and the whole-tone are modal. The most familiar modes today are the major and minor. The original modes were those of the ancient Greeks. On the piano the Aeolian mode runs downward on the white keys from A to A, the Dorian from D to D, etc.

MODULATION: A smooth harmonic transition from one key

to another.

MOTET: A polyphonic form invented in the 13th century, in which a three-or four-voice composition is built on a previously selected melody called a "tenor."

MOTIF: A small, distinctive group of notes, often synonymous with SUBJECT (but not with THEME).

MUSIC: The apparent shaping of time and space by use of sound-patterns. The broader the definition, the more accurate it can be. Brahms defined music as "The organization of disparate elements," a definition which correctly allows it to include such widely diverse examples as a Balinese gamelan and a Greek monody. A common definition describes music as a "pleasing combination of sounds," incorrectly, because the word "pleasing" forces upon it the listener's reaction.

MUTE: A mechanical device used to limit the tone of certain musical instruments. A mute for stringed instruments is a pronged clip that is slipped onto the bridge to damp the vibrations. A brass mute is an acoustical plug that is inserted into the bell of a brass instrument to choke the tone and thus alter its timbre. Woodwinds cannot be effectively muted, since the tone emerges from the perforations all along the pipe. The only workable piano mute is the type used on uprights, consisting of a felt ribbon that drops between hammers and strings.

NATURAL: The musical sign ♮ that restores a note to its orginal position (always in the scale of C) after alteration by a sharp or flat.

NOTE: (1) A musical sound of specific pitch. (2) The mark on a musical staff whose shape indicates the duration of the note, and whose position indicates its pitch.

OCTAVE: An interval of eight scalewise degrees whose two notes sound virtually the same and have the same name.

A man's voice is usually about an octave below a woman's. On the piano keyboard, notes an octave apart look the same in the pattern of keys.

ORATORIO: A type of opera without stage sets or action. Its growth paralleled that of the dramatic opera, and it reached its greatest popularity during the time of Handel's years in England. It consists of a religious or epic poem, set for soloists, chorus and orchestra or organ.

OVERTONES: The progressively higher sounds that can be sensed above any tone. They are caused by an instrument's shape and sound-producing method; they add up to give it its characteristic tone color. See HARMONIC SERIES.

PEDAL POINT: A continuing note in a composition (usually in the bass) above which the higher parts may move into clashing harmonies before they resolve.

PERFECT INTERVAL: A two-note chord in the simplest acoustic ratios. Only octaves, fourths and fifths can be perfect; when inverted they do not change their quality.

PIANO: (1) The familiar keyboard instrument, developed in the late 18th century and first called *piano and forte* (soft and loud). (2) (Italian, *soft*): In music, the quieter half of the dynamic range from mezzo-piano (*mp*), meaning fairly soft, to pianissimo (*pp*), softest. Berlioz, Tchaikovsky and Verdi wrote *PPPP* and even *PPPPP* to startle musicians into playing softly. See FORTE.

PITCH: The quality of a musical tone which specifies its apparent highness or lowness. Pitch is raised by increasing the number of vibrations per second of a string or column of air. Common pitch of musical instruments varied noticeably from country to country until 1939, when middle A was set at 440 vibrations per second. It has since risen still higher because higher pitch seems more brilliant to the ear. The Boston Symphony uses

A-444, the Vienna Philharmonic, A-446.

PIZZICATO: Plucking rather than bowing a string.

POLYPHONY: The style of music, dominant from the 9th to the 16th centuries, that combined two or more human voices contrapuntally and was conceived as horizontal rather than vertical movement.

PORTAMENTO: Sliding between notes on the violin or in singing.

PRELUDE: (1) A short composition that sounds improvised; (2) the music that precedes a drama or opera.

RELATIVE PITCH: The ability possessed by nearly all musicians to hear the interval relationship between one note and another. No relation to ABSOLUTE PITCH.

RESOLUTION: The progression from a point of harmonic tension to one of less tension. In tonal music, a dissonance resolves to the consonance demanded by contrapuntal procedure.

RHYTHM: Any aspect of the rate of musical flow, from its basic meter to the patterns of accents over a whole work. Next to MELODY, music's most important component.

RONDO: One of the basic instrumental forms, characterized by the periodic return to the first theme. A common rondo alternates new themes with the original, one after the other (A-B-A-C-A, etc.); a more tightly packed rondo brings back the second subject, too (A-B-A-C-A-B-A); the most complex rondos also disguise the main theme by variation when it returns.

ROOT: The fundamental note of a common chord or triad.

RUBATO (Italian, *robbed*): A free treatment of tempo, in performance, for expressive effect.

SCALE: A succession of consecutive ascending or descending notes. Most common today are (1) diatonic scales, which are in the standard major or minor modes; (2) chromatic scales, which include all twelve half steps in order; (3) whole tone scales, which have each note separated by two half steps, and which are sometimes thought of as chords rather than scales. The diatonic scale-tones in ascending order are named the tonic, supertonic, mediant, subdominant, dominant, submediant, leading tone, tonic.

SEQUENCE: A popular device for extending a melodic-harmonic idea by repeating it several times while moving it gradually up or down the scale.

SHARP: (1) The musical sign ♯ that precedes a note to be raised a half step. If it is to be raised two half steps a double sharp ✕ is used. (2) Also to sing or play out of tune above pitch.

SINGSPIEL: An opera in German, usually of a comparatively light nature, and always containing spoken lines as well as singing. One of the most famous *Singspiels* is Mozart's *The Magic Flute*.

SONORITY: A catchall term used to describe the acoustical effect of a combination of tones and colors. Often used in describing contemporary music, where composers achieve unique colors by extremely complex means.

SONATA: Originally, a composition for instruments (as distinct from one for voices). Since the time of Haydn, the word usually applies to a three- or four-movement form for solo instrument or for two instruments.

STAFF or STAVE: The five horizontal lines on which music is written. Two staffs are required for piano, harp and organ; other instruments require only one.

STEP: The interval between adjacent notes. A whole step contains two chromatic intervals or half steps. See INTERVAL.

STRETTO: (1) In fugues, crowding or overlapping of themes; (2) in opera, a climactic speed-up, as at the end of an overture.

SUBDOMINANT: The fourth tone of any scale and a key's third most important focal point (see TONIC, DOMINANT). Receives its name from the fact that it is five notes downward from the tonic. The subdominant harmony is known as the "Amen chord" because it usually precedes the final tonic in congregational "Amens."

SUBJECT: The brief, succinct collection of notes that forms the musical idea of a fugue.

SUSPENSION: The delay of one or more notes while the harmony moves on. The result is a dissonance or series of dissonances that demand resolution.

SYMPHONY: A three- or four-movement (rarely more or less) composition for full orchestra. Strictly, it relates only to music of the classical period, but the form has been successfully used since.

TEMPERED PITCH: A method of tuning keyboard instruments so that all chromatic intervals are equal. Commonly used since mid-18th century. Opposed to "Natural" pitch.

TEMPO: The Italian word "time" which refers to speed of playing. It is indicated precisely by metronome marks (e.g., ♩ = 120 means that the quarter-notes should move at the rate of 120 per minute, or in march tempo); tempos are indicated less precisely by such Italian words as *Adagio* (slowly), *Molto Adagio* (very slowly), *Presto* (fast) *Prestissimo* (very fast), *Moderato* (moderate speed) etc.

TESSITURA: The general range, high, medium or low, in which a vocal line lies.

THEME: The melodic idea that dominates each movement of classical and romantic music. It is characteristically tuneful, as distinguished from the fugal SUBJECT (q.v.).

TIME SIGNATURE: Numbers placed at the beginning of a composition, and sometimes elsewhere, indicating the number of notes per bar of the stated value, or their equivalent.

TONALITY: The harmonic locus called "key-feeling" generated by most music between 1700 and 1900 (see KEY).

TONIC: The root or home-tone of any key.

TRANSCRIPTION: Also called "arrangement." A recasting of music from one medium into another, often, for convenience, into piano score. Bach arranged Vivaldi concerto grossos for clavier, Mozart arranged Bach keyboard pieces for strings, Wagner arranged Beethoven's ninth symphony for piano, and Debussy made piano arrangements of Wagner operas. In popular music, an arrangement is a mixture of orchestration, harmonization of the melody and actual composition.

TREMOLO: In the orchestra, a rapid repetition of the same note, commonly used in the strings to produce a sense of unrest or mystery. Also said of human voices in a derogatory sense to indicate that the tone is unsteady.

TRIAD: A chord made up of two intervals of a third.

TRILL: A rapid alternation of two adjacent notes, usually for ornamental purposes.

TRIPLET: Three notes played in the time allotted to two.

TUNING FORK: A two-pronged metal fork which rings with a constant pitch when tapped.

TURN: Next to the trill, the most popular ornamental device in vocal and instrumental music before the 20th century. It decorates the melodic note by entwining it in neighboring notes; e.g., a turn on C runs C, D, C, B, C, and then proceeds to the next melodic note.

TWELVE-TONE TECHNIQUE: The compositional method of Arnold Schönberg, Alban Berg, Anton Webern and a large number of mid-20th century composers. Originally, it was designed to negate key-feeling and thus required that all twelve notes of the chromatic scale be stated (either melodically or in chords) before any one note could be repeated. See ATONALITY.

VARIATIONS: One of the oldest means of extended musical design. Each section derives from either the thematic or harmonic content of the original theme or from some more subtle form of association. Almost every age has developed its new musical language through some kind of variation technique: Bach excelled at the passacaglia and chaconne types, Beethoven and Brahms made variations into introspective spiritual essays; such moderns as Schönberg and Stravinsky have pushed the technique into mysterious realms of subtlety and mathematical exactness. Improvised jazz is also a variation technique.

VIBRATO: Rapid variation in the intensity (sometimes also the pitch) of a tone to make it more pleasing to the ear. Commonly heard in strings and human voices since mid-19th century but still not standard in the winds of concert orchestras.

SOURCE BOOKS

More details on subjects covered in *A Popular History of Music* may be found in the following volumes:

General

Chase, Gilbert: *America's Music*. New York, McGraw-Hill, 1955.

Einstein, Alfred: *Music in the Romantic Era*. New York, W. W. Norton & Co., 1949.

Feather, Leonard: *The Encyclopedia of Jazz*. New York, Horizon Press, 1955./

Ferguson, Donald N.: *A History of Musical Thought*. New York, Appleton-Century-Crofts, 1948.

Lang, Paul Henry: *Music in Western Civilization*. New York, W. W. Norton & Co., 1941.

Loesser, Arthur: *Men, Women and Pianos*. New York, Simon and Schuster, 1954.

Salazar, Adolfo: *Music in Our Time*. New York, W. W. Norton & Co., 1946.

Slonimsky, Nicholas: *Music Since 1900*. New York, Coleman Ross Co., 1949.

Thompson, Oscar: *International Cyclopedia of Music and Musicians*. New York, Dodd, Mead & Co., 1949.

Biographical

Anderson, Emily (Tr.): *Letters of Mozart and His Family*. London, Macmillan, 1938. 3 Vols.

Barzun, Jacques: *Berlioz and the Romantic Century*. Boston, Little, Brown, 1950.

Berlioz, Hector: *Memoirs*. New York, Tudor, 1935.

Burk, John Naglee: *Life and Works of Beethoven*. New York, Random House, 1943.

Corle, Edwin: *Igor Stravinsky*. New York, Duell, Sloan and Pearce, 1949.

Debussy, Claude: *Monsieur Croche,* New York, Viking Press, 1928.

Einstein, Alfred: *Schubert*. New York, Oxford University Press, 1951.

Geiringer, Karl: *The Bach Family*. New York, Oxford University Press, 1954.

Geiringer, Karl: *Brahms*. London, G. Allen and Unwin, Ltd., 1936.

Geiringer, Karl: *Haydn*. New York, W. W. Norton, 1946.

Newman, Ernest: *Life of Richard Wagner*. New York, A. A. Knopf, 1946.

Parry, C. Hubert H.: *Johann Sebastian Bach*. New York, G. P. Putnam's Sons, 1909.

Riezler, Walter: *Beethoven*. New York, E. P. Dutton, Inc, 1938.

Schönberg, Arnold: *Style and Idea*. New York, Philosophical Library, 1950.

Schumann, Robert: *On Music and Musicians*. New York, Pantheon, 1946.

Seroff, Victor: *The Mighty Five*. New York, Allen, Towne and Heath, 1948.

Stravinsky, Igor: *Poetics of Music*. Cambridge, Harvard

University Press, 1947.

Thompson, Oscar: *Debussy, Man and Artist*. New York, Dodd, Mead, 1937.

Toye, Francis: *Giuseppe Verdi*. London, W. Heinemann, 1931.

Turner, W. J.: *Mozart*. New York, Alfred A. Knopf, 1938.

Wagner, Richard: *My Life*. New York, Dodd, Mead, 1911.

INDEX*

---

* Definitions of musical terms may be found in the GLOSSARY, pp. 318-332.